MAKING
PLAY
WORK

MAKING PLAY WORK

*The Promise of After-School Programs
for Low-Income Children*

ROBERT HALPERN

TEACHERS
COLLEGE
PRESS

Teachers College, Columbia University
New York and London

Published by Teachers College Press, 1234 Amsterdam Avenue, New York, NY 10027

Library of Congress Cataloging-in-Publication Data
Halpern, Robert, 1951–
    Making play work : the promise of after-school programs for low-income children / Robert Halpern.
        p. cm.
    Includes bibliographical references and index.
    ISBN 0-8077-4370-4 (cloth : alk. paper) — ISBN 0-8077-4369-0 (pbk. : alk. paper)
        1. School-age child care—United States.   2. School-age child care—Activity programs—United States.   3. Child development—United States.   4. Poor children—United States.   I. Title.

    HQ778.6.H35 2003
    362.71'2—dc21

                                                                                          2003040292

ISBN 0-8077-4369-0 (paper)
ISBN 0-8077-4370-4 (cloth)

Printed on acid-free paper

Manufactured in the United States of America

10   09   08   07   06   05   04   03   8   7   6   5   4   3   2   1

This book is dedicated to Shirl,
whose love and support sustain me,
and whose courage is a miracle.

Contents

Acknowledgments

I would like to acknowledge the assistance of David Klassen, at the Social Welfare History Archives, University of Minnesota; the archival research assistance of Connie Van Brunt, the helpful feedback of Carol Horton, and the financial support of the Annie E. Casey Foundation and the Ewing Marion Kauffman Foundation. Additional thanks go to the Erikson Institute for sabbatical support that was critical to the final stages of writing and editing, and Catherine Bernard and Lori Tate of Teachers College Press for their assistance in preparing the manuscript for publication. Finally, I am grateful to the numerous program directors and staff in Boston, Chicago, New York City, and Seattle, who allowed me to spend time with their programs.

Introduction

*As adults, we feel far removed from the play concerns of children, so we
... experience some annoyance when this culturally distinct phenomenon
of theirs interferes with the work we must get done in educating them.*
            —Brian Sutton-Smith, *The Useless Made Useful*

Over the past decade, politicians and policy makers, the media, child development professionals and parents have focused increasing attention on the after-school hours of children aged 6 to 14, coming to view this daily time period as one of both heightened risk and unusual opportunity. The risks perceived for these hours range from boredom, worry, and idleness to self-destructive and antisocial behavior; the opportunities, from caring relationships with adults to participation in arts, sports, and other enriching activities, to extra time for academics. The new calculus of risk and opportunity for the after-school hours has led in turn to renewed interest in a long-standing child development institution, after-school programs, particularly those serving low- and moderate-income children of elementary and middle school age. About 25% of such children—some 4 million children—now spend 3 to 5 afternoons a week in after-school programs, and participation rates appear to be growing each year (Capizzano, Tout, & Adams, 2000; Halpern, Spielberger, & Robb, 1999).

Given the new societal interest and growing participation in after-school programs, it is an appropriate moment to step back, examine the evolution of their role in low-income children's lives, and reflect on what that role ought to be in the coming years. That is the purpose of this book; I will examine the rationales for and objectives of after-school programs in a sequence of historical eras, and how those were shaped by prevailing ideas about children and their needs and by broad societal preoccupations. I will describe patterns of sponsorship and staffing, describe the daily life of programs, and explore the nature of children's experiences in different kinds of programs. I will examine why children have responded to after-school programs as they have and where after-school programs have fit in the broader array of low-income children's out-of-school activities. Also to be explored is the historical relationship between after-school programs and schools and how after-school programs have both been shaped by and contributed to their local communities. In a later chapter I will discuss the challenges inherent in supporting and, as necessary, strengthening after-school programs. In conclusion, I review the achievements and struggles of after-school programs, summarize their distinctive qualities as a developmental resource, and address the question of appropriate expectations of them.

A history of after-school programs raises broad questions about growing up under conditions of poverty in the United States, and these will be examined here as well. How, for instance, have views of what low-income children need from different child-rearing institutions evolved over time? How have the roles of different institutions in children's lives been sorted out? How ought we think about schooltime and out-of-school time in relation to each other? What are the developmental implications of an ever increasing adult appropriation of children's everyday experience and of an increasingly institutionalized childhood? How much intentionality on the part of adult institutions is needed for children to grow in a healthy way? Finally, why has it been so hard for American society to provide normal developmental supports for low-income children? Why have such supports always had to have some instrumental purpose?

MAJOR THEMES

A STRUGGLE FOR IDENTITY

As the historical account will reveal, the after-school field has a rich and interesting tradition of service to children. Yet it is also a field that has struggled to define, and has sometimes seemed ambivalent about, its own assumptions and purposes. After-school programs have defined themselves in terms of protection and care; opportunity for enrichment, self-expression, and play; and also in terms of socialization, acculturation, training, compensation, and remediation. Providers have argued that program activities should be shaped not only by children's interests and preferences, but also by what they as adults thought children needed. Proponents have sometimes found it easier to define after-school programs by what they were not—family, school, the streets—than by what they were.

What might be called the struggle for identity within the after-school field derives in part from its unusual institutional, social, and temporal "location." After-school programs are neither purely local nor purely national institutions, and neither purely informal nor purely formal. They have often stood—or found themselves—at the intersection of ideological crosscurrents in American society: between romantic and instrumental views of children, between play and work, between the traditions of local communities and those of the larger society, and between a view of low-income children as vulnerable and a view of them as threatening. Because after-school time has been somewhat undefined, a variety of stakeholders have claimed a voice in shaping it. These have included philanthropists, social reformers, elected officials, parents, and educators, as well as after-school providers and children themselves.

The struggle for identity has given after-school programs a mixed or in-between quality and kept them malleable, with both positive and problematic consequences. After-school programs were able to become a different kind of institution from most others in low-income children's lives, one that mostly avoided pathologizing them, and one that could identify gaps in children's lives and try to fill them. After-school programs became an adult-directed institution in which the adult agenda was relatively modest and in which children could re-create their own communities as well as find new ones. They have managed to serve as a bridge between such intimate institutions or settings as family, ethnic group, and neighborhood; and more distant ones, such as schools and juvenile authorities. Yet, lacking a defensible alternative (or conviction in their own convictions), after-school programs have also found it difficult to resist pressures to contribute to the often instrumental, and occasionally harsh, societal agenda for low-income children. And they have been unable to resist pressures to promise more than was commensurate with their means and especially to promise to compensate for what other child development institutions should have been, but were not, providing low-income children.

CONTINUITY AND CHANGE

The after-school field emerged in the late 19th century and would grow idiosyncratically but with some consistency in philosophy, purpose, and approach. The characteristic qualities of after-school programs would change little over the course of the 20th century, though like all institutions they were shaped by their times. Today's sponsors probably continue to see their work as did early ones: as about "the making, rather than the remaking of lives" (Marshall, 1912, p. 315). They would probably agree that their focus remains on what the 1931 Hull House yearbook described as children's "struggles, needs and possibilities" (cited in Kirkland & Johnson, 1989, p. 19). They would agree with the early boys' club director who noted that after-school programs should be fun, but fun with a purpose. As did their predecessors, today's after-school programs continue to help children negotiate the demands of other settings and institutions.

The basic activity structure that emerged early on among after-school programs changed little over the decades, with clubs and classes, arts and crafts and table games, indoor or outdoor physical activity, cultural activity, and occasional field trips. Participation in the visual and expressive arts has been a constant. Specific emphases have risen or fallen. Prevocational activities such as metalwork declined over time. Yesterday's radio clubs have been replaced by today's computer clubs. Academic concerns emerged in the 1960s, and since then most programs have included homework time, perhaps some tutoring, and reading time. A historic pattern of club- or class-based enrollment, complemented by dropping in for gym or game room time, continued through the 1960s. Since then, child care has become a more persistent issue, and programs have moved toward a "closed enrollment" model, especially for younger school-age children, with defined groups of children participating daily in a more or less common program. After-school programs have also become steadily more integrated by gender and (where housing patterns supported it) by race.

There was always some variability in philosophy and emphasis among after-school programs, and that persists. In the course of a recent research study in Boston, one program director noted that his main goal was "to keep kids off the street and alive." Another, working in an equally rough neighborhood, described her program as offering the opportunity to explore interests and discover talents in the arts (through such activities as mask-making, dance, drumming, stilt-walking, puppetry, ceramics, theater, and silk screen—all taught by local artists). Still another described a mission of increasing girls' interest in sports. Some programs make sure to leave time for free play in their schedules; others do not (Halpern, Spielberger, & Robb, 1999).

After-school programs obviously have not evolved in a vacuum. They have been influenced by major historical events and circumstances, prevailing social preoccupations, ideas about childhood, and developments in other institutions and settings, especially families, schools, and neighborhoods. Each generation has had its own fears and preoccupations—child labor and child safety, the temptations of popular culture (and the threat of an autonomous peer culture), economic upheaval, threats to democracy, mobilization for war, youth deviance, and youth violence. Each has had its own views of what children, especially low-income children, needed from adult institutions. At times low-income children have been seen to need more freedom, at times less; at times more opportunity to play, and at times greater engagement in "useful" and "productive" tasks (Zelizer, 1985).

After-school programs started out and remain a fragile, fragmented human service institution. They have been sponsored by diverse organizations, from youth-serving organizations such as boys' and girls' clubs and YMCAs, settlements, and other community-based agencies, to churches, ethnic self-help organizations, schools, and public housing authorities, among others. This diversity has had both benefits and costs. Different sponsors bring different strengths to the work. Each local community has its own most trusted local institutions. Diversity of sponsorship increases parents' and children's choices. And it increases the chances that some institution will step forward to fill local gaps in service. At the same time, it has complicated the task of creating a clear identity for the field and impeded collective action. While different sponsors have occasionally worked together, they have often worked separately.

After-school programs have never been part of any major public system, nor governed by any particular public policies, organizations, or standards (although governance mechanisms are beginning to emerge in a handful of cities, and proposed standards beginning to be promulgated). Frontline staff, if not program directors, have always been mostly nonprofessional, with little or no formal preparation for the work they do with children. After-school programs have always been, and remain, inadequately funded, reliant on community chests, United Ways, and local philanthropy. Modest public funding has emerged over the past decade, as public interest in after-school programs has grown; but the majority of programs still have limited access to this funding.

AFTER-SCHOOL PROGRAMS AND OTHER DEVELOPMENTAL SETTINGS

After-school programs have not just been an "in-between" institution. Their story has been partly one of struggle to define an educating, socializing, and identity-shaping role in relation to that of other institutions, notably children's families, the schools, and the streets. At various times after-school programs have sought to complement, supplement, counter, and even supplant each of these. After-school programs have mediated between families and other institutions, especially the schools (a function that continues) and sometimes mediated between children and their parents, especially in immigrant families in which the rapid acculturation of children created rifts with their more slowly acculturating parents.

After-school programs and schools have a particularly complicated history. At times, the two institutions have worked together, and at times they have competed. Schools and after-school programs have viewed each other as allies in their respective efforts to counter the influence of the streets on children's development. At the same time, a number of factors have constrained the potential of schools and after-school programs to work together. School leaders have proved unwilling or unable to reconceptualize learning in school, as well as ambivalent about an expanded role for schools in meeting children's nonacademic needs (Hawes, 1997; Tyack & Cuban, 1995).

More often than not, after-school sponsors have defined their own role by differentiating themselves from and contrasting themselves to schools. If schools were going to inculcate efficiency, rationality, and a competitive ethic, then they could focus relatively more on creativity, cooperation, and civic-mindedness. If schools were going to focus on the "economic" child, they would focus on the whole child. If schools were going to ignore and even trample on individual differences between children, after-school programs would create space for such differences.

Although the historic pattern of ambivalent, and often strained, relations between schools and after-school providers continued throughout the 20th century, it took on new meaning in the 1990s. During this decade the notions of schools as an ideal base for after-school programming, and after-school programs as an ideal vehicle for helping schools address low-income children's academic difficulties, were promoted aggressively by major foundations and public officials. These twin ideas brought schools and community-based institutions into much closer contact, highlighting philosophical differences as well as a range of practical problems. They also served to demonstrate again how difficult it is for schools to develop equitable, reciprocal relationships with other institutions in low-income children's lives.

AFTER-SCHOOL PROGRAMS AND UNSTRUCTURED CHILDHOOD

The history of after-school programs is interwoven with the history of American adults' ambivalence about the role of play and the use of time in middle childhood and with the related history of children's own efforts to create physical and social space for themselves in urban environments. In spite of many adults' wariness of unsupervised outdoor play, it was an important element in low-income children's lives throughout the first two thirds of the 20th century, an element centered in playgrounds, playlots, and especially the streets. Children's creative and at times subversive use of public space has long contributed to the life of urban neighborhoods. Yet the streets have also been a figurative, and sometimes literal, battleground for control over children's play.

Some observers have viewed the work of after-school programs as one expression of a larger effort to control what, where, how, and with whom low-income children played, and as an example of adult appropriation of children's everyday experience (Finkelstein, 1987; Goodman, 1979; Suransky, 1982). At a practical level, after-school programs have had to compete with both the peer group and the streets for children's allegiance. Although some children have always sought out after-school programs—for respite from stresses elsewhere, as a place to try out drama or dance or music, as a place to develop a different "self," for adult supports, or for access to a gym—

many others preferred spaces where they could create and control their own activities (Nasaw, 1985).

For many decades, at least through the middle to late 1960s, streets, playgrounds, and playlots in fact provided a largely, though not unambiguously, positive developmental context. By the 1960s, intensifying residential segregation, job loss, capital disinvestment, and destructive public policies (such as urban renewal) were seriously undermining inner-city neighborhoods as developmental contexts. Critical changes included the thinning out of institutional networks; a decline in informal social control, in particular a growing unwillingness among neighborhood adults to serve as surrogate parents; the breakdown of traditional social organization; and changes in the nature of gang life. Parents increasingly restricted the freedom of movement and outdoor play of their children during the after-school hours. The decline in neighborhood conditions and related trend toward a restriction of low-income children's out-of-school experience intensified in the 1970s and 1980s.

THE SHIFTING MEANING OF ADULT INTRUSION

As the balance of benefits and risks in unstructured outdoor play and unmonitored after-school time shifted, the valence of after-school programs seemed to shift as well. For most of the 20th century, adult preoccupations with, and efforts to control and shape, children's after-school time were circumscribed, remaining a family and community issue. Philanthropic and, beginning in the 1960s, government initiatives tended to focus on the pre-school years or on older youth. If middle childhood was perceived as both a quiet and an important developmental period, most observers emphasized the former. By the 1990s that was no longer the case. There was a renewed awareness of how central the tasks of middle childhood are in American culture—acquiring literacy, gaining knowledge of the world, solidifying a sense of competence and agency, exploring interests and discovering talents, becoming more autonomous. And there was growing concern that schools, and to a lesser extent families, were not providing the supports and experiences children needed to master these tasks. Indeed, children seemed more fundamentally unsupported—more on their own—than in the past.

Worries about school-age children and about the key child-rearing institutions in their lives led to a new, and qualitatively different, interest in after-school programs. Out-of-school time suddenly "mattered." Out-of-school experience was described as the "third leg" in child development (Comer, 1992). After-school programs were, suddenly, the "third environment" (Heath, 1999). As after-school programs came to be considered a more important developmental setting, the question of what they could and should be about became more consequential. In fact, the new attention to low-income children's out-of-school time was (and continues to be) *itself* a source of risk and opportunity. It was not just that adults were appropriating one of the last corners of childhood that they had not yet taken control of. The changing context of low-income children's lives had altered the meaning of adult intrusion. It was, fundamentally, that the developmental tasks of middle childhood require a delicate balance from adults and adult institutions. School-age children need to be neither too little nor too much on their own. They need adult attention and access to adult expertise and experience. Yet they also need times and places in which the adult agenda is modest, if not held at bay. That is a balance that adult-created institutions have had a difficult time achieving, especially those providing services and supports to low-income children.

THE PLAN OF THE BOOK

The book is divided into two parts. Chapters 1 through 4 provide a chronological history of the after-school field, with themes and substantive issues woven into the chronology. Chapter 4 also serves as a bridge to the second part of the book, which focuses on the current opportunities and challenges facing the after-school field. Chapter 5 affords the reader a look inside the life of a representative selection of after-school programs, including a handful of exemplary ones. In Chapter 6, I discuss recent experience with efforts to support and strengthen after-school programs. In Chapter 7, I sum up, do some reiteration of major themes, and offer a (modest) vision of what it will take to make the work of after-school programs sustainable in the coming years.

This is the third time I have attempted a historical account of a particular set of human services (Halpern, 1995, 1999). Each time I have been asked (and had to ask myself) to justify so much attention to history. At a basic level, I have written this book simply to reclaim a past, to make it available. Every field has a history, but those working in or promoting a particular field cannot gain access to it unless it is available in a public form. In turn, gaining access means connecting to, and then feeling part of, a tradition, which itself gives greater meaning to one's struggles and achievements. Next, I would argue, less simply, that it is difficult to help support and strengthen a field, to guide its development, without understanding its past. That past provides explanation, warning, reminders, insight, into dilemmas and tensions. It provides the joy of recognition in—and occasionally the frustration of—seeing one's efforts reflected in "a distant mirror."

1

After-School Programs Emerge

To despise the powers and needs of childhood in behalf of the attain-
ments of adult life is ... suicidal.

John Dewey, *Schools of Tomorrow*

The children of the city did not wither and die in the urban air, but were
able to carve out social space of their own.

David Nasaw, *Children of the City*

One boys' club is worth a thousand policemen's clubs.

Jacob Riis, *Boys' Worker Roundtable*

THE CHANGING CONTEXT
OF WORKING-CLASS CHILDHOOD

After-school programs first emerged in the last quarter of the 19th century in the form of small, idiosyncratic "boys' clubs"—often no more than
a storefront or a room in a church or other local building. Two intercon-
nected social trends provided the backdrop for the emergence and expansion of the after-school field. The first was a gradual decline in the need
for children's paid labor, in the urban economy as a whole and in working-
class families' own microeconomies. The second was the growth of schooling, fueled by passage of compulsory education laws, large-scale investment
in school construction, and the greater availability of children to attend
school. At the turn of the century, some 20% to 25% of urban children
were gainfully employed (Zelizer, 1985, p. 57). Paid child labor declined
by half in each decade between 1900 and 1930. That decline was spurred
by, and in turn led to, an increase in school participation rates. In 1900,
59% of children aged 5 to 17 attended school; by 1928, 80% did so (Brenzel,
Roberts-Gersch, & Wittner, 1985, p. 480). During that period the point at
which most children left school shifted from the end of fifth to the end of
eighth grade.

The Decline in Children's Labor

It has been argued that the "expulsion of working class children from the market [was a] controversial process" (Zelizer, 1985, p. 209). Rapid industrialization at first created new work roles and opportunities for children, who were well suited physically and psychologically to factory work. Children were "tractable, reliable and industrious, quicker, neater and more careful" and less prone to strike (Hawes, 1991, p. 41). The role of children in factory work did decline beginning in the 1880s, as a result of studies and newspaper stories documenting abusive working conditions and because of a growing need to provide employment for large numbers of adult immigrants.

Home-based piecework, and among boys street trade, became the principle forms of work done by urban children, not declining significantly until the 1920s. Beginning at as early as 3 years of age, girls and boys worked with their mothers in sewing items of clothing, cutting out patterns, stringing beads, making artificial flowers and decorative feathers, making bedding, and rolling and labeling cigars. One report noted that "tiny children, four years old, can cut out embroideries. As soon as they can manage little scissors they help separate the strips, even if they are unable to cut out the scallops" (Watson, 1911, p. 775). Outside the home, boys picked up materials and delivered finished goods; bootblacked; sold papers, gum, and candy; and scrapped and scavenged (Berrol, 1995; West, 1997). Homes literally became minifactories, which were almost impossible to regulate.

Until the early 1920s, children's wages (or their equivalent in piecework at home) could constitute a third or more of the total income in the family of an unskilled worker. Families' immediate need for that income "outweighed considerations about an individual child's future benefits from schooling" (Walters & O'Connell, 1988, p. 1117). Children's work provided a hedge against the risks of injury, ill-health, death, and the cyclical unemployment faced by adult workers (Zelizer, 1985). Van Kleeck (1908) describes the case of two families living together in one apartment, in which "it had required the combined efforts of a settlement, a relief society, and school officers, to keep [the] children in school even for a few days. Nellie aged six, Josephine aged eleven, and Josie aged nine, worked all day long, often until 10 o'clock at night finishing coats at four to six cents a piece. . . . The [fathers] worked only at rare intervals, and depended upon the women and children to support the family" (p. 3). Even when children's work was not an absolute necessity, many working-class parents viewed it as a constructive activity for children, especially in comparison to "idleness," but sometimes also in comparison to school. The latter seemed to offer a poor substitute for the apprenticed learning of earlier eras: "In place of more numerous older workers, there were vastly outnumbered teachers who had no pay envelope to offer and whose promise of skills and knowledge that would be useful in the workplace had little credibility" (Resnick, 1990, p. 26).

To the extent that children's own views of work and schooling carried weight in the early years of the century, those views also varied, by experience, individual inclination, and gender. While many working-class children put up (surprisingly well) with the rote recitation and drill, harsh discipline, and rigidity of early 20th-century schooling, perhaps seeing these as the price of getting an education, a sizable minority of children experienced school as boring, frustrating, and sometimes humiliating (see, e.g., NUS Archives, Box 45, Folder 7). For girls, schooling provided freedom from home-based work and domestic responsibilities and offered the hint of possible nondomestic identities. For older boys especially, school often seemed less attractive than the streets and the possibilities that came with earning some money through peddling, scavenging, or selling newspapers (Clement, 1997, p. 114; Macleod, 1998). Between family needs and children's own preferences, rates of attendance were low—a third or more of enrolled children might be absent on any given day—and rates of early school-leaving were high.

THE GROWTH OF SCHOOLING

In the end, the decline in child labor turned as much on a changing labor market, changing technology (for instance the telephone reduced the need for messengers), and the growing public influence of school leaders, as on what parents or children themselves wanted. Schooling gradually became a defining socialization experience for urban children, and schools a new kind of child development institution—professional, bureaucratic, centralized, an institution beyond and sometimes set in opposition to control by parents and local communities. Schools shaped themselves in purpose, content, and organization to sort children by ability and social class and to prepare the majority for roles on the assembly lines of large industrial corporations. Since more than half the children in urban schools were from immigrant families, schools assumed a central acculturation role.

Schools also brought large numbers of like-age children together, in turn creating the peer group, with its own norms and behaviors. Further, schooling led to the articulation of different kinds of daily time, which might have different purposes, and in particular to what we now think of as out-of-school time or free time. Girls were nonetheless slower than boys to gain control of their time, many retaining responsibility for home-based work and care of younger siblings. In her memoir *Bronx Primitive*, Kate Simon (1982, p. 21) describes the burden and ambivalence she felt in having to assume care for a younger brother when she herself was just 4 years old: "I could lift him to the pot, clean him and take him off. I could carry him to bed and mash his potato. I knew where he might bump his head, where he might topple, how to divert him when he began to blubber. It was a short childhood."

If the gradual decline in child labor and growth of schooling created out-of-school time, other factors created the immediate rationales for organized programs to fill it. One was overcrowding, lack of light, and lack of privacy in tenement apartments, which pushed school-aged children into the streets and empty lots. Observers during the first decades of the century described the streets as "thronged" or "swarming" with children. The Juvenile Protective Association in Chicago estimated in 1912 that "on any given afternoon almost 6000 children could be found playing within eighteen or nineteen blocks" of its offices (Zelizer, 1985, p. 33).

Children were, nonetheless, not just pushed into the streets but attracted to them, by the richness and variety of street life, the possibility of earning some money, and a few hours of freedom from family responsibilities or conflict. The streets provided ingredients for play, exploration, and mischief. Children used "stoops, sidewalks, alleyways, and the city's wastelands" (Nasaw, 1985, p. 1). Chicago settlement leader Mary McDowell wrote that "the great game for boys . . . was to commit some misdemeanor that would call out the policeman, and then escape under the sidewalks and run for blocks" (McDowell, 1914, p. 25). Simon (1982, p. 2) describes the pleasures of an empty, elevated lot near her childhood home in the Bronx, with its ragged collection of flowers and weeds, assorted discarded objects, and physical challenges. The few girls who made it into this lot through the steeper entrance "were never quite the same again, a little more defiant, a little more impudent." The streets also provided refuge and affirmation: "Sweets tasted better in the streets; a new dress awaited the verdict of the streets; a beating or scolding faded in the noise of all the beatings and scoldings audible and visible through the many open windows" (Graff, 1995, p. 274).

At the same time, some blocks were more amenable to street play than others; some vacant lots better suited than others. Street traffic was growing year by year, heightening the risk of injury and death to children from horses, wagons, street cars, and freight trains. One commentator noted that "teams [of horses] and traffic and the hungry builders have all claimed open spaces for their own" (American, 1898, p. 159). By 1910, accidents were the leading cause of death for children aged 5 to 14; and between 1910 and 1930 half of automobile-related fatalities were suffered by children (Zelizer, 1985, pp. 32, 35). Loss of play space to traffic and real estate development was compounded by the growing use of the streets for commercial purposes. Boys' games, usually sports such as stickball, while not requiring elaborate equipment, did require space. Even less active play was difficult at times: "In the midst of the pushcart market, with its noise, confusion and jostling, the checker or crokinole board is precariously perched on the top of a hydrant, constantly knocked over by the crowd " (Wald, 1915, p. 72).

CONVERTING A PROBLEM TO AN OPPORTUNITY: THE PROGRESSIVE AGENDA FOR CHILDHOOD

The immediate responses of municipal authorities to the conflict between children's needs (and preferences) and adult concerns was to pass curfews and other "street laws" prohibiting fire setting, begging, roaming around, loitering, blocking sidewalks, and playing street games (Goodman, 1979; Nasaw, 1979). These laws, enforced by police and the new juvenile courts, led to large numbers of arrests. Yet the "problem" of working-class children's out-of-school time also began to be reinterpreted as an opportunity to improve those children, and through that effort ultimately to improve society.

The idea of transforming working-class children's out-of-school time from a source of risk to a source of opportunity was rooted generally in the optimism and reform spirit of the Progressive Era, and specifically in an evolving view of children and their needs. Progressive reformers shared a belief that the problems associated with urban life, an industrial economy, and large-scale immigration could be solved through scientific knowledge, social experimentation, and cooperation between contending groups and classes. The city would become a laboratory for the creation of new institutions designed to meet new social needs and demands.

Progressives acknowledged the factors that kept millions of urban families on the edge of destitution, most notably unregulated corporations, abysmal working conditions, and wages for unskilled workers. Yet their reform agenda addressed these issues indirectly at best, by proposing to protect children (and families) from their consequences and to prepare children to compete in an admittedly harsh world. This agenda included maternal and child health services, tenement reform, child labor reform, compulsory schooling, improved child care, and the creation of protected spaces for recreation and play. Progressives rationalized their reform strategies by arguing that they were trying to create a better society and that it was children who would do so. The new institutions designed to care for and educate children would, as John Dewey put it, be "embryos of society."

The child-oriented concerns of Progressive reformers both fed and were fed by the nascent child study movement. In the later years of the 19th century, adults had already begun to consider childhood as a qualitatively different stage of life and to look more closely and systematically at children's behavior. These early, mostly observational and descriptive studies (often involving the investigators' own children or relatives), focused on the question of when particular mental, moral, and physical capacities emerged in childhood. Investigators soon turned to the study of working-class children, finding that such children did not meet developmental norms and that the family and community contexts in which they grew up were disorganized, overstimulating, and physically unhealthy. This led to the argument for creating alternative settings for educating and socializing working-class children and to an ensuing debate about the kinds of supplementary or compensatory experiences that children needed.

Educators and psychologists working in the Romantic tradition of Rousseau, Pestalozzi, and Froebel argued for experiences that fostered creativity, imagination, and inner direction, and experiences that respected "the nature of childhood." As one wrote, school-age children must have time and space for "dreaming, playing, creating" (Patri, 1925, p. 133). Dewey (1915) and other Progressive educators focused on the need for cognitively flexible, socially skilled, and cooperative children. They argued that, especially in middle childhood, children needed opportunities to wrestle with real problems and required interaction with the social environment and its demands. To those working in the emergent psychoanalytic tradition, childhood was more about growing up than about development, more about the repression of childish instincts and an adjustment to the often unpleasant demands of adulthood and adult society.

For working-class, immigrant children the growth of child study and debate about what children needed was a double-edged sword. It would lead to new resources and programs for them. But it did not alter late-19th-century assumptions that they were different, and therefore had different needs, from their more advantaged peers. For these children, the idea of childhood as a special, sensitive, and critical period was combined with the notion that they had to be prepared to take their modest place in an increasingly complex industrial society. This led to the inference that while they needed access to child-centered experiences and activities, such experiences had to be offered with a strong dose of socialization and in a class-specific manner. While working-class children needed to master literacy and understand technology, they needed to do so in a way commensurate with the kind of work they were likely to acquire as adults.

GROWING ATTENTION TO AND CHANGING VIEWS OF PLAY

Of all the ideas about child development that emerged around the turn of the century, those centered around play were the most distinct and the most contradictory. Play became a focus of attention in part because of greater awareness of its role in child development, and in part because the forms it took in urban areas appeared to contribute to social disorder. (Aronowitz [1979, p. ix] argues that attention to play as a distinct phenomenon emerged also because the demands and nature of factory work had "cleanse[d] the work process of its play elements.") Play quickly came to be seen as potentially healthful, educational, and essential to children's development, their most natural form of activity, a right as well as a necessity. Yet, for working-class children especially, play also posed some risks, to them and to society, and it thus became something to be monitored and controlled.

The newly perceived importance of play is reflected in an 1897 pamphlet by the head of the Philadelphia Cultural Extension League, who wrote that "the collective play of children has a greater influence in forming habits of personal and social conduct of life than has school or even home instruction" (quoted in Kadzielski, 1977, p. 176). This theme would be expressed in different ways over the following quarter century. When the Playground Association of America was formed in 1906, its mission was "to secure for urban children their natural birthright—play" (cited in Cavallo, 1981, p. 37). Proponents of play postulated an ideal of 4 hours of school and 3 hours of play for younger school-age children (Gill & Schlossman, 1996).

Opportunity to play was seen as a key to preventing juvenile delinquency. It was argued that play could relieve some of the stress induced by schooling; free children (at least temporarily) from the realities of circumstance; and more broadly, restore some balance to an increasingly alienating, dehumanizing industrial culture (Lee, 1928; Kadzielski, 1977). Play was seen also to provide a counter to the grinding, oppressive environment of the tenement child. Settlement leader Graham Taylor wrote that the tenement child "is in a constant state of fatigue and ennui. It is not capable of physical endurance or mental perseverance. Restlessness, lack of will power and self-control become characteristic. . . . The child cannot conquer these tendencies because its weapon against them is play, and it has no place to play" (1914, p. 4).

While arguing for the importance of play, Progressives criticized working-class children's own autonomous play activity. Children's self-directed play was seen to create a potential for moral contamination. In both their indoor and outdoor play, children were seen to draw on and reenact the worst of the adult behavior they saw around them. Dewey (1915, p. 109) wrote that "in playing house, children are just as apt to copy the coarseness, blunders and prejudices of their elders as the things which are best." Woods and Kennedy (1922, pp. 106–107), wrote that "it would be hard to invent a commentary on [American society] more caustic than the episodes dramatized upon the streets by little children. . . . Lady Bum and Cop, Police Patrol, Burglar, the latest crime or sex scandal."

Although children were extraordinarily imaginative in their adaptation to and transformation of the urban environment—every object was utilized, from stoops, walls, fire hydrants, lampposts, and manhole covers, to the junk and debris in vacant lots—children's self-directed play was dismissed as unimaginative, unproductive, and occasionally a pathway to trouble. Commenting on the game of tag, Jane Addams noted that while it provided exercise and some excitement, "it is barren of suggestion and quickly degenerates into horseplay" (1909/1972, pp. 94–95). Reformers seemed particularly annoyed by children's tendency to waste time fooling around. The authors of a 1913 study in Cleveland found the majority of children spending their spare time on the streets, some playing organized games, some "not doing anything," but many others "gambling with dice and pitching pennies, gossiping and taunting on another, stealing from fruit stands, and writing on the walls of buildings" (West, 1997, p. 25).

Underlying the criticism of children's self-directed play was a deeper worry about the emergence of an autonomous peer culture. For the first time, children were turning as much to one another as they were to adults in deciding how to behave, who and what to emulate. In some respects, the new peer culture not only lay outside the control of adults, but seemed deliberately oppositional. When a bunch of children gathered on a vacant lot, built a fire using whatever junk they could find, and roasted stolen potatoes, they seemed to be doing something vaguely subversive. As Nasaw (1985, p. 20) notes, children's street-based play communities "were defined not only by their commitment to their own rules but by their disregard for those laid down by adults."

ORGANIZING PLAY

As a developmental imperative, a basic right, and a source of worry, children's play came to be a significant theme in the already crowded Progressive reform agenda. The need and right to play became a subtext in campaigns to improve urban space, to control development, and to promote cultural activities of all sorts. Lack of play space became a symbol for many the ills of urban life. Lillian Wald decried "the woeful lack of imagination displayed in building a city without recognizing the need of its citizens for recreation through play, art and music" (1915, p. 80).

To a modest extent, Progressives argued for adapting the city to children's needs, either making the streets safer or creating or protecting play space in vacant lots. A boys' club leader noted that "the streets are the all-year playgrounds. . . . We need better lighted streets, cleaner streets, more yard room for the children of the tenements" (Chew, 1911, p. 6). Sporadic efforts were made, usually through the cooperation of the police, to reduce traffic or close off streets from traffic at set times. Police tried occasionally to direct children to particular lots for play. In the main, though, children's right to play was reinterpreted as a need for "organized" play, in playgrounds, under adult supervision. (Unsupervised playgrounds would be little more than an extension of the streets.)

The idea of organized play attracted a diverse array of proponents and acquired a host of objectives. The latter ranged from safer, happier, healthier, and more cooperative children, to better students, fewer delinquents, stronger communities, better relations between ethnic groups, and reduced class conflict. Thus a police lieutenant in Chicago told Sadie American (1898, p. 163) that "not less than 15 lives have been saved from the electric car since the establishment of the [local] playground, and juvenile arrests have decreased fully 33 1/3 percent." And Charles Zueblin, director of the Northwestern University settlement, noted that "we are welding the people together as in a great melting pot on the playgrounds of Chicago" (cited in Cavallo, 1981, pp. 29–30).

Proponents argued that organized playgrounds would also produce better workers, a promise of particular interest to business leaders. William Polman, director of an institute that helped guide the business community's corporate welfare investments, argued that "the children [of immigrant families] are coming into your shop in a very few years; how much better for you that their bodies have been somewhat strengthened by exercise, and their minds disciplined by regulated play" (cited in Spring, 1972, p. 36). Children who had been socialized in playgrounds, especially through team sports, would be better teammates at work. Guides to playground work also emphasized such business principles as efficiency and punctuality: "Every event should begin on time whether the children are there or not" (cited in Goodman, 1979, p. 103).

Proponents of organized play typically worked through civic associations to pressure municipal governments to provide public funding for playgrounds. In Chicago, women's clubs had playground committees that lobbied the city council for funds. In Philadelphia, the drive for playgrounds, which began in 1893, involved the efforts of the Cultural Extension League, the City Parks Association, the Civic Club, and the College Settlement and later came to include a Public Playground Commission (Kadzielski, 1977). In New York City, the Outdoor Recreation League was formed in 1898 to advocate for playgrounds. In some instances, the movement by elites to promote play space became joined to existing efforts, led by neighborhood organizations, athletic clubs, and machine politicians (Hardy, 1982; Reiss,

1989). Motives varied even here. Residents of working-class neighborhoods fought to prevent open play fields from being developed by outsiders. A playground could also be a reward for votes, and its staff part of the patronage system.

Local governments proved receptive to playground advocates. Cavallo (1981, pp. 2, 45) notes that "between 1880 and 1920 municipal governments spent over one hundred million dollars for the construction and staffing" of almost 4,000 playgrounds. Some of that money came from general revenues, the rest from special taxes levied on individuals and businesses. In addition to financing municipal playgrounds, some based in larger city parks, a few urban school districts sponsored playground programs, and a moderate number of playgrounds were based at settlement houses, churches, and other community institutions. Settlement leaders persuaded and cajoled landowners to lend, lease, or sell their land to the settlement, even to tear down buildings to create play space.

A Playground Program

Playgrounds were supervised by city recreation staff, settlement staff, police matrons, older youth (including gang leaders, a practice renewed in the 1960s), and occasionally teachers. Although a handful of colleges and universities developed courses for budding playground supervisors, most playground workers received little or no preparation for this new work. Playground size and equipment varied widely. In addition to sandboxes, seesaws, and swings, there might or might not be some gymnastics equipment such as parallel bars and horizontal bars and one or more basketball hoops. A few playgrounds actually had bookracks and blackboards for outdoor lessons (American, 1898). Playgrounds based in city parks sometimes had access to field houses, which in addition to gyms and swimming pools, had libraries and recreation rooms for arts and industrial crafts.

The majority of playgrounds had at least a few organized activities, and some had defined daily schedules. A handful of playground directors tried, unsuccessfully, to take attendance. Activities for younger school-age children included quiet games, singing, dancing, sewing , story-reading, drama (e.g., reenacting stories) and supervised free play; for older children, competitive games (e.g., tug-of-war), folk dancing, and athletic activities. Older girls could participate in some sports, but typically they were discouraged from competitive team sports. Playgrounds sponsored play festivals and, space permitting, athletic festivals and competition. They were also a common site for community-wide cultural events. Although children had little input into the choice of activities, there were sporadic experiments in playground self-governance, allowing children to choose some activities and to set and enforce rules. (Hiram House settlement in Cleveland created a "playground city," a self-enclosed community that, in addition to offering recreation, was designed to provide training in "self-government.")

Children's (and Others') Responses to Organized Play

From children's perspective, supervised playgrounds held some attraction and had some drawbacks. Playgrounds provided a protected space for play, at least in their early years. For girls, playgrounds, like schools, provided a place of their own. Finkelstein (1987) argues that the school playground "liberated girls to invent new forms of play." Playgrounds were also frequently used by school-age girls caring for preschool siblings. The playground at the Henry Street Settlement in New York City hung baby hammocks, to relieve "little mothers" of their burden, and gave precedence at set times to girls "as young as six and seven" in charge of younger siblings (Wald, 1915). Although playgrounds sometimes got very crowded, the main drawback from children's (especially boys') perspective was adult intrusiveness. Nasaw (1985, p. 36) quotes an 11-year-old from Worcester, Massachusetts, who told an interviewer that "I can't go to the playgrounds now. They get on my nerves with so many men and women around telling you what to do." A prominent child advocate noted that playground leaders often viewed themselves as "stern drill masters, having children line up and stand up straight" (Patri, 1925, p. 14).

The great majority of children in working-class, immigrant neighborhoods either did not have access to, could not or chose not to use playgrounds. Mothers preferred that children play closer to home, and children themselves felt most comfortable on their home block. At a basic level, there were simply too few playgrounds and too many children. In 1912, on the Lower East Side of Manhattan, for instance, there were "fewer than 16 acres of play space for 237,222 children" (Reiss, 1989, p. 136). Other factors also prevented access. Playgrounds tended to be ethnically defined (and occasionally ethnically contested) space, limiting which children felt safe using them; and they were sometimes controlled by local gangs, leading to intimidation of other children. African American children were generally not permitted into playgrounds in neighborhoods where they might have used them. In 1920 they were permitted into only 3% of all urban playgrounds (p. 147). African American neighborhoods were the last to get their own playgrounds, and those playgrounds had the smallest budgets. (As late as the 1930s, "just two out of 225 new playgrounds" built in New York City were constructed in African American neighborhoods [Reiss, 1989, p. 148].)

Supervised playgrounds were, finally, at least somewhat controversial from the perspective of the larger adult community. As a 1906 editorial in the *Washington Post* (cited in Hardy & Ingham, 1983, p. 295) put it:

> What healthy child we should like to know, would give three straws for a so-called playground if there has to be someone there with authority to forbid this or limit that? Who wants to be watched, and lectured, and restrained, and pulled and hauled about, and slapped and straightened, and washed behind the ears, and tagged and registered, and kept account of and generally browbeaten from the time he or she enters the playground until an escape shall have been achieved?

THE FIRST AFTER-SCHOOL PROGRAMS

The effort to establish indoor programs for after-school play, recreation, and informal education shared many of the same roots as the effort to promote supervised playgrounds. At times in the early years, the two were intertwined. After-school programs, however, would offer a better defined, more fully institutionalized, and more versatile approach to working with children. Their own history begins in the later decades of the 19th century, with individual men and women intent on rescuing children from the physical and moral hazards posed by growing up in immigrant neighborhoods. These first sponsors sought to create protected spaces in storefronts or vacant rooms in churches or other buildings, where children might relax, play board games, read, and be provided as much instruction as they would tolerate. Most early programs had modest aims and were intended as a refuge and diversion from the streets; in fact, some called themselves "off the street clubs." Children could drop in when they wished, expectations were low, and "any youngster who refrained from tearing up the place was welcome" (MacLeod, 1983, p. 66).

A few early programs nonetheless had evangelical aims, wishing to "bring the gospel" to street children; and more than a few attempted to provide moral instruction or behavioral correction. A program at Chicago's Christopher House, organized in 1905 and supported by the First Presbyterian Church of Evanston, was originally intended to be "broadly religious" and "evangelistic" in character (Christopher House, 1914). Schneider (1992, p. 137) describes a program at the North Bennet Street Industrial School in Boston whose goal was to teach "habits of order, neatness, punctuality, honesty, gentler ways of speaking and acting." It served about 300 children after school and in the evenings, providing such classes as clay modeling, carpentry, cobbling, and cooking. Children were not to "get excited, chew gum, spit, swear, cheat or talk Italian."

After-school programs sometimes emerged organically. When a settlement house established itself in a particular neighborhood, children were usually the first to show up, mostly out of curiosity, and "boys' work" by necessity became the first concrete activity. Settlement residents nonetheless were not always sure what to do with boys. John Elliot, founder of the Hudson Guild Settlement in Manhattan, noted that "finding out just what a boys' club should do was for a good many years a matter of serious perplexity" (Elliot, 1921, p. 17). In a few cases, after-school programs were initiated in a desire to continue serving graduates of settlement kindergartens, with groups actually called kindergarten graduates' clubs. Settlement residents' outreach efforts also brought children into the settlement (NUS Archives, Box 13, Folder 10).

A typical developmental pattern for most early programs involved a gradual, room by room, physical expansion, and a corresponding addition of activities, as more boys showed up and as goals became more ambitious. In 1876, for example, businessman Edward Harriman opened up a boys' club, with an initial membership of seven, in a building on Tompkins Square in Manhattan. Its goal was to provide a place where boys could enjoy themselves, "protected from the mischievous pleasures of the street" (Zane, 1990, p. 5). Within a decade, the program had taken over more space and had playrooms, reading rooms, and a "makeshift" gymnasium with parallel bars, a horse and some dumbbells. By the late 1890s, a variety of organized activities were offered, including a natural history club; fife, drum, and bugle corps; singing class, writing and bookkeeping classes, and wrestling. By 1900 the Tompkins Square Boys' Club had 400 regular members between 6 and 18 years of age, and plans were under way to build a large new building. Although still staffed largely by middle-class volunteers, the program now had a paid superintendent.

Starting around 1900, after-school provision was spurred by a new social movement, called boys' work. ("Girls' work" was soon to be added, but almost as a kind of afterthought.) This movement, fueled by anxiety about the decline of masculinity in American society and worry about unsupervised and undersocialized working-class boys, had the support and involvement of politicians and business and civic leaders. Leaders organized meetings and conferences and published a journal (early on called *Work With Boys* and later, *Boys' Workers Roundtable*). Adherents believed they were fulfilling an urgent public mission. One noted that "there has been a sudden, spectacular awakening of the public conscience to the need for boys' work" (Butcher, 1920, p. 20); another, that "the boys' worker should be a fighter, a crusader, one who wears his heart on his sleeve and who proclaims the gospel of boyhood so that the public can hear and act" ("Boys' Work," 1923, p. 24). The rhetoric of the movement had a slightly mystical tone; for instance, adherents sometimes called what they did *boy craft*, and occasionally even used the term *boyology* ("Editorial," 1918, p. 39).

As the after-school field was elaborated during the first 2 decades of the 20th century, it took on the decentralized character that would define it throughout the century. While boys' and girls' work quickly became identifiable as a form of social practice, the after-school field would not develop as one formal system of services. Different kinds of agencies sponsored after-school programs, and each set its own policies and priorities and organized its offerings somewhat differently. The role and importance of specific providers varied from city to city. Leadership within the field was diffuse, informal, and largely self-appointed. After-school programs were also funded almost exclusively by private sources.

Settlements and boys' clubs were the two largest sponsors, although the term *boys' club* was used in a generic way by many agencies. Churches appear to have begun sponsoring after-school programs by the turn of the century. By 1921, some 75 churches in Chicago were providing these programs. Other religiously based organizations also provided programs, as did organizations serving specific ethnic groups. For instance, the Educational Alliance in New York City, which served Jewish immigrants, had "after-school religious classes, domestic science classes for girls, clubs and gym work," and debate and discussion clubs (Goodman, 1979, p. 37).

YMCAs played a very small role in the emerging after-school field. Although they began doing a small amount of boys' work as early as the 1870s, such work, which included religious instruction, was seen primarily as readying boys for membership when they were older. (YMCAs did not begin admitting boys under 12 years of age as members until 1930.) YMCAs also saw their mission as serving the middle class, not the working class, against whom they positioned themselves on economic and labor issues (Pence, 1939). Some of the resistance to serving poor children grew from the fact that members paid to use YMCA facilities and might be unwilling to do so if confronted by socially undesirable children or youth (Zald & Denton, 1963).

Municipal parks and recreation departments sponsored a modest amount of programming, as did schools, although both were more active in the summer. School authorities were ambivalent about after-school programs in part because of reluctance to take on a social welfare role, in part because of the loss of complete adult control inherent in them. Nonetheless, Progressive leaders urged them to take on a broader role. As one noted, "The opportunity is there, the power is there, the buildings are there" (Simkhovitch, 1904, p. 411). Between 1900 and 1920, some school-based after-school programming was provided in the context of a broader movement to transform schools into "social centers." This programming created was sometimes little more than a supervised school playground, but occasionally came to include classes and clubs. Dewey (1915) described the example of PS 26 in a low-income African American neighborhood in Indianapolis, which purchased land and buildings near the school and turned them into a base for a variety of after-school activities, with club rooms, classes, and workshops and with tutoring of younger children by older ones. Dewey notes the girls' classes and clubs as a particularly important feature of this program; they provided an unusual opportunity for girls to talk with teachers and one another about individual problems and worries.

As more sponsors entered the after-school field, different institutions sought to differentiate themselves, and in fact each had strengths and limitations. Boys' clubs strengthened their visibility and identity by creating a national confederation. In 1905 the superintendents of about 50 local clubs had met in Boston to form a national organization, to be called the Boys' Clubs of America, with Jacob Riis as the first president. (The meeting had originally been called to consider, and reject, an offer from the national YMCA to merge boys' clubs into the YMCA movement.) By the late 1910s, there were 120 boys' clubs in the national Boys' Club Federation, in 87 cities. Each was largely responsible for raising its own budget, planning its program and governing itself. Boys' clubs nonetheless evolved a common approach to after-school work, characterized by informality; an "open door" policy (i.e., a willingness to serve any and all children in a community, with an emphasis on reaching out to and serving the hard to reach); and, as boys got older, a focus on leadership development. Although many local clubs began serving girls soon after they opened, there was general agreement that boys' clubs could not have girls in "common membership" with boys. Rather, they had to have their own separate programs.

By around 1910 the concept of the "mass club" emerged. Many boys' clubs began campaigns to raise money for their own buildings, which usually meant space for a gym, industrial arts rooms, studios, a library, a kitchen, and occasionally an auditorium or swimming pool or both. These new buildings greatly enlarged the reach of boys' clubs, which began serving as many as 200 to 300 or more children a day, but also greatly increased operating expenses, making fund-raising a growing part of the role of superintendents and boards.

Settlements viewed themselves as more selective than boys' clubs in how many and whom they served, on the grounds that "it is better to know a few children well than many superficially" (Woods & Kennedy, 1922/1970, p. 73). They served well under 100 children daily, typically somewhere between 30 and 60. Philosophically, settlements were more attuned than boys' clubs to such "feminine ideals [as] social cooperation, empathy, [and] loyalty" (Cavallo, 1981, p. 111). Practically speaking, settlements usually had more restricted space than did boys' clubs. They were designed along the lines of more a home than an institution, and their club meetings might take place in dining rooms, library rooms, parlors, and even residents' bedrooms. Because of space limitations, settlements tended to have less physically expansive and active offerings than did boys' clubs and were in some ways better suited to, and more comfortable, serving girls than boys. The necessity of smaller groups had some benefits, allowing club leaders to come to know children better—their worries and concerns as well as their hopes and aspirations.

Schools' great strength was their facilities, and in some cities they opened these for programs run by other community agencies that lacked space. Dillick (1953) estimates that about a quarter of school-based after-school programs in the 1920s were privately organized and run, with settlements the most common partner. Like schools, municipal parks and recreation departments sponsored a modest amount of programming, although they were more active in the summer, and sometimes provided facilities for programs run by settlements or boys' clubs. They also served as an occasional funder of after-school or summer programs. For example, in the early 1920s, the city recreation department in Indianapolis worked with boys' clubs to run summer programs, using boys' club facilities.

RATIONALES AND GOALS

As the after-school field grew between 1900 and 1920, it proved difficult to keep purposes simple and expectations modest. One reason was simple accretion. Each restatement of goals echoed existing ones and led to the addition of new language. In addition, there was a desire to secure a place in the emerging human service system. Throughout this period, institutional roles and boundaries were still in flux. Schools flirted with a broad role in children's lives (through visiting teachers, social centers, and summer programs), as did various family agencies, ethnic organizations, and even local juvenile courts. After-school providers wanted to be taken seriously. This meant claiming some responsibility for a broad array of opportunities and experiences that children were thought to need, traits to be nurtured or inculcated, negative influences to be countered, and problems to be prevented. As early as 1914, a boys' club director noted that "in the evolution of boys' club work the idea of mere play is fast losing ground" ("Tieing Activities," 1914, p. 223). Yet providers also wanted to attend to children's preferences, if for no other reason than that after-school programs were voluntary.

In the context of such tensions, most after-school programs came to share a set of (slightly contradictory) aims: to protect children and to control their activities, to provide order and a safe space in which to be slightly disorderly, to socialize children and to enrich their lives, to Americanize children and to support their pride in "home" cultures, to reinforce the work of schools and to counter their damaging effects on children, and to nurture children's individuality and to help them to adjust to societal demands. Additionally, many sponsors sought a mediating or bridging role, between the more intimate institutions or settings in children's lives, such as family, ethnic group, and neighborhood, and more distant or national ones, such as schools, police, and the juvenile courts.

Although the children's play movement gradually lost steam between 1910 and 1920, the majority of after-school providers remained committed to providing children opportunity for play. There was, nonetheless, a growing tendency to rationalize this goal in instrumental terms, such as fostering creativity and self-expression, strengthening group skills (e.g., cooperation, turn-taking, and setting and following rules), and even building character. Play was sometimes also seen as the hook to draw children in to programs. John Witter, an early superintendent of the Chicago Boys' Clubs told a reporter that "school is not the most important matter in a boy's life usually; on the other hand, play is. . . . our object is to take advantage of it" (CBC Archives, Box 1, Folder 1).

The emphasis on care and protection among after-school programs derived from concern about the pressures resulting from maternal employment. A Chicago Boys Club report described many working-class children as "half-naked, under-sized, uncared for" (CBC Archives, Box 1, Folder 1). Henry Street Settlement director Lillian Wald (1915, pp. 111, 133) noted that some children whose mothers worked all day were "locked out during their absence [and were] expected to shift for themselves," with nowhere to go and no money for meals. More generally, she saw the settlement's after-school programs as protecting children "from premature burdens, to prolong their childhood." Working-class girls were seen to need particular attention and support in the years preceding adolescence. A study of preadolescent girls by the National Federation of Settlements noted, among other findings, the sexual risks associated with family boarders and the enormous stress many girls experienced in their (often complete) responsibility for the care of younger siblings (NUS Archives, Box 44, Folder 4).

After-school providers liked to see their work as about "the making rather than the remaking of lives" (Marshall, 1912, p. 315). They nonetheless sometimes linked their work to the amelioration of problems, especially crime and delinquency. They quoted police officials, who noted that "crime increased nearly 50 percent in poor city wards at the end of the school day" (Cavallo, 1981, p. 86) and they argued that after-school programs were the most effective means of reducing those figures. Prevention of crime was argued to have economic as well as social benefits. Proponents compared the small cost of serving children in after-school programs to the much higher cost of holding young criminals in jail. A Children's Aid Society proposal for a new boys' club on Manhattan's West Side argued that the "underprivileged boy is an economic problem" and that "every dollar spent upon boys' work is an insurance policy in favor of the future" (BWR2.3, 1922, p. 31).

Gender-specific goals were conventional yet reflected the shift in gender ideals just beginning to occur in American society. After-school leaders, believing that too many boys were moving into adolescence without a sense of their vocational talents and unequipped for a particular vocation, argued that after-school programs had a responsibility to meet this need ("A Visit," 1923, p. 20). They wished to teach boys to "think with their hands as well as their heads" (Marshall, 1912, p. 317). As noted earlier, after-school programs were part of a movement to renew a sense of masculinity in boys, tinged with moral uprightness, a cooperative spirit, and compassion (for those who were weaker than oneself). The widely circulated "Message to the Boys of America" from Theodore Roosevelt, an active proponent of boys' work, described the ideal boy: He "must not be a coward or a weakling, a bully or a shirk or a prig. He must work and play hard. He must be clean-minded and clean-lived, and be able to hold his own under all circumstances and against all comers" (Roosevelt, 1920). In a typical refrain, the boys' work department at Northwestern University Settlement described its emphases for the 1919–1920 program year as "clean speech, clean sports and clean habits" (NUS Archives, Box 13, Folder 10).

For girls, programs typically focused on bringing out artistic abilities and on preparation for domestic responsibilities and family life. In girls' sports, the focus was on grace, individual skill, and learning to be appropriately noncompetitive. After-school providers nonetheless supported girls' wish to participate in intellectually and physically demanding and competitive activity, such as debate and team sports. More generally, girls' work staff recognized that they were creating social space in which girls could become more independent.

The large majority of children served by after-school programs in the early decades came from immigrant families. As such, "Americanization" was a major objective. A 1908 Chicago Boys' Club report noted a total membership of "1741 street boys, 30 percent of whom are Italians, another 30 percent are Jews, about 15 percent are Negroes . . . while only about 3 percent are Americans" (CBC Archives, Box 1, Folder 1). The writer goes on to ask, "Is not this a foreign missionary work?" Americanization would occur partly through simple contact with American staff. A speaker at the 15th Annual Boys' Club Federation Conference told his audience that the best way "to impart Americanism to children of alien birth or parentage is to put an American heart up against their hearts" ("Midwest Division," 1921, p. 7). It would occur partly through teaching middle-class mores and practices; for instance, teaching little girls to make beds "in the American manner" (Crocker, 1992, p. 128). The goal here was both to change the children's own values and behavior and to use children to change the values and behavior of their parents, as new practices were brought home. And Americanization would occur partly through a process of deracination. As one writer noted, the boys' club is "a crucible in which various races are melted down into Americans" ("Meeting," 1912, p. 90).

After-school programs were not completely insensitive to children's home cultures. Staff tried to tread a fine line, aware of the derision that immigrant children experienced at the hands of teachers, police, and other adults (Berrol, 1995). Some after-school leaders were ambivalent about particular American values, such as unbridled acquisitiveness. Some were ambivalent about the role asked of them by the business leaders who supported after-school programs, in particular the inculcation of such habits as "regularity, punctuality . . . obedience, and self-control" (p. 31). Yet after-school sponsors were firm in the belief that it was in children's best interest to learn to conduct themselves like Americans and value American ideals.

In general, after-school providers viewed the specific activities they sponsored, the relationships children developed with staff, and the values inherent in their settings, as combining to provide what Wald (1915) described as "incidental education" and Bellamy (1912) as "teaching by indirection." Adults had a clear role in guiding and shaping children's experience, but it was a hidden one. Thus children would do useful things in a fun way. More broadly, after-school work was seen as a "support" for "lives unfolding" (GH Archives, Box 3, Folder 6). Children were seen to need time for talk about wishes and worries, help with personal problems, and linkage to resources outside a program. Club leaders were asked to keep an eye on children, looking for signs of problems and letting head workers know of anything they saw or heard. Speaking of her participation at Hull House as a child, Dorothy Sigel noted that "you didn't realize you were being observed or that someone was really caring about you personally. There must have been, in all the residents' duties, sort of an unspoken assignment, each of them choosing a few [children] that they were following up on" (quoted in Silberman, 1990, p. 54).

Not Family and Not School

After-school programs defined their role in part by distinguishing themselves from other child development institutions, particularly home and school. In their rhetoric they usually tried to suggest a complementary role, positioning themselves, for example, as "a supplement to the home" (GH Archives, Box 3, Folder 3). Graham Taylor, founder of Chicago Commons, wrote that every room at the settlement was "really an addition to every home in the neighborhood. The family without a nursery or play space at home can find both here for the children" (Chicago Commons, 1909, p. 2). At the same time, while proclaiming a commitment to supporting the family, after-school sponsors commonly cited family inadequacy as a rationale for their work (see, e.g., Marshall, 1912). They viewed themselves as providing attention to children whose parents neglected them (because of work demands), and as offering structure for children whose parents could or would not control their children. Lillian Wald (1915, p. 93) wrote that "the extreme difficulty of maintaining orderly home life in the tenement makes it important to supplement the home training, or to supply what it can never give." Immigrant parents were perceived to be incapable not just of controlling their children and meeting their developmental needs, but also of preparing them for the demands of a complex, industrial society. By holding on to "separatist religious traditions, alien languages and dialects," they blocked their children's (and thus society's) progress (Lasch, 1977, p. 7).

With respect to the schools, after-school sponsors were decidedly ambivalent. After-school programs would never "usurp the place of school," but at the same time provided "opportunity for experimentation [with educational methods] not possible in a rigid system" (Wald, 1915, p. 106). Such experimentation in turn might influence schools' own methods. Settlement leaders Woods and Kennedy (1922/1970, p. 414) noted that " a real danger is found in the confusion sometimes caused by lack of harmony between the teaching in public schools and in settlements." In a few cases, for example that of the Educational Alliance, which served Jewish immigrant children, after-school programs took it upon themselves to help prepare children for the demands of school (Goodman, 1979).

To an extent, Progressive educational thought, with its emphasis on following children's interests, practical learning experiences, plentiful but carefully orchestrated play, and the group as social and learning unit, provided a conceptual link to after-school work. Dewey (1915, pp. 31, 71, 85) argued for the importance of "games, handwork and dramatizations" in education and for regular field trips to observe the real world. He also emphasized the importance of nonschool institutions to children's learning. After-school sponsors, particularly settlements, interacted with Progressive educators in meetings and sometimes adopted Progressive education rhetoric. Karger (1987, p. 18) notes that "Dewey's principle of learning by doing became the second commandment" of the Unity House settlement in Minneapolis.

Yet as after-school staff learned of children's school experiences from parents, from children themselves, and through their own work with schools, they found a discouraging picture. Of a group of 124 children who around 1911 or 1912 were surveyed at Chicago Commons, 98 were behind a grade or more in school. School climate was mechanical and stifling, classroom activity mostly rote recitation and drill. Children, in classes of up to 50 or more children, "sat at desks bolted to the floor, obliged to keep still and silent" (Macleod, 1998, pp. 81, 88). In most schools, children were forced to "take on the stiffness and deadness of age" (Patri, 1925, p. 14). After-school proponents cited the work of child psychologists who argued that schooling damaged children's confidence and mental health. The inordinate quantity of homework assigned to children ate into time for enrichment, play, and rest (Gill & Schlossman, 1996).

After-school programs, by comparison, were settings in which children might come to feel valued and successful and be recognized for who they were. A settlement-based group leader noted in his plans for the year that "I should like to make the boys feel that everything they do and say does make some difference" (CC Archives, Box 6, Folder 1). Older children were free, and in fact encouraged, to assume responsibility for running activities. Learning in after-school programs was hands-on, flexible, creative, and focused on the whole child. In some respects, play, even in its organized form, was perceived as the antithesis of schooling. Since schools were "too busy to give much time to play," after-school programs would provide that function (Chew, 1913, p. 333).

In general, proponents argued that after-school programs would fill in whatever gaps appeared in children's lives at particular moments because of strains on family or school. During World War I, for instance, after-school programs positioned themselves to meet the special war-related problems of children, especially a purported rise in delinquency attributed to parental neglect. (Data from juvenile court statistics in some cities actually suggested a decline in delinquency during the war years; "Editorial," 1918, p. 12.) A 1917 report from one settlement noted that "the war spirit, irregularity of school work, and reduced family resources make the work with boys more necessary than ever" (CC/NB Archives, Box 1, Folder 10). After World War I, providers noted again that many working-class families were in stress and upheaval, affecting their children's behavior and making the providers' work crucial to children. Some of this rhetoric was necessary to secure the continued support of financial backers feeling donor fatigue. But it was also rooted in a belief that after-school programs had a unique role in children's lives.

STAFFING AND STAFF TRAINING

Most after-school programs relied heavily on part-time workers, and on middle- and upper-class volunteers to lead clubs and classes, and might have

5 or 10 volunteers for every paid staff member. Men and women skilled in specific trades or crafts might receive some payment for teaching classes or might donate a few hours a week. For many volunteers in those early years, motivated by religious or civic feeling, after-school work was a calling. For college students who worked as club leaders it was a form of service, field-work, or practicum. After-school work was sometimes simply a way station for young adults not sure where they were heading professionally. Programs also used former participants and "graduates" as staff.

Training opportunities were scarce. There were a handful of practical workshops at conferences and meetings, but these were mostly for program directors. There were occasional college courses for those interested in boys' and girls' work. For example, in 1918–1919, Columbia University had two courses titled "Boys' Clubs Outside of School" and "Boys' and Girls' Clubs as Part of the School Program." Northwestern University had one or more courses for students wishing to pursue boys' and girls' work. Most after-school staff simply brought to the job their own beliefs and typically limited knowledge of immigrant, working-class children.

Although program directors envisioned a one-way socialization process, in which club leaders' middle-class character and perspective influenced those of children (Carson, 1990), the actual process was more mutual. Some staff were genuinely open and grew enormously as they came to know the chil-dren they worked with; others changed little. Some club leaders liked and respected the children they worked with and others simply did not. The lat-ter tended to use their reports to complain of children's laziness, unruliness, impulsivity, inability to attend, or lack of truthfulness. Most staff who lasted any length of time came to recognize that they had to share control and re-press any instincts to lecture and indoctrinate, if they wanted children to continue coming to a program.

Monthly and annual reports by program directors noted regular wor-ries and struggles with staffing issues, particularly the limitations imposed by part-time staff, difficulty finding specialists, and high rates of turnover. In 1916 the boys' work director at Chicago Commons wrote in a report that some of his group leaders lacked initiative and some the ability to establish and maintain discipline. A October 1920 boys' department report at the Northwestern University Settlement noted that "the handicap of [club] lead-ership is already apparent [early in the program year] and is a problem." During much of the 1920–1921 year, club work at Northwestern University Settlement was "almost at a standstill" because of staff turnover and absence (NUS Archives, Box 13, Folder 10). Describing settlements' heavy reliance on (often young) volunteers to lead club activities, Woods and Kennedy (1922/ 1970, p. 436) noted that it could place "a heavy burden on the administra-tors of the settlement."

ORGANIZATION, ACTIVITIES, AND DAILY ROUTINES

Most after-school programs operated 5 or 6 days a week and were open in the evenings as well as immediately after school. Saturday activities were common, and there were occasional special programs on Sunday. A majority of programs operated throughout the year, although the venue typically shifted to out of doors in May or June, and schedules were different. Participation was either free or almost so, although there was occasionally a charge for materials.

Group Structure. The bulk of activity in after-school programs was organized in classes and clubs. Yet there was also time and opportunity for informal activity, for example, a group of girls sitting in a room sewing and listening to a settlement resident reading a book (Jackson, 2000) or children hanging out in a game room. Classes and clubs might have anywhere from 4 or 5 to as many as 30 children. Most were scheduled once or twice a week and might continue from 10 to 12 weeks to as much as 10 months. Although the two terms were sometimes used interchangeably, there were characteristic differences. Classes focused on a particular skill or activity, and children typically enrolled as individuals. Clubs were more socially oriented and their composition was determined by age, friendship, interests, and occasionally ethnicity or nationality. Clubs elected officers (i.e., a president and secretary), chose their own name, set their own rules, and chose (or had a hand in choosing) the projects and activities they engaged in.

Groups of children not infrequently asked to be allowed to create their own clubs and sometimes arrived at a program as a defined group. Wary of reproducing gangs, many programs tried to break up these natural groupings. In a 1915 report a boys' work leader at Chicago Commons describes his struggle with a group of boys who wanted to do everything together "as a bunch." He tried to divide them up, but they would not have it. Eventually, staff in most programs came to see that at some level the majority of children were members of gangs, and that "not all gangs were bad" (Woods & Kennedy, 1922/1970). In other words, children's loyalty to one another and desire to belong could be viewed as a strength. The gang as a natural social group could be used and directed by adults ("Boys' Work," 1923).

A Range of Activities. Collectively, the range of activities offered by after-school programs was enormous, though any one program would offer only a handful of choices at a particular point in time. On a typical day there might be three to five separate clubs or classes meeting. For girls, choices included sewing, knitting, dressmaking, doll making, embroidery, etiquette, elocution, housekeeping ("domestic science"), little mothers' clubs, even "quiet" clubs for "frail" girls. Activities for boys included metalwork and woodwork; cobbling; radio signaling and radio repair; wireless telegraph, electricity, and camera work; printing; and barbering. Activities for either or both boys and girls included the area of debate, parliamentary law, health and hygiene, cooking, stenography, drawing, poster making, photography, home culture, bookbinding, ceramics, toy making, basket making, hammock making, drama, dance (usually folk dancing), choral singing, band, playing instruments (e.g., mandolin or guitar), and perhaps taking music lessons.

Programs had Scout troops, and some had hiking or explorers clubs, which took weekend day trips around and out of the city. Children visited museums, parks, the seashore, newspaper-printing plants, factories, and local universities. Many programs served meals or milk and snacks, a smaller number provided health and dental checkups, and a few had Saturday baths for children. Many programs had libraries, and some had part-time librarians. (In keeping with other settlement-based service innovations, the settlement library acted as a spur and model for the growth of public libraries.) Programs with adequate space set some aside for reading activities, including book discussions, and study. As early as 1907, for instance, New York City's Henry Street Settlement provided study rooms, where children could do homework and receive assistance from residents and volunteers. On Fridays, time was set aside for book selection and reading. In 1909 Chicago Commons started a "study hour" in which children "of the 6th, 7th and 8th grades can bring their homework and study in a quiet place" (Chicago Commons Newsletter, 1910, p. 3).

Some programs had newsletters that were written and produced by participating children. Articles covered a range of topics, from descriptions of activities and trips, to poetry, announcements, and social commentary. For example, the September 7, 1920, issue of *US Boys*, the Northwestern University Settlement newsletter, included a commentary on the start of the new school year: "The parochial schools opened last week and public schools today, and most of us have returned—to tell the teachers how much we love them. Words fail to express our feelings. We shall just have to make the most of it and get the most out of it. Anyhow, there are the clubs and classes and gym that we can enjoy even while we go to school."

Drama was a common activity in after-school programs in the early decades, especially in settlements. There was usually a production in some stage of development. Drama clubs reenacted stories, staged fairy tales, wrote and staged their own plays, and did dramatic readings of contemporary and classic plays. Drama was seen to provide a range of functions for children, from cultural enrichment and literacy development, to escape from the drab realities of working class life, to opportunity for children to work out fears. It also linked the after-school program to parents and other community members, who came to watch and occasionally helped with productions.

Settlements and other community centers (but usually not boys' clubs) offered distinct programming for younger children, based on the kindergarten, with its structure of games, music, artwork, and social, imaginative, and dramatic play. Special programs for younger children included story reading, "fairy play," and doll clubs. Local Child Study Associations occasionally also worked with after-school sponsors to create "play schools" for younger children. (The play school concept originated with Caroline Pratt, who developed it at Hartley House, a New York City settlement, and later started her own private school [Beatty, 1995].)

Classes in after-school programs combined a belief in the dignity of craftwork and a belief in the value of planning and carrying through "projects." Craftwork was meant to tap children's artistic spirits and to serve as a counterpoint to the loss of dignity and meaning in factory work. Children designed and built complete "products"—bookracks, brooms, chests, chairs, kitchen utensils, baskets, birdhouses. Industrial crafts, sometimes called manual training, had vocational aims as well. It was intended to familiarize boys with the basic concepts of specific trades, introduce them to a variety of tools, teach specific skills such as "precision and patience," and not least give boys useful vocational skills (CC Archives, Box 6, Folder 1). A report on one month's activity for a radio club noted that "instruction was given in the theory of the apparatus; code practice and construction of simple sets, and work continued on the house receiving station" (NUS Archives, Box 13, Folder 11). A description of the activities of a printing class in the Somerville, Massachusetts, Boys' Club captures the seriousness of some classes: "There are six boys in this class striving their best to learn how to set up a job, how to throw back type, and how to feed a press correctly" ("Somerville," 1915, p. 57). The author also reported the club to be self-supporting, soliciting orders from the public.

The Game Room: Important and Problematic. After-school programs typically had one or more game rooms, where children dropped in to play board games, read magazines, talk, and hang out. A 1915 report by a boys' work leader at Chicago Commons notes, "In the game room I shun the noisy games, and have the boys play checkers or dominoes, question and answer games and picture puzzles" (CC Archives, Box 6, Folder 1). Game rooms tended to be gender segregated (and sometimes racially segregated), and girls' work staff often had to fight for a game room, even though "the girls like to play games just as well as the boys do" (Abraham Lincoln Center, 1916, p. 38).

The game room typically was the first stop for children newly enrolled in a program, and it could get very crowded. At the Northwestern University Settlement, some 450 boys used the game room during one typical month in 1920, many coming more or less regularly (NUS Archives, Box 13, Folder

10). A 1918 visitor to the game room for "juniors," at a new boys' club on Avenue A and 10th Street in Manhattan, noted that "upward of two hundred tykes, with very little supervision, were playing a variety of table games, mostly caroms" (Editorial, 1918, p. 9). Space was occasionally set aside for more active play. A few local Chicago Boys' Club branches, for instance, had rough-and-tumble rooms, where boys were free to wrestle, punch a heavy bag, and make as much noise as they wished. Boys were sent to this room from activity rooms when their behavior became too wild, "to step over and rough it for a while in the room where roughing is good" ("Other Workers' Plans," 1918, p. 27).

Program reports suggest that game rooms were a source of stress for staff, who debated what purpose they should serve, how to limit the number of children at any one time, what the rules should be, what to do when children broke rules, and how to keep children from becoming bored by the limited choice of activities and materials. One boys' club director noted with frustration that "games were practically useless because of missing pieces, lost, strayed or stolen" (Chew, 1913, p. 336). Again the room leader complained to Lea Taylor, head resident at Chicago Commons, that the game room was serving more as a "dumping ground for surplus boys" than as a "feeding ground for our various clubs" (CC Archives, Box 6, Folder 1). Issues of control also arose. At one point, the girls participating in the Northwestern University Settlement asked for the restoration of noisy and more active games in the game room (apparently successfully).

Athletics as a Lure. Opportunity to use the gym and related facilities was the main attraction of after-school programs for many boys, although they sometimes discovered other activities once they enrolled. Most boys' clubs and a few settlements had gyms, some boys'clubs and settlements had playgrounds, and both might also have rooms or other space for boxing, wrestling, and free weights. The gym was typically the center of gravity in boys' clubs, and basketball a central activity. Other common sports included indoor baseball, boxing, wrestling, gymnastics, and track (where indoor tracks were available above the gym).

Program staff viewed with ambivalence time spent in the gym. The director of physical education at the Henry Street Settlement in New York City called the gym a "manhood factory" (Carson, 1990, p. 174). Yet staff struggled with children, boys especially, to turn athletics to character-building ends. Woods and Kennedy (1922/1970, p. 79) noted that the goal of athletics had to be to help the boy learn "to curb his impulses, control his appetites, respond to orders quickly, accurately, thoroughly." Boys mostly wanted to curb adult interference in their games and control their own time in the gym. For girls, the question was how competitive athletics should be. There was some room and support for girls to express athleticism. For instance, Chicago Commons had a girls' basketball team as early as 1910. Yet Carson (1990, p. 175) cites the consensus opinion at a 1924 meeting of girls' leaders at United Neighborhood Houses in New York City, that girls' athletics should not focus on competition but on "the development of general physique."

Lack of a gym, and lack of space generally, at times placed constraints on physical activity and was one of the most frequent complaints in annual reports (see, e.g., NUS Archives, Box 13, Folder 10; "Midwest Division," 1921, p. 25). The 1914 Annual Report of Christopher House noted, for example, "We now have, besides a room in the basement, only a small room, transformed for that purpose from an old frame stable, which is totally inadequate" (Christopher House, 1914, p. 5). Space limitations also heightened struggles over control of behavior, especially in settlements. Commenting on boys' "superabundant energy," Woods and Kennedy (1922/1970, p. 79) complained about their a tendency to "break into something which approaches anarchy."

PATTERNS OF PARTICIPATION AND OVERALL COVERAGE

Children used after-school programs in different ways. Maybe a quarter of participants came regularly, 3 or or more days a week. For some of these children, the after-school program, its staff, and sponsoring agency were literally a second family. Most children used after-school programs as one more resource to explore and exploit, depending on the activity on a particular day; on the weather; on what else was happening in school, on the playgrounds, or in the streets; and on work patterns. Overall attendance rates, recorded through sign-in sheets (or at boys' clubs sometimes by turnstiles), fluctuated by season, by day of the week, and for no apparent reason. Turnover in participants during the course of a particular session varied widely. Program reports suggest that turnover of 25% to 50% was common in the vocationally oriented classes of after-school programs and was somewhat lower in most clubs (NUS Archives, Box 13, Folders 10 & 11; "A Visit," 1923, p. 21).

It appears that in the early decades of the century, after-school programs reached about 5% to (at most) 10% of school-age children in their neighborhoods, on a more or less regular basis. A 1920–1921 Chicago survey reported that, altogether, the boys' work agencies of the city—"clubs, settlements, scouts, YMCAs, community centers, church clubs, recreation centers"—were reaching 1/12 the population of "underprivileged" boys, who themselves constituted 2/3 of all boys in the city (reported in "Midwest Division," 1921, p. 24). In the late 1910s and early 1920s, Chicago Commons reported annual enrollments (in at least one club or class) of between 300 and 500 boys, and a similar number of girls. This constituted close to 10% of children in the immediate neighborhood.

Part of the reason for the modest coverage was the population density of many immigrant neighborhoods. The blocks surrounding an after-school program might be home to between 3,000 and 10,000 children, and occasionally more than that (Philpott, 1978). One annual report of the period noted, "Last winter the demand for club privileges was so much greater than we could supply that we had to station a guard at the gate to keep out the boys who tried to force their way in" (CC Archives, Box 6, Folder 1). At the same time, programs tended to recruit primarily from the immediate neighborhood, prompting sponsors to use various strategies to extend their reach. Boys' clubs, for instance, developed branch clubs and outposts, sometimes no more than a storefront with a few rooms. Settlements negotiated with schools to use their facilities, with the settlement supplying and paying the staff.

One group that after-school programs hardly reached was African American children. Practices nonetheless varied from city to city, and sponsor to sponsor. New York agencies, for example, were somewhat open to integration, Chicago agencies much less so. Boys' clubs were more likely to be integrated than settlements. (The leadership of the boys' club movement nonetheless included few African Americans.) Settlement houses feared that racial integration would lead White ethnic families to pull children from integrated programs, and while they would not usually turn African American children away, they did nothing to encourage their participation (Philpott, 1978). Christamore House in Indianapolis actually "moved—rather than desegregate its facilities—when the surrounding neighborhood became predominantly black" (Borris, 1992, p. 219).

Settlement leaders tried to justify their actions by making token efforts to support the development of African American settlements. For instance, the Henry Street Settlement in New York City helped start and supported the Stillman House for Colored People on West 60th Street. As Philpott (1978, p. 314) notes, "Whites committed just enough resources to Black Belt settlements to ensure a 'margin of safety' in neighborhood relations." African American community leaders also established their own settlements. For example, Fannie Emanuel established Emanuel House on Chicago's South Side in 1908. The settlement offered "youth clubs, classes in domestic science and manual training," and other services (Philpott, 1978, p. 319). Few African American settlements survived very long, being both underfinanced and understaffed. Emanuel House survived for only 5 years. Old-line African American churches, such as Chicago's Olivet Baptist Church, provided a small amount of programming, but such programming rarely reached the poorest children (Spear, 1967). The network of more than 100 African American

YMCAs that emerged in the first decades of the century also provided a modest amount of after-school programming, but it too did not reach the most disadvantaged urban children.

CONCLUSION

In their formative years, after-school programs came to reflect many of the strengths, tensions, and limitations that would define them throughout the century. In one sense, they were part of a broader effort, reflected in the schools and the juvenile courts, to institutionalize and domesticate working-class childhood, and boyhood in particular. The effect, if not the goal, of this effort was to bring a wider range of children's behavior and activity under the influence of nonfamilial adults. At the same time, after-school programs emerged as one of the few new children's institutions that struggled to view working-class children in a positive light and that mostly avoided pathologizing them. The police, juvenile courts, and school authorities recognized this, and sometimes turned to after-school programs for help with children who were in legal trouble or were truant. They asked after-school staff to informally monitor and supervise children, to talk to parents, and to help with personal problems. In this capacity, after-school programs walked a fine line. Schneider (1992, p. 6) argues that in collaborating with public authorities, community agencies such as settlements blurred "the line between private and public and voluntary and coercive institutions." Yet in numerous instances they provided a means to reduce the consequences of problems.

A handful of social historians have been critical of after-school programs' role in undermining immigrant children's street play and street life (see, e.g., Goodman, 1979). Just as time and opportunity for play emerged for children, it was corralled by adults: "Playmasters . . . 'discovered' children's play, revealed its educational possibilities, tried to confine it to school yards, parks and recreation facilities" (Finkelstein, 1987, p. 26). Such criticism was present from the outset. A. H. Fromerson, an editor of the *Jewish Daily Forward*, wrote, "The settlements have conspired with the big city to rob the boy of his inalienable right to play: the city by means of ordinances and prohibitions; the settlement by means of sit-up-straight-and-be-good social rooms, literature clubs, civic clubs, basket-weaving and scroll iron works" (Fromerson, 1904, p. 120).

Holding aside the fact that after-school programs barely made a dent in immigrant children's street play, sponsors were sensitive to criticism that they were constraining children's play. In discussing the attraction of the streets to children, Thomas Chew, a boys' club director, wrote that "there is a democracy about the street that no [supervised] playground, no club, can equal"

(Chew, 1911, p. 6). Although reports by after-school staff suggest that they sometimes struggled with children's silliness, foolishness, and resistance to adult wishes and priorities, it also appears that staff made a serious effort to reconcile themselves to behavior that they did not always understand. Children themselves not only wanted freedom, but also sought support, opportunities for engagement, and a place to be protected from life's demands. Moreover, the streets provided a mixed blessing: safety and comfort on the one hand—children were often surrounded by familiar adults—and genuine risks on the other, in that some adult activities endangered children. Children adapted both because they chose to and because they were forced to. As Hawes (1997, p. 21) notes, "Children's lives were not protected in the way that adults wanted, but kids tried to control their world so that the risks they took were acceptable."

For girls especially, after-school programs were places of respite and self-development. Although girls were slower than boys to gain control of their after-school time, by the late 1910s and early 1920s, as many as a third of participants in some programs were girls. (This estimate derives from a perusal of class and club membership records in program archives.) After-school programs provided girls a base from which they could not only discover talents, but also gain a measure of independence, some control over time, and room in which to develop an autonomous identity (see Brenzel, Roberts-Gersch, & Wittner, 1985). Girls predominated in the drama and music groups of after-school programs, but the opportunity to engage and compete in debate and athletics, from gymnastics to basketball, was also important. To their surprise, after-school staff discovered that not all girls were interested in traditional domestic activities—sewing, cooking, child care. Rather, they were as interested as boys in traditionally masculine pursuits (and more interested than boys in literary matters).

The cultural aspirations of after-school programs were as objectionable to critics of that era (and of the present one) as was their role in institutionalizing childhood. After-school programs, particularly settlement-based programs, unquestionably played a role in a broader effort, led by the schools, to enculturate immigrant children. This effort, which minimized the struggles of immigrant parents to balance maintenance of traditional ways and adaptation to a new world, sometimes set after-school programs in opposition to children's families and may have contributed to undermining, or at least diluting, family authority. Parents' own attitudes toward and relationships with after-school programs varied. Some reportedly urged sponsors to develop more after-school programming, to get children off the streets (Wald, 1915); others were indifferent, and still others suspicious. Suspicions (especially of settlements) centered on religion and on the belief that children were being encouraged to question family and group traditions and values (Carson,

1990, p. 62). Parents and after-school staff also disagreed at times about the appropriateness of children's work responsibilities, especially when these responsibilities undermined school attendance.

After-school programs may also have seen their role—here the evidence is murkier—as helping inculcate in working-class children the traits they would need as factory workers. This effort could be seen in the emphasis on industrial craftwork and use of team sports to shape identity. As Nasaw (1979, p. 103) puts it, the new industrial order needed young people who were not so much "self-made men and women as team players . . . ready to sacrifice their personal dreams, hopes and aspirations for the good of the productive unit." Yet after-school sponsors also viewed their programs as protective institutions, designed to compensate for, if not fight actively against, working-class children's continuing exploitation in the labor market. Sponsors were aware of the need to balance the societal belief that children benefited from engagement in useful activity with their own sense that children needed safe places for play, recreation, and enrichment.

2

Becoming Established

It is not what the boy does to the wood but what the wood does to the boy.
—Anonymous participant in a 1936 meeting of Chicago boys' clubs

Most fascinating (to the girls) was the sculpting and modernistic painting.
—Report on a visit to the Art Institute of Chicago,
Abraham Lincoln Center, 1930

In the period between 1920 and 1950, after-school programs and their sponsoring agencies became part of the solidifying human service system in the United States and established themselves as a child-rearing institution. During these decades, providers faced the task of navigating a turbulent external environment. This environment was marked by rapid cultural change, two major societal crises—the Great Depression and World War II—and growing competition for social welfare resources, in the context of a social service system becoming more treatment- and problem-oriented. Broad social processes and events affected ideas about what children needed from different child-rearing institutions, exacerbating after-school programs' continuing struggle for identity.

A MODERN SOCIETY

By the 1920s, Americans were adjusting to the idea that theirs was an urban society; at the same time they were worried by the complexity, choice, and impersonality characterizing urban life. Across social class, growing up was becoming more complicated. Fewer urban families were living on the edge of destitution, although many were still hard pressed. The economic and cultural ties binding working-class children to family and local community were loosening. Children had more discretionary time, and with the rise of popular culture, including motion pictures and the penny arcade, they had more options for using that time. Like their more advantaged peers, working-class children faced the task of cobbling together a set of values and an identity from diverse sources—parents and relatives, teachers, friends, and entertainers and other public figures.

Worry about "youth," a stage of childhood that began about age 9 or 10 and continued through the adolescent years, emerged as a social preoccupation Youth seemed to be taking over everything, from playgrounds to American culture as a whole (Wolfson, 1927). Older children were described as alienated from an increasingly impersonal, mechanistic society and seen as seduced by popular culture—as the group that signaled the decline of American life and the group that would bring American society into the modern era. Adult society seemed most concerned that children no longer looked to it as a source of values and behavior, but rather conferred "identity and status upon themselves" (Sochen, 1988, p. 16). The notion that "young people could arrive at their own codes of behavior seemed at best troubling and at worst threatening to the very foundations of society" (Hawes, 1997, p. 4). A few of the new child development professionals warned against the view of urban life as a solely negative influence on children (see, e.g., Bowman, 1929). Most argued that children needed more guidance than they were getting from contemporary institutions. Juvenile court judge Franklin Hoyt (1927, p. 5) wrote that "very seldom do I find a child deliberately a law breaker. He simply lost himself in the maze of man-made civilization, which takes no account of youth's desire to have an active share in the life of his community."

The first detailed observational studies created a clearer portrait of the tasks and support needs of middle childhood. Susan Isaacs (1932) described school-age children as becoming less egocentric, better able and more motivated to cooperate as part of a group, and discovering other children as allies. She also described them as becoming gradually less interested in fantasy (although still interested in adventure) and more interested in mastery of practical skills and in understanding how the world worked. Barbara Biber (1942), also drawing on observational work, described middle childhood as a period in which interests were being explored and defined, a time in which children were striving to understand, developing basic dispositions toward, and seeking mastery over the major tasks of their culture and the social world they inhabited.

The implication for educational and socializing institutions was clear. School-age children needed a balanced menu: They needed opportunities to identify and express interests, to create and make things, and to see the product of their efforts; they needed to experiment independently, to become aware of their own errors, and to draw their own conclusions, including those about right and wrong. Adults had to validate children's interests, offer appreciation for children's aesthetic expression, and at the same time to emphasize the functional and relational aspects of experience. They had to provide children with the opportunity for constructive and challenging group activity and to help children learn to be sensitive to the needs of the group, for example, taking turns, helping out, and considering the needs of other group members. Not least, adults had to recognize that they could no longer take their authority for granted, but rather had to earn it, by being fair, judicious, firm, and sensible (Isaacs, 1932; Biber, 1942).

What was unclear was which institutions could and should take responsibility for guiding children through a more complicated world and for providing the subtle adult scaffolding and guidance children needed. Working-class parents continued to be perceived as incapable of meeting their children's needs. This long-standing perception was reinforced by the pervasive parent-blaming that characterized the psychological movements of the 1920s and early 1930s, especially the mental hygiene movement and John Watson's behaviorism. According to proponents of these two movements, mothers were either negligent or overinvolved. Fathers had abandoned their traditional role and responsibility as family disciplinarians, through absence or overindulgence. Some argued that power in the family now resided as much in children as in parents; others that children needed "liberation" from their parents and required new sources of guidance and control.

Although schools were now a central child-rearing institution, those who studied or worked with children outside school doubted that schools were fit for the task of helping children adjust to and prepare for a more complex society. Nor were they capable of recognizing and supporting children's interests, or of providing the wider range of experiences that growing children needed. Most urban schools continued to be rigid, regimented, boring, and alienating institutions that overemphasized conformity and failed even to meet children's academic needs. Truancy remained widespread. In one study of children's progress within the Chicago school system between 1924 and 1931, 61% of children were found to be performing below grade level (cited in Rivlin & Wolfe, 1985, p. 128). Psychiatrist Adolph Meyer described schools as "pathogenic," because of the stresses they induced (Cohen, 1999). Educators themselves sometimes worried about the growing monopolization of school over children's lives. As one superintendent argued, school should not "so dominate the life of the child or youth that worry makes his play time anxious" (Holmes, 1929, p. 7). There was debate about the appropriateness of homework, with some educators (as well as parents) arguing that it robbed children of enrichment, play, and rest (Gill & Schlossman, 1996).

A ROLE FOR THE AFTER-SCHOOL FIELD

The newly identified needs of working-class children, the persistent worries about them and the apparent limitations of other institutions, reinforced the rationale for after-school programs. The middle decades of the 20th century were in fact a period of growth, albeit fitful growth, for the field. During the 1920s, the number of local programs expanded steadily, as more funding became available through community chests, corporate welfare programs, and private philanthropy. Growth was reversed during the depression of the 1930s, as after-school programs scrambled to survive on slashed budgets. It was renewed again in a modest way during the 1940s, as the neglect of school-age children became a widespread concern and as after-school programs joined other institutions in the mobilization of American society in the war cause. And it continued in the 1950s, amid intensified concern about juvenile delinquency and a renewed belief that children needed respite from the pressures of the world around them.

REFINING A PURPOSE

The rationales and goals articulated in the early years became a basic vocabulary for the after-school field, while new problems and social conditions shaped the story lines by which after-school programs lived. In broad terms, providers continued to see their work as supporting "lives unfolding" (GH Archives, Box 3, Folder 6), and helping children "learn to live" (CBC Archives, Box 50, Folder 1). Providers continued to describe their role as discovering and nurturing children's talents, providing opportunity for self-expression, and broadening cultural horizons. A report on a visit to the Art Institute of Chicago by the Brush and Palette Club of the Abraham Lincoln Center noted, "Most fascinating [to the girls] was the sculpting and modernistic painting" (Abraham Lincoln Center, 1930, pp. 27–28). Providers continued to emphasize the teaching of "Americanism," but with a new emphasis on political and ideological loyalty, deriving from the growth of socialist and communist political movements during the 1930s (Olivet Items, 1936).

For boys, providers talked of fostering prevocational and trade skills (what one program report described as "trade beginnings"). For girls they continued to emphasize preparation for family life and fostering strength to "bear the burdens" of life (CC Archives, Box 6 , Folder 2). For younger children, providers emphasized the developmental value of adult-supervised play; for older children, the dangers and temptations of unsupervised play in the streets, and the benefits of organized activity in preventing truancy, delinquency, and gang formation (Robinson, 1932). In discussing the arts, sports, and clubs offered by after-school programs, Jones (1943, p. 87) argued that "any clever adult who appreciates the value of this kind of activity . . . has at hand possibilities for preventing and curing delinquency."

New goals were overlaid on existing ones. As American society became modern, children needed not just safe places, but also sensible ones, to help them sort out new options and possible identities. After-school programs enlisted themselves in the struggle to help children make sense of—and resist—the images and messages of popular culture, including earlier exposure to sexual matters. In a 1925 report, the drama instructor at Chicago Commons complained that boys mostly wanted to act out everything they saw at the movies and burlesque shows (CC Archives, Box 6, Folder 1). A 1925 report of the Minneapolis Women's Cooperative Alliance noted that an important function of settlement-based after-school programs was to help immigrant children learn to distinguish the "true American ideals from the cheap and unwholesome" ones (cited in Karger, 1987, p. 63).

Beginning in the late 1920s, after-school providers began to include psychological rationales, such as better adjustment and mental or emotional health. One speaker at an annual meeting of Chicago Boys' Club directors noted that "recreation in a game room is just as necessary to the mental hygiene as is sleep to the physical tissues" (CBC Archives, Box 50, Folder 1). A few sponsors used psychodynamic concepts in talking about their work. Karger (1987, p. 93) cites the comment of a girls' worker in a Minneapolis settlement in the mid-1930s: "A settlement is there to meet all disclosed needs [of the girls] and to sense and anticipate those which are dormant and not disclosed." Lambert (1944), arguing for the importance of play in after-school programs, noted that it was children's mode of expressing needs and feelings and of working out inner conflicts, fears, and worries.

After-school sponsors continued to define their work in contrast to that of schools. In a 1932 talk, Ruth Canfield of the Henry Street Settlement told fellow art instructors that, since school focused on producing conformity, it was their role to help children see that they were unique individuals who could create something original (UNH Archives, Box 6, Folder 54). In a discussion of schooling at a 1935 conference, Charles Hendry of the Boys Club of America noted that "those close to Boys' Clubs know how sterile and how futile much of the education of the school is" (CBC Archives, Box 1, Folder 1). One writer reminded after-school staff to be sensitive to what children might be feeling after a long day at school: "For many hours they have been obeying orders, completing definitely assigned tasks. Most of the time they have not been allowed to speak or move about without permission." For this reason, "schedules must be flexibly implemented, staff should refrain from lecturing and telling" (Franklin & Benedict, 1943, p. 23).

More broadly, sponsors continued to debate the traits they were trying to nurture and what children needed from them. Some argued that children most needed guidance; others, recognition as unique individuals; others, respite from external demands; and still others, hands-on work with useful tasks. A few program directors argued for after-school programs to be more child-centered, by which they meant responsive to children's own agendas;

others claimed that children did not know what they wanted or needed. A few directors argued that playing and having fun were important ends in themselves; most others, that they were only legitimate to the extent that they served other goals. The director of Chicago's Abraham Lincoln Center claimed, "I think play is its own justification. . . . [P]lay as such is highly worthwhile" (Reese, 1930, p. 19). Meanwhile, a Chicago boys' club director noted that play should be an important part of the program, but "we should have motive in play" (CBC Archives, Box 50, Folder 1). In practice, many staff appeared to strive for balance. The leader of a play club for 9- to 12-year-old girls at the Northwestern University Settlement in the early 1930s captured the duality of most after-school work, stating that she wanted to "leave [the girls] to their own whims as much as possible, but to demand a certain amount of orderliness" (NUS Archives, Box 45, Folder 9).

DIVERSITY IN SPONSORSHIP

As the after-school field grew, sponsorship remained diverse, with boys' clubs and settlements the two largest sponsors, but with churches and ethnic associations; assorted other community and neighborhood centers; family service agencies; and more selectively, schools, park districts, and newly established public housing developments all playing a role. By the 1930s, YMCAs began serving a few more working-class boys, while making sure to keep those boys from overrunning facilities intended for middle-class, Protestant men, their bread and butter. YWCAs, historically more socially committed than YMCAs, also began extending their programming downward to school-age girls.

School authorities continued to waver on a role in children's after-school lives, in favor of the idea but worried about costs and loss of control. Proposals for school-based after-school programming were periodically put forward by superintendents and school reformers, typically suggesting that teachers be used to design and run activities distinct from those found during the school day (Holmes, 1929). Proponents argued that it was better to have some influence on children's out-of-school lives than to have none, even if such influence meant allowing children greater control over after-school activity. Schools and community agencies continued to collaborate in running programs, sometimes uneasily. One study noted various problems in using school space, including teachers putting a variety of restrictions on after-school providers and school administrators being uncomfortable with active and boisterous behavior inside the school building (Lambert, 1944).

Settlements and boys' clubs offered their experience in after-school work to new providers. The Hiram House settlement in Cleveland, for instance, set up and staffed after-school programs at a number of local elementary schools during the late 1920s and early 1930s. It made itself appear to be relevant to school staff by helping parents respond to their children's school-related problems. Settlements and boys' clubs also established outposts in a growing number of new public housing developments, in some cases lobbying during the planning phase for space to be set aside for indoor recreational facilities. A handful of local housing authorities funded their own positions for recreational specialists (although more commonly for playgrounds than for after-school programs).

PROGRAM AND ACTIVITY STRUCTURE

The activity structure of after-school programs, established in the prewar years, changed little in the ensuing decades. Most programs maintained the dual class and club-based structure, with children typically participating in one or two classes a week, perhaps belonging to a club, and sometimes dropping in for less formal activity in the game room, library, or gym. Although gender integration was gradually increasing, especially at settlements (which wanted boys and girls to "grow up together"), the majority of activities remained separate. A smaller settlement might have 25 to 50 children in attendance on a typical day; a larger one, as many as 80. Boys clubs' reported daily attendance that ranged from less than 100 to 400 or more children. The game room, and to a lesser extent the gym, continued to be the points of entry for many children at boys' clubs, with the goal of eventually interesting them in more structured activity.

The content of activities also remained more or less unchanged during this period. For instance, in the 1920s and 1930s, Grosvenor House, a settlement in New York City that served between 25 and 50 children daily, had classes in metalwork, carpentry, cobbling, basketweaving, beadwork, cooking, sewing, poster work, dance (folk, rhythmic, and tap dancing), decorative arts (e.g., designing and painting lampshades, making sconces), clay modeling and pottery, bookbinding, block printing, weaving, and drawing. Children typically signed up for two classes at a time. Time was set aside each afternoon for free play in the game room or outdoor playground. There were once- or twice-monthly outings, weekend activities, a library that was "thronged with young people daily," health and dental clinics for children, and a hot-lunch program. Some participating children also joined age-based social clubs, "which choose their own work for the year" (GH Archives, Box 3, Folders 3–6).

Other reports of the time note similar activities, with variations depending on what specialists could be found (and perhaps induced to volunteer), space, and what was more and less popular with children. In announcing a new camera club, a writer in a March 1936 newsletter from the Olivet Community Center in Chicago noted, "We are to have as leader a most exceptional 'find,' a man who has taken many prizes in amateur photography and who is donating his services" (Olivet Items, 1936). One program might have boxing and wrestling for boys; another, an orchestra or band; another, a debate club. Programs had classes and clubs for nature study and urban study. Puppetry remained popular, as did drama, and children worked with staff to turn stories into plays, and sometimes wrote and staged their own plays. An early 1930s survey of crafts work among programs in New York City noted leatherwork, bookbinding, batik, oilcloth dolls, wrought iron work, and puppet making, among other activities (UNH Archives, Box 55).

Facilities improvement and expansion led to wider offerings in some programs. Sponsors grew by taking over neighboring space, or occasionally securing capital grants or loans to build new buildings. The University of Chicago Settlement, for instance, grew to include two gymnasiums, a boxing room, a handful of club rooms, a game room, a library, manual training and sewing rooms, and two playlots (one on the roof). Some sponsors had either or both dental and medical facilities and gave children examinations upon enrollment (and annually thereafter).

Clubs remained an important program element, providing time to talk and plan. A club leader's report on the Chicagoettes, a club at Chicago Commons, reported that the girls "knitted and played concentration and guessing games. They discussed new members and planned to ask two more girls to join them." Another club of 10- to 13-year-old girls, mostly Polish, spent weeks planning a holiday party, during that time also having a variety of discussions about boys, school, and parents' discipline practices, among other topics. One discussion involved a club member who was unable to go on a day trip during Christmas break because she needed to help her mother wash clothes, providing income for the family. Although the date of the trip could not be changed, the members decided to try to be more aware of such family demands in planning future trips (CC Archives, Box 6, Folders 3 and 5).

Clubs and some classes continued to be staffed partly or mostly by volunteers. These included college students; junior league members; older youth from the neighborhood; and as noted, specialists in specific arts or crafts. A 1928 survey of 12 after-school programs on Chicago's Northwest Side found that more than two thirds of all staff were volunteers, with most of the rest being part-time paid staff (CC Archives, Box 6, Folder 1). Program reports describe different clubs as having distinct characters and reputations. When possible, programs tried to match group leaders' characteristics to club profiles. For instance, a club consisting of preadolescent girls at Chicago Commons, the Peoria Street Gang, was thought to need a leader who was strong, yet likeable and easygoing.

ISSUES FACING AFTER-SCHOOL PROVIDERS

This second phase in the development of the after-school field brought a measure of reflection and self-questioning. Staff debated what and how much clubs should be expected to accomplish. Class and club leaders' reports reflected struggles to understand why children did not respond more enthusiastically to their ideas and plans. Common problems noted in reports included eliciting interests, sustaining engagement, controlling acting up, and responding to children's desire for some ownership of space and activities (UNH Archives, Box 24, Folder 480). Discussing boys' principal desire to hang out and to use the game room and gym, a boys' work director noted that "the functions of these rooms is still principally negative. That is we are providing a better place for the boys to hang out than they would otherwise have" (CC Archives, Box 6, Folder 2). With patience, it was nonetheless possible to encourage boys to embrace activities, particularly art and drama, that were outside the realm of what would be considered masculine on the streets.

Although some issues that had arisen during the formative decades of after-school work dissipated, others gradually became characteristic of the field. Program reports began to reflect worry about the quality of children's experiences. A mid-1930s study of arts and crafts in Chicago after-school programs by Edith Kiertzner, a local leader in the after-school field, described them as uninspiring: "Typical crafts programs consist largely of a series of dictated lessons in folding, cutting and pasting." She noted a lack of opportunity for children to use their creativity (CBC Archives, Box 1). Worry about quality was tied to worry about staffing. One report noted that club leaders who only came once a week for the meeting of their club failed to connect with or understand the larger program (CC Archives, Box 6, Folder 4). The majority of programs experienced a chronic struggle to retain club leaders, as well as staff with specific vocational and artistic skills. Reports indicated about a 50% year-to-year turnover rate for frontline staff, with some turnover occurring during the year, affecting the momentum of clubs, participants' morale, and attendance (see, e.g., CC Archives, Box 6, Folder 5). The basic problem was that it took time for class or club leaders to figure out their roles, as well as to come to know and understand children. Those who stayed with after-school work for more than a year or 2 often came to see low-income children very differently from when they began, viewing them in a more complex way, seeing resilience and humor, as well as the effects of family insecurity and conflict (CC Archives, Box 6, Folder 5).

Neighborhood change unsettled some after-school providers. As the boundaries between different ethnic groups shifted, they found themselves caught up in the resulting conflict. Ethnic transition in neighborhoods required providers to gain the trust of new groups of families and learn to work with new groups of children. In his 1927–1928 annual report, the boys' department director at Chicago Commons complained that the Polish families moving into what had been a predominantly Italian neighborhood did not "understand the functions of the settlement" and were reluctant to let their children attend (CC Archives, Box 6, Folder 2). The following year, boys' and girls' workers from the settlement made home visits to describe their programs and answer parents' questions.

Expanding African American populations continued to confound sponsors, including those ostensibly committed to serving their neighborhoods rather than particular populations. The pattern of finding ways not to serve African American children, established between 1900 and 1920, continued. At a 1927 meeting of girls' workers in New York City, one participant noted that "we tactfully discourage some races [from participating] and make it appear acccidental" (UNH Archives, Box 7, Folder 63). By the mid- to late 1920s, as Chicago's African American population grew, Hull House found itself bordering the South Side Black Belt. Its solution was to redefine its southern boundary for boys' work, from 16th Street to 12th Street (Philpott, 1978, p. 332). Settlements and some boys' clubs set quotas for African American children, typically 10% to 15%, and sometimes provided separate club rooms and other facilities for them.

PROFESSIONALIZING AND DEFINING A METHOD

During this period, the leaders of the after-school field felt a need to improve the status of the field. Despite the fact that most staff had little preparation for work with children, and despite the reality that many were volunteers, leaders within the field began to describe boys' and girls' work as a profession and debated the formal knowledge that was central to it. One writer argued that "those natural bents which qualify some of us boys' workers must also be buttressed with a knowledge of psychology, both as it relates to the individual and to the mob; [also] psychiatry [and] sociology" ("Boys' Work," 1923, p. 23). There was some internal debate about the extent to which volunteers could and should be formally supervised and held accountable for their work with children. A few universities also began offering course sequences in boys' and girls' work, typically in their sociology or social work departments.

Professionalizing meant articulating the relevant theory and methods for after-school work. Some sponsors argued that group work, then being fleshed out by social workers, was the most appropriate choice. Group-work proponents noted that the group, not the individual, was the key unit in after-school programs, with the staff member as de facto group leader. An understanding of the stages in group development provided the leader a helpful framework for understanding what was happening with his or her children. The group process was well-suited to teaching such values as cooperation and teamwork, leading and following, and commitment to a larger cause, as well as the skills needed for joint problem-solving and promoting democracy.

Other leaders and sponsors preferred to describe what happened in after-school programs as informal education, recreation, or recreational arts. Others argued that apprenticeship was a better model for describing the method of after-school programs, with the paradigm of skilled craftsperson (or artist) and apprentice as a useful way of viewing at least some the work of classes. Still others resisted the equation of after-school work with a particular method, preferring to describe boys' and girls' work as primarily about adults exerting influence, through example of character (i.e., indirectly). At one of the Chicago Boys' Clubs' annual meetings, a speaker reminded his audience that "character is caught more often than it is taught" (CBC, Box 50, Folder 1).

There was some effort to promote the principles and methods of Progressive education as a guide for after-school work, partly because these offered a balance between individual and group orientations, partly to find a home for ideas that were not being taken up by the public schools. Some proponents emphasized the continuity between group-work principles and the more group-oriented Progressive principles, such as cooperative learning and re-creating democracy in the small group. Others emphasized the value of the "project method" or such Progressive notions as building on the interests of the child, and a nondirective adult role, defined by offering suggestions and subtly guiding the child (rather than dictating). The latter emphasis is reflected in the recollections of painter Jacob Lawrence. Describing his experience in the early 1930s at Utopia Children's House, an after-school program in Harlem for "children of women working as domestics," Lawrence noted, "They didn't tell me what to do, how to draw or what to paint. They gave me materials and ideas on how to experiment, and left me alone to create out of my imagination" (Rothstein, 2002, p. A22).

Debate about methods was partly about the nature of adult-child relationships in after-school programs. For Progressives, for instance, discipline was secured through the child's commitment to and interest in a project, rather than through the will of the adult group leader. It was also about means and ends and about the right lens through which to view after-school work. Was the purpose of engagement in specific activities to develop skills, to foster self-expression, to provide psychological release, to nurture passion and appreciation for particular cultural forms, or to develop positive personal qualities, whether self-discipline, attention to detail, following orders, planning and completing a project, or self-realization? Almost any activity could be viewed from different angles. Thus one settlement activity report noted that drama was useful for helping children understand the variety of human nature. A participant at a 1936 regional boys' club meeting in Chicago commented, "It is not what the boy does to the wood but what the wood does to the boy" (CBC Archives, Box 50, Folder 1). The means-ends issue was important because it was not easy to hold on simultaneously to different basic purposes. As one drama instructor explained, when you tried to combine the methods of drama and group work, you got the worst of both (UNH Archives, Box 3, Folder 27).

THE PLAY SCHOOL AS A FRAME FOR AFTER-SCHOOL WORK

One distinct approach to after-school work was the play school, embodying elements of play theory, Progressive educational theory, and psychoanalytic theory. Between 1920 and the late 1950s, local Play School Associations and Child Study Associations helped design and establish after-school and summer programs within settlements, schools, churches, the new public housing developments, and other community centers; trained and occasionally supervised frontline staff; provided consultation; held conferences for after-school providers; and developed program guides.

The basic idea behind the play school was that of play as the school-age child's natural mode of learning; striving for mastery and control; exploring the physical and social world; expressing feelings; and working out inner conflicts, fears, and worries. The play school approach placed "less emphasis on the acquiring of skills and techniques and more upon what the experience means to the child" (Franklin & Benedict, 1943, p. 13). Lay school staff would be good observers of individual children and interpreters of their behavior, and would make the play school a setting in which "the child feels safe and accepted, and where he can express his own needs through the medium of play" (Lambert, 1944, p. 18). Some play school materials also stressed regular opportunity for group process, such as group discussions.

Perhaps the best-known play school was the Chelsea Recreation Center, based at PS 33 in Manhattan. It was started in the late 1930s by a local child study association, with the goals of providing "recreation—but with a difference" (Franklin & Benedict, 1943, p. 1) and of serving children with special needs who were, referred by teachers. These included "restless children, troublesome children, children who had language difficulties" (p. 4). The activities of a typical after-school program—play, artwork, craftwork, and even industrial crafts—would become the basis for helping children address their difficulties. Dramatic play was an especially important vehicle for the "natural expression of emotions that would otherwise become bottled up." But any activity could be therapeutic: "The action of hammering and sawing helps release emotional tension; a child who is angry or who seethes with resentment can often quite effectively work off steam in this way" (pp. 5, 13, 48).

Within a few years, the therapeutic focus of the program had declined, not least because of difficulty finding staff with the appropriate training. The Chelsea Recreation Center became a more conventional after-school program, with the usual mixture of clubs and classes, while retaining the play school philosophy—helping children master a complex world, come to terms with strong feelings and difficult experiences, acquire a sense of efficacy, and learn democracy. The presence of the recreation center apparently had some effect on daytime practices at PS 33 itself: "Play began to make its way into the classroom. Desks were unscrewed[;] the long, silent marching lines of children were done away with; [and] the pupils began moving freely and purposefully through the halls" (Franklin & Benedict, 1943, p. 5). During the 1940s, the Chelsea model was adopted by other elementary schools in New York City, with support from the board of education (and later from the Mayor's War-Time Committee), starting with a school in Harlem, which appointed six teachers to act as club leaders. The local Play School Association, by then the nation's most active, provided training and consultation to these programs.

In addition to keeping play alive as an element in after-school programming, the play school approach added a child development perspective to the after-school field. This perspective would in turn take the edge off some of the harsher agendas that emerged for after-school programs in the second half of the century. It would also create a channel between early childhood and after-school programming, through which flowed a variety of the child-centered ideas and practices that would shape after-school practice.

AFTER-SCHOOL PROGRAMS IN TIMES OF CRISIS

After-school programs were powerfully shaped by, yet also worked actively to respond to, the profound events of the 1930s and 1940s. As the Great Depression began to take hold in 1929 and 1930, after-school providers sensed that something cataclysmic was happening before they clearly understood its import. Within a few years they had come to be shocked by the fragility of core American beliefs and ideals that was revealed by the depression, by families' complete loss of confidence and security, and by government's initial denial (Halpern, 1999). Like other human services providers, after-school providers found a new sense of purpose and identity in helping children cope with their families' economic stress. World War II brought a completely different set of demands, as mothers entered the labor force and millions of families experienced war-related social and physical dislocation. After-school providers again carved out a role in helping children cope with new stresses and contribute to the war effort.

THE GREAT DEPRESSION

The depression of the 1930s brought both challenges and some new roles. After-school staff observed children's physical and psychological well-being deteriorate before their eyes. A 1931–1932 girls' department report at Chicago Commons noted that "this spring 75 girls were weighed for camp, 48 were underweight. During the past two years we have seen the children get thin and pale in our classes." The report also noted that in one third of neighborhood families, "no member is employed" and that children in these families were restless, distracted, and irritable because of home conditions. Two years later, reports from the same agency noted that in 161 of 284 children enrolled, no member of the family was working; children's clothing was deteriorating, "causing intense humiliation"; and many more children had "bad teeth" (CC Archives, Box 6, Folder 3).

After-school staff observed children once again assuming significant economic responsibility within (and for) their families, taking on the worries and cares of adults, and in some cases reluctantly dropping out of school. One program report noted growing evidence of conflict at home resulting from fathers' unemployment, "causing children to look at Grosvenor House as a place of refuge and sanctuary" (GH, Box 3, Folder 8). As the depression continued, program reports noted disillusionment, anger, and rebellion in children: "The terrible conditions of poverty and privation [experienced by neighborhood children] have caused them to believe with their elders that nothing can be regained or re-secured except by open revolt" (GH Archives, Box 3, Folder 9). Providers tried to reassure children who were worried about their parents' well-being, and struggled to figure out how to respond to those who felt compelled to quit school to help their family. Children themselves appeared to seek out after-school programs for their stability, facilities, meals, and preoccupations. Severe winters in the mid-1930s further filled game rooms, gyms, and classes.

As budget pressures forced schools to eliminate art, music, manual training, physical education, and health services, after-school sponsors tried to compensate here as well. Yet the budgets of youth-serving and community-based organizations were perhaps more decimated than those of schools. Workers at the Chicago Boys' Clubs, for instance, took pay cuts of 25% or more and sometimes were not paid at all. Between 1931 and 1935 the number of art instructors in settlements in Manhattan declined from 61 to 21 (UNH, Box 6, Folder 54). Funding problems were exacerbated by the belief among some funders that the activities of after-school programs—especially play and enrichment—were superfluous, even absurd, in the face of mass unemployment.

By the second half of the 1930s, modest public funds and resources became available to programs, primarily through the Works Progress Administration (WPA), the Federal Arts Project, and the National Youth Administration (NYA). Many programs became temporarily dependent on WPA workers (some of whom were laid-off teachers) and visual and performing artists funded through the Federal Arts Project and provided classes in whatever areas these new staff had expertise. About 10,000 NYA-subsidized youth, aged 16 to 24, also worked in after-school and related recreational programs in urban areas. In New York City, for instance, the United Neighborhood Houses helped place 1,700 NYA youth in after-school and other recreation programs in 175 agencies (UNH Archives, Box 24, Folder 452). NYA youth typically received a week or 2 of initial training, in such areas as art, music, drama and storytelling, and general curriculum planning and were supervised (more in theory than in practice) by "teachers, playground supervisors, recreation directors, and settlement house workers," some of whom were themselves funded through the WPA (Lindley & Lindley, 1938, p. 49).

The NYA also supported new program development. In Birmingham, Alabama, the NYA cooperated with community leaders to establish a boys' club in a low-income African American neighborhood, in a building donated by a local citizen. NYA youth led classes at the club in athletics, choral, manual training, and art; led study groups, and helped establish a library (Lindley & Lindley, 1938). On Chicago's South Side, NYA youth rehabilitated the South Side boys' club, which had long served African American youth but had fallen into disrepair due to lack of funds, and then helped staff the club after it reopened.

MOBILIZING FOR WAR

During World War II, after-school programs were part of a society-wide mobilization affecting virtually every social institution. Like schools, they were asked, and took it upon themselves, to help children cope with the stresses associated with the war. In this regard, after-school providers defined three principle roles: providing care and supervision to children of working mothers, helping children cope with psychological stresses of the war, and providing a means for children to contribute to the war effort.

The Struggle to Provide Adequate School-Age Care. At the height of World War II, 6 million women with children under 14 years of age were working in factories and other "essential" jobs (Meyer, 1943). While that number constituted only about 20% of all mothers of children in that age group, it was composed disproportionately of mothers with school-age children. Mothers mostly worked because they had to, especially in families with servicemen. Some worked because they found they liked the work or at least the freedom it offered. Rural women generally and African American women especially valued new opportunities to escape farm labor and domestic work (Rose, 1997).

Although women's labor was critical to the war effort, working mothers were still criticized. Tuttle (1993) writes that "the American latchkey child was one of the most pitied home front figures of the Second World War, and his or her working mother was not only criticized but reviled" (p. 69). Children whose mothers worked were seen to lose their psychological "anchor," especially in the after-school hours (Fredericksen, 1943, p. 161). One writer noted that "children will not stay home after school, but they feel safer when their mothers are at home" (Lambert, 1944, p. 7). Mothers working long hours were exhausted, irritable, and inattentive (Tuttle, 1993, p. 67). There were reports of malnutrition linked to maternal neglect. With fathers away and mothers working, social control was weakened and family routines disrupted. As in World War I, reports suggested that school truancy and delinquency were on the rise, although the former may have been the result of an increase in child labor among children 10 to 14 years of age. Increased childcare responsibilities probably kept some girls out of school. Meyer (1943), who visited war production communities throughout the United States, wrote that "from Buffalo to Witchita it is the children who are suffering the most from mass migration, easy money, unaccustomed hours of work, and the fact that mama has become a welder on the graveyard shift" (p. 60).

The decline in parental availability and the emergence of the latchkey child led after-school programs to assume a more explicit child care function and led day nurseries, kindergartens, and other early child care centers to serve more school-age children, before as well as after school. Defense Day Care and Defense Recreation Committees, set up by local governments, stimulated some after-school care. For instance, in Detroit the state Day Care Committee used war chest funds to set up after-school "canteens" in schools and other facilities. In New York City the Mayor's Committee on War-Time Care asked the Play Schools Association to supervise after-school centers established under its authority. The Los Angeles committee developed an array of "nursery schools, playgrounds, community halls, gymnasiums, libraries, clubrooms, handcraft and educational classes, and good recreational leadership at the housing projects" (Meyer, 1943, p. 158). School-based extended-day programs sponsored by local school districts, and sometimes operated by community agencies and private groups, appeared in dozens of cities. Funding came from parent fees, local community chests, war chests, and local school districts. At one time or another, close to 300,000 children participated in such extended-day programs, staffed primarily by college and high school students.

Although creative, local efforts were inadequate to the demand for after-school care and were further hampered by staffing and facilities shortages. In Mobile, Alabama, for instance, a local YMCA started a boys' club, but found itself overwhelmed by a combination of too many boys and the impossibility of finding staff and quickly gave up (Meyer, 1943). Yet the federal response to the need for all kinds of care was extremely modest. WPA-subsidized workers were still available through mid-1943 to work in a handful of after-school programs. In 1943, the U.S. Office of Education began a short-lived program called Extended School Services, which set aside modest funds for start-up, coordination, and purchase of curricular materials, but not for ongoing program operations. Some funding for new and expanded facilities was provided in 1943 and 1944, through the Community Facilities Act (commonly called the Lanham Act). This funding went mostly to schools, a few recreational facilities, and a few day care centers, only slightly easing extreme facilities shortages in many communities.

The limited, and in most ways inadequate, federal response to school-age child care needs resulted from ambivalence about maternal employment and the belief that child care provision was not an appropriate government role. Prominent figures such as Grace Abbott, Katherine Lenroot (of the Children's Bureau), and J. Edgar Hoover warned against the social damage potentially caused by working mothers (Tuttle, 1993). To some extent, the family was also reidealized as the cradle of democracy and a bastion against fascism and communism (Rose, 1997). The lack of federal response nonetheless led to harsh criticism of the government, by labor leaders, working mothers, and even normally conservative corporate executives, such as Henry Ford. Cities around the country were paralyzed by expectations of federal funding that never materialized, leading local officials to feel strung out and angry. Meyer (1943, pp. 156, 371) stated that "I must in all candor report that [the administrators of the Lanham Act are] criticized from one end of the country to the other." Instead of leading the way, the federal government created an atmosphere of "confusion and antagonism."

Responding to the Psychological Effects of War. School-age children residing in cities were affected to differing degrees by the climate of fear, worry, and anger created by the war and by the civil preparations made for enemy attacks, especially in coastal cities and war production centers. Children were literally bombarded with endless patriotic messages and figuratively bombarded by enemy attacks that never came. (These phantom attacks took on a measure of reality through blackouts, air raid drills with sirens blaring, and construction of bomb shelters.) Children were affected more directly by family disruption and dislocation. They worried about fathers and brothers sent off to fight, and they struggled to adapt to strange communities, as millions of families made what became permanent moves, primarily from rural areas to war production centers in or near urban areas.

In trying to help children cope with these war-related stresses, after-school programs, like parents themselves, were buffeted by the contradictory opinions of child development experts. Advice ranged from reassuring children that they were safe, to keeping them busy (i.e., diverting them from their fears and worries), asking them to summon their courage, and asking adults not to let children see their own fear (Kirk, 1994). Some experts encouraged play that incorporated warlike themes; others discouraged it. It was suggested that children would feel less helpless if they were better prepared for air raids and other emergencies, so schools and after-school programs taught and rehearsed routines for the air raids that never came. After-school staff created games that were supposed to help children express their war-related aggression in healthier ways. For example, in one game, called Blitzkrieg, children swung on ropes, dropping beanbag bombs on imaginary targets (p. 27).

After-school programs joined a broader effort to reinforce American ideals and values in the face of external threats to them. Children recited oaths, sang patriotic songs, and talked about democracy and tolerance of racial diversity. Programs sometimes had to help children cope with animosity toward their own ethnic group or family. A report from Greenwich House, a settlement serving primarily Italian American children, noted that staff had to help children cope with and make sense of issues of loyalty, as well as the hatred expressed toward Italian Americans (UNH Archives, Box 24, Folder 480).

Creating a Role for Children in the War Effort. As with the question of how to help children cope psychologically, there was disagreement about the extent to which children should be expected to contribute to the war effort. Child labor opponents reminded other government departments and the public about the need to protect children from exploitation. The U. S. Children's Bureau "wanted to make certain that the rights which only one or two generations of children had enjoyed thus far were not forfeited" (Kirk, 1994, p. 58). A few leaders in the after-school field argued for a continued emphasis on "normal peace time activities in order to offset the constant impact of war" on children (UNH Archives, Box 24, Folder 480). A few worried about the loss of childhood and of simple opportunity for play. Lambert (1944, pp. xi, 25) noted that the need for play "in a world of terrific pressures, turmoil and frustrations, is often ignored or considered of small importance." It was through play that children "fit the incomprehensible segments of the world around them into an understandable whole."

By and large, sponsors accepted the task of mobilizing children to support the war effort, not least because they believed it would help their programs secure financial support. The 1941 annual report of the Chicago Boys' Clubs stated, "It is boys who will defend America from its enemies." One settlement's 1942–1943 annual program report was titled "We Build America" (GH Archives, Box 3, Folder 17). After-school programs organized scrap collection campaigns, had children make bandages and service flags, knit clothing for soldiers, and cultivated "victory gardens." Children salvaged old clothes, rags, paper, rubber, and metal. They learned first aid and telegraphy and studied airplane design. Children were told that they were "citizen soldiers" in a "total war" in which "nobody is left out" (Tuttle, 1993, p. 122). They received military titles such as "paper trooper," and cloth insignia to attach to their clothing (they could even advance in rank [Kirk, 1994]). Providers' arguments for mobilizing children varied. At times they argued that it helped children feel valued, a part of the war effort; at times that their aim was to make such tasks fun as well as useful. What was clear was that after-school programs were trying once again to reconcile conflicting instincts.

THE POSTWAR YEARS

The end of World War II brought a return to prewar boundaries and roles for after-school programs, as for other child-rearing institutions. The focus within the after-school world, as throughout society, was on a return to normalcy. Thus a visitor to a 1947 exhibit of children's artwork from settlement-based after-school programs in New York City commented that "the machinery of destruction so dominant in children's art work during the war" was no longer present (UNH Archives, Box 3, Folder 27). Yet the postwar period was also marked by a host of social tensions and worries and the beginning of major change in the population of low-income neighborhoods. These various pressures would require after-school providers to define themselves once again and to adjust long-standing approaches to new demands.

The need for after-school care for children of working mothers was not that much less than it had been during the war years, especially for low- and moderate-income families. Yet with the close of the war, American society returned quickly to its traditional position of seeing child care as a private responsibility. (The Korean War, which led to a renewed defense mobilization in 1951, briefly stimulated renewed government commitment to child care, including for school-age children.) Proponents of what had come to be called "school-age child care" thus tried different arguments. They argued for the need to serve veterans' children and children in the growing number of single-parent families. They argued that after-school programs prevented delinquency. For instance, in the late 1940s, the New York State Youth Commission funded some child care centers in "high delinquency neighborhoods" to provide school-age care (UNH Archives, Box 24, Folder 236). Proponents argued that, as one put it, "the graduates of [day care and preschool] centers still have the same problems that made them eligible for preschool care" (Folder 247) Responding to pressure from parents and civic groups, a handful of schools in a handful of urban school districts also continued their extended-day programs.

Emphases and practices within the after-school field continued to evolve, although many changes were incremental. A portrait of the Pittsburgh Boys' Club in 1948 finds much continuity with the situation in earlier decades. The club had its own three-story building, with rooms for woodworking, photography, art and printing, music and drama, model aeronautics, a hobby shop, and games. On the main floor there was a kitchen, gym, and library, and in the basement a swimming pool and bowling alley. Chicago's Lincoln Boys' Club listed among its regular activities wood shop, "handcrafts," plaster painting, making lanyards, shell craft, building battleships, cooking, gym, and swimming. Programs continued to attend to children's basic needs. The Pittsburgh Boys' Club noted earlier also housed a medical and dental clinic. When children first enrolled, they received an exam, and a report with exam results was sent home to parents. A 1949 newsletter of the Olivet Community Center in Chicago described children dropping in to wash up before going to school, particularly in the winter: "Surprising how much hot running water can mean to youngsters who do not have this luxury in their homes" (OCC Archives, Box 2).

As in earlier decades, activities rose or fell in popularity, and new activities were added to the core. For example, boxing became especially popular, while classes in social graces and manners waned. Service clubs for older boys and girls became more common (although they had existed before the war). Homework time was beginning to become a more regular feature in some programs. In general, program activities were becoming more gender integrated, although boys' clubs continued to be ambivalent about serving girls. (The number of independent girls' clubs, although beginning to grow more rapidly, remained small, perhaps 30 to 40 nationwide [Phelps, 1995].)

THE STRUGGLE TO ATTRACT CHILDREN

The 1950s were in many respects a golden era of street play. Children went outside after school and played until darkness forced them indoors. In this context, after-school sponsors continued to struggle to lure children to their programs, and keep them coming, even as they struggled with oversubscribed facilities and chronic financial insecurity. Sponsors developed new outposts or extension clubs, in order to reach out to children not coming in or living close enough to the main site. During the 1949–1950 program year, one such newer club, the Marshall Square Boys Club in Chicago, had a staff of four, plus six volunteers, and an annual budget of $20,000—consisting of $5,000 from the Community Fund and $15,000 raised from individual donors and other sources—to serve 600 members. The immediate neighborhood held another 5,000 unserved children (CBC Archives, Box 73, Folder 13).

In reflecting on why it was so difficult to attract and engage children, especially boys, after-school sponsors sometimes ignored the obvious fact that children preferred the spontaneity, variety, and freedom of self-directed play in the streets and playgrounds. One report noted that "proud and sensitive" low-income boys were [*sic*] "suspicious of efforts to reform them"; moreover, engagement was not "cool" (CBC Archives, Box 73, Folder 12). Program leaders continued to try to convince themselves that boys could have just as much fun "through expertly directed play as when running wild" (GH Archives, Box 3, Folder 20). Yet they also sensed that their traditional structures and activities, such as crafts, were no longer working to attract children older than 8 or 9, a theme that would become increasingly common over the following 2 decades.

Continuing quality problems contributed to difficulty in retaining children. Russell Ballard of Hull House wrote that "while school attendance is compulsory, no one has to come to Hull House, so there is the ever-present problem of retaining staff who possess the skill and understanding to work successfully with youth" (Ballard, 1947). In a study of reasons for the high drop-out rate in one local Chicago Boys' Club, Murao (1954) reported that they ranged from family responsibilities to bullying to parents' concerns about foul language and rough behavior. Children generally liked the staff but found them alternatively, and arbitrarily, too strict or too laissez-faire, failing to control children who misbehaved. There were also complaints about older boys running the clubs. Erratic staff were partly a reflection of erratic staffing. Between 1950 and 1952, the boys' club studied by Murao had four directors and lost four group workers, five physical education instructors, and four swimming instructors.

NEW PRESSURES

The postwar years were marked by ideological crosscurrents that strongly affected all child-rearing institutions, including after-school programs. The cold war (and the threat of a nuclear war) fostered a public climate of paranoia, competition, and uncertainty. At the same time, there was a renewed emphasis on recreation in society, perhaps as a form of release from the pressures and worries of the era. There was debate about authority and authoritarianism, a response to the rise of fascist regimes in the 1930s and 1940s (as well as to concerns about communist dictatorship), and debate as well about the tensions between conformity and individuality. Each of these broad issues left tracks in the after-school literature and shaped the work of programs themselves.

After-school programs promoted themselves as sources of security for children, "havens" in a stressful world (GH Archives, Box 3, Folder 26). Sponsors described after-school programs as "democracy at work," democracy learned in small groups of children "working and playing together" (GH Archives, Box 3, Folder 24). Program reports of that era include numerous descriptions of projects intended to encourage children to work together to plan neighborhoods or cities, or to develop solutions to real and simulated urban problems. After-school programs tried to contribute to "readiness" in the competition with Russia, by, for instance, providing more science activities. The Chicago Boys' Clubs had an annual science fair, to which children from different local clubs brought projects they had worked on during the year.

Yet after-school staff also worried about sacrificing children's individuality and creativity in the service of the group, children's self-determination in the service of societal needs, and their play time in the service of instrumental aims. A report to United Neighborhood Houses in New York City noted that "the importance of play in the life of the [school-age] child" was still "not as yet generally understood" (UNH Archives, Box 24, Folder 236). Providers debated the appropriate degree of adult structure in activities. Participants at one meeting argued about whether to "teach" technique to children in art classes or to let children express themselves freely. Lillard McCloud, an art instructor at Willoughby and Colony House in Brooklyn, argued that too much instruction would kill children's creativity, frankness, and simplicity (UNH Archives, Box 3, Folder 25).

REACHING OUT TO ALIENATED CHILDREN AND YOUTH

One distinct societal theme emerging in the late 1940s and early 1950s was that of low-income children growing up in a world to which they felt they did not belong. In school, they were treated, and thus came to feel, like failures. As one settlement official argued, schools were incapable of providing the kind of attention and support "which allows each child to find himself" (UNH Archives, Box 24, Folder 333). In the community, children were harassed by police and pushed off street corners and were unwilling to seek out organized recreational resources, which they perceived to belong to the society that was rejecting them. A "new" kind of child appeared in low-income communities: hard to reach, resistant, alienated, and oppositional.

Such children learned to reject opportunities before opportunities rejected them. They took perverse pride in "insubordination at home, truancy from school, assignment to a probation officer" (Nightingale, 1993, p. 37). Concern about at-risk and alienated children extended to girls as well as boys. Girls were forming gangs of their own. Petty crime, school problems, and family conflict among girls were reported to be rising, as was loss of belief in a positive future.

Worries about low-income children crystallized eventually as a national obsession with juvenile delinquency. The federal government sponsored commissions on delinquency, and Congress held special hearings. A mid-1950s article in the *Saturday Evening Post* described delinquency as "the shame of America" (Clendenen & Beaser, 1955). Older children and youth were thought to have staked out territory "outside the dominant social and moral order" (Gilbert, 1986, p. 15). Blame for the delinquency epidemic was placed variously on absent fathers, the rise of disorganized "multiproblem" families, comic books, the breakdown of neighborhood social controls, lack of order in schools, and the frustration of blocked opportunity. A few claimed that, at heart, delinquency was a moral problem: "As a society we cannot hold up examples of hate, crass materialism, greed and corruption" to children, and "expect pious precepts to counter their effects" (UNH Archives, Box 24, Folder 333).

In some respects, long experience with low-income children allowed after-school providers to take the new worries about alienation and delinquency in stride. One agency report described low-income boys as "just boys—boys whose natural inclinations toward gangs, hero worship and showing off can easily find dangerous outlets" (CBC Archives, Box 1, Folder 1). Yet, in their chronic quest for funding and legitimacy, after-school providers had to join the delinquency fray. After-school programs thus declared themselves the first line of defense against delinquency, uniquely positioned to catch children "on the way to trouble" (Hall, 1971, p. xiv). They would provide a sense of belonging and recognition not found elsewhere in children's lives, provide constructive alternatives to negative or oppositional identity, and not least provide outlets for children to express and explore their alienation and worries.

Art activities came to serve as a key outlet for such self-expression. A brochure for the settlement-wide children's art exhibit in New York City described earlier noted that "Here [in this exhibition] is war on prejudice, discrimination and juvenile delinquency. . . . The peaceful tools of the studio and workshop are providing the means to a new and richer life experience for young citizens" (UNH Archives, Box 3, Folder 27). Group work also gained renewed purchase as a vehicle for staff (preferably skilled social workers) and children to examine feelings of self-doubt, alienation, and anger and to explore issues of self, identity, affiliation, and attitudes toward authority (Bernstein, 1976). Any group activity could have a therapeutic dimension and be used for therapeutic purposes.

After-school programs recognized that they had to reach out physically to some children; thus a new role, the detached or street corner worker, was created. This role actually had long precedent—in settlement outreach work and later in the street corner work of indigenous workers and college and graduate students, which was part of the Chicago Area Project. This juvenile delinquency prevention initiative was conceived by Clifford Shaw and carried out in three low-income neighborhoods during the 1930s (Schlossman & Sedlak, 1983). The first aspect of the detached worker's role was to study the neighborhood, to identify nonschool programs and activities, and to establish relationships with providers, as well as with police, truant officers, and teachers, and to learn where children hung out. He would then engage children on their own territory, address their fears, gain their trust, "interpret" existing community resources for them, and become a "channel for the expression of [children's own] ideas on recreation" (UNH Archives, Box 24, Folder 277). In some cases, the detached worker concentrated on a particular block, in effect becoming part of the residents' daily life.

Another approach to outreach was the storefront center, reminiscent of the earliest boys' clubs. One local initiative, the East Harlem Youth Project, established such a center on a block in Harlem. It was staffed by a social work intern, whose job was to get to know (and gain the trust of) children who lived on the block, and then link them to existing institutional resources, including a nearby settlement house and boys' club. As with the original clubs, children's curiosity brought them to the front door. The intern soon discovered that the children, at first mostly 10- to 13-year-old boys, wanted a place that they could feel was theirs, and that the storefront suited that purpose. She organized a few activities, including painting, drawing, and simple woodwork, but set few behavioral rules and mostly let the children control the setting. In response, they took responsibility for it, monitoring one anothers' behavior and contributing their own materials and supplies. The father of one boy told the intern, "It's amazing that these kids bring things instead of rob things from here."

Changing Neighborhoods

Ethnic and racial change had always been a fact of life in low-income neighborhoods, and after-school programs had always struggled with the question of whether their commitment was to the neighborhood itself or to specific populations. Beginning in the 1950s, urban renewal, public housing development, and racial transition in scores of older neighborhoods made this question more acute than ever. In some cases, such as that of Boston's

West End, wholesale land clearance caused neighborhoods to literally disappear around particular agencies. Racial transition led agencies to try to hold on to populations they had served historically, typically children from White ethnic families. And providers found themselves once again helping migrants and immigrants adjust to urban life. In a letter to a funder, the director the Olivet Community Center noted that a "constantly increasing [group of] newcomers" from Puerto Rico and the south "don't understand Chicago and they can't understand each other . . . few belong to anything, none are 'at home'" (OCC Archives, Box 3).

Providers also tried to carve out space in the new "vertical neighborhoods" being created through massive high-rise public housing developments. Private agencies often had to fight both for a role in planning and providing services in new developments and for indoor space to be set aside for recreation programs, even when there was a clear lack of outdoor play space (Halpern, 1995). In some cases they had modest success; in others they found much greater hospitality. In the early 1950s, for example, the Chicago Boys' Clubs established two outposts in new Chicago Housing Authority developments. New York City's Housing Authority welcomed community agencies, and by 1959 there were 69 community centers operating in local public housing developments (Trolander, 1987, p. 83).

As the balance between African American or Puerto Rican and White, ethnic families shifted in some neighborhoods, after-school providers found themselves on the wrong side of invisible boundaries that children whom they had been serving would not cross, or right on the boundary between two groups, and thus at the heart of conflict. The author of a report on children's out-of-school lives in East Harlem commented that the degree to which children from different ethnic backgrounds "hate and suspect each other on sight alone defies exaggeration" (UNH Archives, Box 24, Folder 277). A report of an April 1947 meeting of head workers at Grosvenor House in New York City noted that "racial and inter-racial tensions are terrific at the moment, with gangs organized on distinct [racial] lines . . . with fights going on so long that in the end the participants no longer know what they are fighting about" (Box 3, Folder 29).

Most sponsors took on the task of addressing friction between ethnic and racial groups, creating opportunities for children from different groups to get to know one another and once again building trust between new populations. They held social and athletic events designed to bring children from different groups together under controlled circumstances. They created occasions to celebrate the culture and customs of new groups. They made a point of hiring African American and Latino staff. At the same time, some agencies started screening children at the door, to keep those youth known to cause trouble out of the building, or to monitor for weapons.

At a broader level, the leaders of long-standing social agencies worked to establish relationships with new community leaders, to ensure that their agency would continue to be seen as relevant. Even when it came to after-school programs, a less obvious form of social control or cultural imposition, providers were sometimes surprised to discover that they had to make their case for relevance once again. Thus, for instance, the leadership of the East Harlem Youth Project had to contend with a local Urban League director who told them that the community needed new housing and jobs, not "tiddlywinks."

CONCLUSION

Throughout the middle decades of the century, a time of extraordinary social events, after-school programs sought a balance between responding to external pressures and maintaining their particular identities. The field grew, solidified, and took the form it would maintain in coming decades—identifiable yet diverse in sponsorship and decentralized, with hundreds of local programs defining and shaping themselves in relative isolation. Many schools of thought continued to influence after-school practice, including play theory, progressive education, group work, and prevocationalism. Providers continued to search for reasonable goals and the right rationales, and especially struggled over a role for play.

In the upheaval and insecurity of depression, war, and then cold war, after-school programs served as a source of respite and stability for some children. Providers struggled with the neighborhood change, racial turnover, and ethnic tensions of the late 1950s, but so did almost every urban institution. These powerful events and social processes made it clear to after-school providers that the tasks of caring for and helping rear children were distinct to each time and place. Yet they also led providers to reaffirm the value of their approach and activities. After-school programs proved themselves to be at once conservative and mildly, if inadvertently, subversive. In a conservative objective such as broadening low-income children's cultural horizons, they exposed children to modern art and literature. Although they still prepared girls for traditional social roles, they also provided a base for independence and questioning of those roles.

In the literature of these decades, one sees a gradually strengthening sense of accomplishment. The 1931–1932 annual report of Grosvenor House in New York City noted of the changes in children in its after-school program: "Mothers tell us how different their boys and girls are at home. . . . they don't fight so much and try to help. . . . school teachers and welfare workers add their testimony to the difference between those who come to the settlement and those who do not." In November 1952, the director of a new boys' club in the Julia Lathrop Homes, a public housing development in Chicago, reported, "The management of the Julia Lathrop Homes . . . see a great improvement in the boys' behavior. . . . the window-breaking has been reduced to a new low, and there has been far less property damage than in the past" (CBC Archives, Box 87, Folder 5).

After-school programs continued to have to fight for the attention and allegiance of children, especially boys. And providers continued to struggle to understand and accept that children needed different things from after-school programs and used them and benefited from them in different ways. For most working-class children, after-school programs remained another neighborhood resource, used for sports, arts, crafts, socializing, and hanging out in cold weather. For a few children, they were an important source of support, recognition, help with problems, or respite from pressures elsewhere: "Kate may feel an urge to work off tensions by squashing clay between her fingers, without making anything at all. Or Concetta, who lives in a crowded home and is responsible for many brothers and sisters, may need to sit quietly for a while, simply looking out the window" (Franklin & Benedict, 1943, pp. 24–25). Children's own testimonials indicate that some were drawn to after-school programs by the very order and structure that kept others away. Girls were not drawn to the streets as strongly as boys were, and in that sense found after-school programs more hospitable than boys did.

Carmen Vega Rivera, director of East Harlem Tutorial, and a leading figure in the after-school field today, describes "growing up" at the Henry Street Settlement on New York City's Lower East Side (personal interview with the author, January 26, 2001). She lived three blocks away, and started coming to the settlement at age 5. During her elementary years she participated in sewing, woodworking, and cooking clubs ("whatever you made you ate") and took classes in the arts. Her friends were the other children who came to the settlement almost every day. As she grew older she joined Aspira, a leadership club for Hispanic youth, and became active in its community projects. Beyond retaining the strong physical memories of the settlement, Vega Rivera emphasized the fact that the staff listened to her, took her seriously. She felt that "she had a voice." She noted that, for many children from Hispanic immigrant families, the settlement's after-school programs were a safe, approved way to branch out and explore the broader world. For a few children, whose families were overwhelmed or preoccupied, they were "a salvation."

3

The Struggle for Relevance

Our children are having a hard time growing up because our civilization itself is experiencing an identity crisis.
—J. Sommerville, *The Rise and Fall of Childhood*

[After-school providers] are not straitjacketed by assumptions about how these programs ought to run; neither do we have in most instances sufficient resources to design and run them in harmony with our dreams.
—D. Fink, "School-Age Child Care: Where the Spirit of Neighborhood Lives"

The period between 1960 and 1990 offered little respite for an institution trying to maintain its footing. During these decades the social fabric of the United States, and especially its urban areas, was torn apart and never fully rewoven. In the 1960s, the federal War on Poverty created a seemingly promising new funding environment, scores of new service initiatives, and a brief moment of optimism about the potential of services to solve social problems. Within a few years, optimism had turned to disillusionment (accompanied by an attack on services and service providers), in the context of an increasingly militant minority rights movement. In spite of (and, some claimed, in part because of) the efforts of the federal government, the inner-city neighborhoods in which after-school programs operated were becoming increasingly isolated from the social and economic mainstream of society, leading to a deterioration in the quality of life, a decline in social organization, and new threats to children's well-being.

The 1970s and 1980s brought new purposes to after-school programs. A rapid growth in maternal employment across social classes led to renewed interest in these programs' child care function. The growing involvement of the early childhood community in after-school provision renewed the commitment to the importance of play. The women's movement focused attention on the distinct needs and rights of girls. At the same time, a smaller rights movement, focused on the general condition of children in society, raised questions about the growing institutionalization of childhood. Moreover, a decade and a half of urban fiscal crisis led after-school programs to scramble constantly for funding just to keep operating.

THE WAR ON POVERTY YEARS

Although after-school programs had always adapted as necessary, they had basically been operating in the same way for more than half a century. In the 1960s they found that this was no longer possible. They had to find a niche among the scores of new programs and initiatives stimulated by the War on Poverty. They had to respond to sometimes militant criticism of their approaches and relevance. They had to contribute to the new societal task of improving educational success among inner-city children. And they felt compelled to respond to the basic needs of children who increasingly seemed too much on their own, psychologically as well as physically.

By the early 1960s, both the demographics and the structure of urban poverty were changing. Jobs were permanently leaving the central city, now predominantly African American and Hispanic, for the white urban periphery and the suburbs. In 1940, unemployment among African Americans was 20% higher than among Whites. By 1953 that figure had climbed to 71% higher; and by 1963 to 112% higher (Marris & Rein, 1973, p. 11). Inner-city residents, many of whom had migrated to the central city during the previous 10 or 15 years, were "left behind" and "left out." The majority of inner-city children would remain poor throughout their childhood; and close to a majority would live in families with no or only intermittent wage earners, and therefore forced to rely on welfare.

As a result of unemployment, disinvestment, and changing family structure, low-income urban neighborhoods were changing in ways that made them far less supportive settings for child development (Nightingale, 1993; Silverstein & Krate, 1975). For many decades, the streets, stoops, and other public spaces had offered a largely positive developmental context for children. They had provided ingredients for play, opportunity for conversation, and lessons in self-government. Clark (1985, p. 269), for instance, argues that the stoop had an impact on children "no less enduring than [that of] the school, the church and perhaps even the family." It was a home port, safety valve, and learning center. Informal outdoor play taught children quickness of mind, self-confidence, and the abilities to cope with all kinds of people and situations and to sort out and respond to complex demands. Adults, meanwhile, had provided "a safety net, a web of sociability and unobtrusive guidance" (Dargan & Zeitlin, 1990, p. 170).

Now critical changes included the breakdown of traditional social organization, a decline in informal social control, and the beginning of a shift from ethnically based or turf-driven gang conflict to drug-related violence. The idea that inner-city children were raising themselves—an idea that would be echoed with increasing regularity in subsequent decades—first appeared in the literature. Mays (1965, p. 7), for instance, noted that "the whole business" of growing up too often "goes by default." Community adults were observed to be withdrawing (mostly out of fear) from monitoring children's behavior and letting children know when such behavior was wrong. At the same time, some inner-city parents began to place more restriction on their children's movements. In a mid-1970s study in East Harlem, Boocock (1981, pp. 98–99) found that more than half of a sample of children she talked to were not permitted to leave the house on their own to play outside.

Observers began to document the effects of community isolation on children's life experience. In describing the childhood of a boy who had grown up in a low-income minority neighborhood in Pittsburgh during these years, Williams (1985, p. 22) remarks that "these were the days when Ray did not know what a library or a museum was. . . . He was never taken downtown, and his parents subscribed to no newspapers or magazines." A study of the daily lives of elementary-age inner-city children in New York City found that "they do not read, they do not study, they do not take lessons, they do not get instruction in any of the things that interest many children at these ages" (Keller, 1963, pp. 829, 826). The author went on to worry that such "constriction of experience" undermined children's school success. In testimony before the National Advisory Commission on Civil Disorders in the wake of ghetto riots in a number of cities in the mid-1960s, the Cleveland school superintendent described social isolation as one part of the equation of poor educational outcomes among inner-city children. The other two parts were poor-quality schools and unsupportive family environments.

Criticism of the schooling provided to low-income children intensified. Old themes were reiterated. Schooling was marked by rote learning, rigidity, pointless rules, and failure to respond to children's individual interests or support needs. New themes emerged. Low-income children had less opportunity than more advantaged peers to explore, construct, problem solve, and create. Inner-city schools were underfinanced, overcrowded, and dilapidated; lacked textbooks; had less experienced and less qualified teachers; had high teacher turnover; and were thoroughly segregated (National Advisory Commission on Civil Disorders, 1968, pp. 236–252). Schools were held to ignore and belittle low-income, minority children's language, culture, and community, and to be little more than sorting machines.

At the same time, the home environments of inner-city children also were noted to be unconducive to educational success. Observers described overcrowded homes where lack of space, light, and quiet, and lack of books and other learning materials, made it difficult for children to study. Parents were accused of raising their children's anxiety about school by threatening punishment by school staff for misbehavior (Moore, 1969). Whether or not this portrait was an exaggeration, another aspect of the gap between home and school was real. Children, beginning as early as fourth or fifth grade, were losing faith in the value and purpose of public education. They were coming to see it as irrelevant to their lives and, more than ever, as someone else's institution. That led them to a feeling even more destructive than the alienation of the 1950s, that of being completely blocked, at once shut in and shut out. As one observer noted, the inner-city child was "caught in a cage in which there is not even the illusion of freedom of action to change his situation, except, of course, in activities outside the law" (Ward, 1978, p. 17).

SEEKING A NICHE IN THE WAR ON POVERTY

Although the War on Poverty had a variety of conceptual underpinnings, one study is often cited as key to the work of that decade. In 1960, Lloyd Ohlin and Richard Cloward of the Columbia University School of Social Work published a book in which they argued that delinquency was caused not by bad parenting, community disorganization, comic books, or general moral breakdown, but by exclusion from opportunity to employ socially approved means (i.e., education, "extracurricular" activities, part-time jobs) to strive for socially approved goals (Cloward & Ohlin, 1960). "Blocked opportunity" led older children and adolescents to seek deviant means of achieving their goals, led to alienation from social norms (already noted in the 1950s), and would ultimately lead to a "social explosion." Lack of opportunity quickly became a key organizing concept for the problem-solving efforts of the decade, and education became the principal arena for re-creating it.

A New Educational Role for After-School Programs. Along with the historic role in preventing juvenile delinquency, equalizing educational opportunity provided the main rationale for modest new investments in after-school programming during the 1960s. The latter goal was new for after-school providers, who were asked for the first time to help foster low-income children's basic literacy and academic achievement. This new task derived from a growing conviction among policy elites that, while reforming schools was critical, the full range of community institutions had to be mobilized in efforts to improve the lives and life chances of low-income children (Halpern, 1995). It derived also from research findings suggesting that children's home and community environments, and experiences outside school, were as important as, or more important than, their school experiences in determining educational success (Coleman, 1966).

The goals of addressing delinquency and equalizing educational opportunity were brought to the attention of President John F. Kennedy's domestic policy advisors by academics, including Lloyd Ohlin, family members such as Sargent Shriver (who had been involved in delinquency prevention in the 1950s), and staff of the Ford Foundation, who had just funded one delinquency prevention initiative on New York City's Lower East Side, called Mobilization for Youth, and were planning their own educationally oriented initiative, to be known as the Gray Areas Project. After-school programming was a modest element of both, but was more developed within the latter.

After-School Programming in a Major Foundation Initiative. The Ford Foundation's Gray Areas Project was a four-city effort premised on the ideas that inner-city residents, particularly the coming generation, needed to be made better prepared for the demands of a complex industrial economy; that mainstream public institutions had to be turned toward this goal and made more responsive to the needs of inner-city residents; and that at times it would be necessary to work around these institutions, to "create new instrumentalities" (Ford Foundation, 1967). In the service of these ideas, local Gray Areas Projects funded a variety of services to children, including preschool; enriched educational services (reading initiatives, tutoring, summer school, and teacher training); and, more selectively, after-school and "youth development" programs.

The Oakland project, for instance, developed after-school study centers in which high school youth helped elementary school children with homework. In discussing the rationale for the centers, project staff noted that "some children are from families of nine or ten people crammed into three rooms, a television set blares, babies cry, distracted parents lose their tempers, and school work goes undone" (Ford Foundation, 1967, p. 8). The New Haven project created seven community schools, with after-school programs that included "play groups," classes in visual and performing arts, crafts, athletics, and tutoring. New services to children were conceived in part as an indirect way of getting at parents. In commenting on the after-school programs of the New Haven Gray Areas Project, Mayor Richard Lee remarked that "we tried getting at the children first. We started afternoon and evening programs in recreation and tutoring. Sometimes, through these kids, the message began going home to the parents—simple messages, like the importance of washing hands or balancing a diet" (Ford Foundation, 1967, pp. 8, 13).

In order to better serve children, agencies funded by Gray Areas were required to work together. After-school providers, for example, were asked to work with schools, housing authorities, and police departments. This expectation and role was not as new to them as was perceived by Ford Foundation staff. Nonetheless, in a staff report on the Oakland project, it was noted that "the police began to change their views of probation officers as a bunch of 'bleeding hearts.' Probation people, sitting across the table from police, had to stop thinking of them as 'skull-cracking cops.' Recreation officials no longer thought dogmatically, 'If I had hold of that kid first, he wouldn't have gotten into trouble'" (Ford Foundation, 1967, p. 7).

Local Gray Area staff discovered, nonetheless, that it was difficult to alter the values and behavior of public institutions, especially schools. They had expected that the innovative, holisic and positive approaches to children demonstrated by preschool or after-school programs would influence core school practices. Yet education "was extended into holidays, evenings, or early childhood by summer school, after-school and preschool programs, without challenging the everyday classroom routines." Innovation was limited to whatever the schools were willing to tolerate (Marris & Rein, 1973, pp. 63, 66). Other factors also complicated efforts to improve services for children, diverting administrators' attention and draining participants' energy. These included a new philosophical commitment to community participation in designing and implementing problem-solving efforts, and growing political conflict between residents of low-income communities and institutions charged with providing services to those residents.

Fighting for Scraps from the Federal Larder. Even as private initiatives such as Gray Areas were struggling to define a workable yet sufficiently ambitious approach to addressing urban poverty, they became the blueprint for the government's War on Poverty. President Lyndon B. Johnson inherited the goals of preventing delinquency and equalizing opportunity and, in the face of political obstacles to a more direct attack on poverty through job creation and improved wages, made these ideas (especially the latter) a centerpiece of his poverty-fighting program. Although President Johnson's indirect War on Poverty dramatically increased federal funding for services to children, most of that funding went either to early childhood services, especially Head Start; compensatory education programs; or initiatives for older youth. The actual disbursement of federal poverty funds was controlled by the new agencies set up to administer the community action programs, by mayors and other local politicians, and to a modest extent by the schools. Established after-school providers had to figure out where control of funds resided, develop relationships with the new funders, and fight for scraps from such federal programs as the Neighborhood Youth Corps, Title I compensatory education, and general community action budgets, adapting their rhetoric and adjusting their emphases to the priorities behind those programs.

Most new federal funding also came with strings attached—a particular objective, strategy, or population or a requirement to collaborate with other institutions. One funder might encourage after-school providers to extend themselves beyond the boundaries of their buildings, to do street work and outreach, on the assumption that the children who most needed after-school services were not being reached. Another might emphasize educational tutoring; another might require greater community participation. An initiative in Chicago called STREETS, for instance, used outreach workers to identify "unreached" children and link them to existing community resources. It required the Boys Clubs', YMCAs, Chicago Youth Centers (a multisite network of after-school programs), and the local federation of settlements to develop a common plan and work closely together, something none of these agencies were accustomed to. (Indeed, this initiative fell apart after just a few years due to conflict over goals and philosophy among the participants.)

Since a good deal of federal money was available for school reform, after-school providers had to discern and respond to the currents swirling around that embattled institution. Long-standing philosophical and curricular battles among school reformers took on explicitly political dimensions, in the context of the civil rights movement. Some argued that learning, in school and out, had to be built on children's life experiences, culture, and language; others that children needed compensatory experiences that reduced their social and cultural isolation. Some argued for less adult coercion in the learning process and for more respect for individual differences; others for methods of learning that helped children come to see the inequities of their society and that encouraged them to become politically conscious. A few reformers argued for the "deschooling" of society, in order to eliminate the institutions that oppressed low-income children (see, e.g., Illich, 1970).

Balancing Independence and Relevance. After-school providers viewed new War on Poverty–related opportunities and ideas ambivalently. Most valued the relative independence that historically had come with private funding. Yet most providers also believed that they were well placed to meet the new societal goals for low-income children. Their agencies were rooted in and oriented toward their communities; their programs were child centered; and in some cases they already had initiatives in place to address delinquency and educational problems. Most providers were also exhausted by the difficulty of having to sell themselves and raise their budgets anew each year, a task that had become more difficult after more than a decade of institution building. Between 1954 and 1964, for instance, the overall budget of the Chicago Boys' Clubs had tripled. The costs of federal funding—becoming more project-oriented, writing proposals using the rhetoric demanded by particular initiatives, demonstrating that one could collaborate, defining measurable outcomes to be achieved—seemed worth the benefit of a predictable funding stream lasting 3 or more years.

Providers tried to seek a balance between long-standing philosophies and changing demands. A 1964 review by administrators of the Chicago Boys' Clubs reiterated that most of the activities of the local clubs were provided and enjoyed "for the sake of the activities themselves without any great focus on . . . later productivity" yet goes on to note a new element of "utility" in some activities. The authors write that "what is still basically a recreation program is moving toward one of education; of counseling" and that the boys' clubs were "in process of becoming community action directed" (CBC Archives, Box 193, Folder 11). As ethnic pride became a more prominent feature of low-income communities, providers created clubs and specific activities that built on ethnic identification. In Chicago, the American Friends Service Committee ran the Pre-Adolescent Enrichment Program for children in the Garfield Park neighborhood, a program that included "cultural education, creative expression, community service and inter-group relations" (CBC Archives, Box 171, Folder 8).

New Roles for After-School Programs

The historic core of most after-school programs remained intact. The 1967 program guide to the Hudson Guild, located in Manhattan's Chelsea district, included arts and crafts, miscellaneous clubs (including a chess club), ceramics, gym, music, and dance lessons, among other activities. New emphases and activities were simply added on to existing frameworks. Like other providers, Hudson Guild began offering various forms of "educational enrichment." It developed and ran a program called Operation Brainstorm, which provided tutoring and enriched educational and cultural activities for seventh to ninth graders; and also a Study Den, providing homework help and tutoring for elementary and junior high children. Program reports from this era more commonly noted literacy-related activities, such as spelling bees, Scrabble tournaments, and book clubs, and science activities and projects. Traditional activities were sometimes provided under the cover of academic enrichment. Metal or crafts or electricity shops now did "science experiments" (CBC Archives, Box 177, Folder 9). Programs took advantage of federal funding for at-risk youth to employ them as tutors for school-age children. The assumption was that giving such youth responsibility would bring out or develop qualities that the schools had been unable to stimulate. In fact, tutors, often with limited basic skills and marginal literacy themselves, were reported to benefit more than those they tutored.

As after-school providers attended more to academic concerns, school systems dabbled with after-school programming, occasionally to innovative effect. In 1967 the Dayton, Ohio, public schools initiated a program called the Living Arts, focused on nurturing artistic talent. It was housed in a remodeled school warehouse, with space created for music (primarily instrumental but including conducting and exploring sound), drama, creative writing, literature, visual arts (including welding and weaving), and dance. It employed guest artists as well as regular, part-time instructors. In San Diego, a third-grade teacher started a program called the Elementary Institute of Science, for fourth through sixth graders, situated in a house that belonged to the city. It included chemistry, electronics and geology labs; beehives; a terrarium; an aquarium; astronomy and space study; and a photography studio. Staff included public school teachers and volunteers, including graduate students in the sciences (Ford, 1977).

The War on Poverty's emphasis on community participation strongly affected after-school programs' staffing approaches. Providers began hiring more indigenous workers from the community, and from that time forward most staff in after-school programs would be from the same ethnic, racial, and social class backgrounds as children served. The shift in staffing was not accompanied by improved training or supervision, the lack of which continued to cause major problems. A few observers wondered where the new workers, often having had mediocre and stultifying educational experiences themselves, would find the "models" needed to provide interesting, enriching experiences to children: "Creativity is inventiveness, imaginativeness, ability to cope in new ways with given factors. It's a process. It can only be 'taught' to children by people who have it, and people who have it, have it because they have experienced the process themselves while growing up or while in one kind of program or another" (Greenberg, 1969/1990, p. 43).

Meanwhile, social workers recommitted themselves to after-school work, drawing on traditional group-work theory, but also trying to use after-school programs as a vehicle for deeper relationships with vulnerable children and families. One program in New York City, Interfaith Neighbors (based in its early years at Lennox Hill Neighborhood House), combined tutoring with group work, on the assumption that inner-city children's educational and psychosocial difficulties were intertwined. Educational and social work staff focused together on such problems as truancy, petty theft, conflict with parents, and (among older children) drinking: "The difficulties we see in our children do not go away with the passing of time, but in most instances get worse and more complex as adolescence approaches" (Interfaith Neighbors, n.d.). Girls and boys met once or twice a week individually with tutor/mentors and had their own groups, led by social workers, which also met weekly to discuss daily life, concerns, and worries. Participants would then join in the regular recreational activities at the settlement.

By the late 1960s, after-school providers, like the members of the communities they served, felt as if they had been through fire. Most had struggled through the late 1950s and early 1960s to figure out a place and identity in what had become largely minority neighborhoods. Now, having joined a historic, but fundamentally limited, effort to improve the lives of the residents of those neighborhoods, they were attacked whenever that effort was attacked—and in the latter part of the decade the War on Poverty, particularly its community action program, was attacked regularly in the media, by politicians, and by the poor themselves. In 1966, the four largest after-school providers in Chicago—the boys' clubs, settlements, Chicago Youth Centers, and YMCA—actually felt compelled to issue a joint public statement describing how the federal funding they had received had not been wasted or misused but had helped them reach more children and had encouraged them to work together more effectively (CBC Archives, Box 177, Folder 6).

Perhaps most painfully, after-school providers were criticized by the new community leaders and residents with whom they were trying to collaborate. Although they believed in their missions and philosophies, they inevitably lost some faith in themselves when they heard their traditional activities and methods described as stale and their overall efforts as irrelevant, even as part of the problem (Moynihan, 1969). Along with other discrete services, after-school programs were criticized as Band-Aids and sops. Meanwhile, brand-new community organizations, led and staffed by nonprofessionals, assumed the mandate to provide a range of services, including after-school programming, sometimes competing directly with established providers. Yet as one participant in the work of these new organizations noted, they were "long on polemics and ideology, short on specifics and soundly based practice" (Taylor & Randolph, 1975, p. xi).

THE NEW LATCHKEY CHILD AND SCHOOL-AGE CHILD CARE

The 1970s and 1980s brought renewed interest in the child care function of after-school programs, as a result of growth in maternal employment (across social class), and of newly emergent women's organizations, which pushed for programs to meet women's and families' needs. The after-school field reclaimed an old symbol, the latchkey child of World War II, and gained a new dimension, called "school-age child care." Most proponents of school-age child care were concerned with, and talked about, the needs of middle-class families, and were thus able to garner the kind of political attention that those who had historically been committed to serving low-income children had not managed to receive. At the same time, both new and long-standing proponents were unable to secure increased public funding for after-school programs, because of a sustained fiscal crisis in urban areas, a federal government preoccupied with devolution and spending caps, and a meandering (and ultimately fruitless) debate about public responsibility for child care.

While the new interest in after-school programs was driven by the fact that middle-class mothers were entering the labor force in significant numbers, there was some residual attention to the support needs of low- and moderate-income families, including growing numbers of divorced and single-parent families. It was pointed out that the children most negatively affected by these three social trends resided in low-income communities (Hedin, Hannes, Saito, Goldman, & Knich, 1986) and that in many cities, close to a majority of school-age children lived in or near poverty. The image of the worried, neglected latchkey child was revived, and the popular media reported stories of children locking themselves in bathrooms or closets; walking around their apartments with baseball bats; or in the case of one child, getting trapped in the chimney while trying to get into his house. Echoing the rhetoric of the 1940s, the writer of a 1981 article called latchkey children the "new orphans of today's harsh economic world" (Wellborn, 1981, p. 42). The writer reported a growing number of locked-out children, forced to hang around school yards or stay on the streets, subject to harassment by gangs, until parents arrived home.

Academics debated the effects of "self-care" after school. Some argued that children who spent considerable time in self-care were at risk for lower grades, psychological distress, accidents, and inactivity (Core, 1978; Golden, 1981; Seligson, 1984). Others saw a more complex picture. A child's age, gender, social class, and personality; the family situation; parental rules and monitoring strategies; and neighborhood conditions all influenced the self-care experience and its effects, as did the number of hours of self-care daily and weekly and the presence or absence of siblings, friends, nearby neighbors or relatives (Miller & Marx, 1990; Robinson, Rowland, & Coleman, 1989; Steinberg, 1986). In one study, which included children from diverse socioeconomic backgrounds, children described self-care as a mixed experience, characterized by both worries and pleasures (Hedin et al., 1986). There were clear social class differences in findings: While 80% of all fourth through eighth graders reported liking being home alone, only 50% of those from low-income single-parent families did. Low-income girls were especially likely to report a variety of fears, including that of being victimized.

AFTER-SCHOOL PROGRAMMING AS CHILD CARE

The reintroduction of a child care dimension to after-school programming complicated the task of long-standing proponents and providers. Interest in child care appeared to create new opportunities for after-school funding. Yet the child care debate was strongly ideological and was not for the most part a poverty-related one. Child care was more about meeting the needs of working families than about meeting the developmental needs of low-income children The funding structure of child care and after-school programming were very different. Child care was perceived as a fee-based service, with parents paying what they could and government or private funders subsidizing the rest of the cost. Most after-school programming historically had been provided free of charge (or virtually so). Participation patterns were different in child care and after-school programming. Also, child care was perceived primarily as an early childhood service.

After-school providers tried to link their work to the child care and latchkey debates, in part by using a delinquency prevention argument. The director of a California program remarked, "Before we started, there was a lot of vandalism in the neighborhood. Kids ran in gangs, broke windows, destroyed plants and made messes. . . . we can't prevent it all, but by giving the children a loving environment and something interesting to do, we're better able to get a handle on it" (cited in Wellborn, 1981, p. 47). A Cambridge, Massachusetts, city councilwoman noted that latchkey children "have the freedom to get into whatever they want, and with peer pressure they may wind up in the courts or on dope" (Saundra Graham cited in Golden, 1981, p. 24).

Although public and government debate about day care increased in the 1970s, little was accomplished in terms of legislation or new public funding. The most significant piece of federal legislation was the 1971 Comprehensive Child Development Act, sponsored by Senator Walter Mondale and Representative John Brademas. It would have created a broad national child care policy for children from birth to age 14, a mandate for federal support, and an administrative agency under the aegis of the federal government. But though passed by both houses of Congress, the act was vetoed by President Richard Nixon. In 1972 the U.S. Department of Health, Education, and Welfare established an interagency School-Age Day Care Task Force. The task force appears to have accomplished little beyond a survey of 58 selected programs, whose findings were never released, but which reportedly found financial and facilities problems, among other obstacles to provision of care. Subsequent child care legislation introduced by Senator Alan Cranston, which included language on the need for after-school programs, did not pass Congress, a victim of growing financial pressures facing the federal government and of declining public interest in social reform. In 1985 an authorization for a "school-age child care and dependent care resource and referral" block grant was passed by Congress and signed by President Ronald Reagan, but funds were not appropriated for it.

A few states, such as California, provided a modest amount of state funding for "latchkey" programming. California's program, operated by the schools, was designed to serve low-income children. For the most part, state governments saw the development of new after-school programming, whether for child care, delinquency prevention, or other purposes, as a community issue. In his January 1983 Message to the Legislature, New York governor Mario Cuomo argued that "the state must assist families as they work in their communities to develop local after-school services" (p. 23). Mayor's offices, city planning departments, and social service or child welfare agencies did surveys that demonstrated a need for after-school care, as did local day care councils and task forces and women's commissions. Yet growing fiscal pressures on municipal governments were leading to cutbacks, not growth, in funding, and these fell disproportionately on what were viewed as nonessential programs: "libraries, parks, recreation, school sports and extracurricular activities" (Medrich, 1983, p. iv).

Most new program development in "school-age care" was in fact generated locally and sustained with minimal public resources. Working mothers whose children attended child care or preschool centers suddenly discovered a lack of options when their children reached school age. In some cases they went back to those centers and pleaded with directors to offer school-age care. Reports began appearing of children sent to libraries after school by working parents with no other options (Children's Advocate, 1987). Families with modest incomes were willing to take a chance with self-care, rather than pay unaffordable fees for after-school care.

Urban school systems continued to shy away from formal after-school programming. The comments of a New Haven school administrator captured the prevailing sentiment of his colleagues: "What is the prime purpose of the schools? Is it to provide all these social services or is it to educate kids? We have to draw the line somewhere" (Schneider, 1982, p. B1). One skeptic suggested that the schools had "a lot to do just to clean up their own act and take care of their original mission" (WSACCP, 1985). Yet under pressure from parents and women's groups, a handful of school districts and individual schools flirted once again with extended day and drop-in programs. Proponents argued that after-school care made a school more attractive to "working" (i.e. White, ethnic) families, and that this might help dissuade them from fleeing the school district (an emerging correlate of court-mandated desegregation efforts [Seligson, 1984, p. 5]). They focused on underutilized space, especially during a time of declining enrollment. Excess space was described as an "albatross" around the necks of school administrators and taxpayers (Scofield & Page, 1982). Proponents noted that the presence of organized activities after school reduced school vandalism, and they argued for schools' general responsibility as community institutions.

Small after-school initiatives popped up all over the country, sometimes involving a public-private partnership using school space. The Shreveport (Louisiana) Women's Commission (appointed by the mayor) started an initiative called the Youth Enrichment Program, based in 18 elementary schools. In addition to the typical mix of daily activities, the program included weekly arts classes led by regional artists, supplied by the Shreveport Arts Council. In New York City's Chinatown the community planning council ran programs using school space. In the mid-1980s, a program called the After-School Partnership was developed by the Houston Committee for Private Sector Initiative. Using a mix of corporate funding and in-kind contributions (of space, janitorial services, and a few teachers for homework help and tutoring) from the school district, the partnership sponsored after-school programs operated by community-based agencies (including the Campfire Girls, YMCA, YWCA, and the local Child Care Council) in 14 elementary schools serving low- and moderate-income children.

A handful of local school districts ran their own after-school programs, with mixed consequences. One local Queens, New York, school district designed an after-school program that put teachers' aides in regular classrooms with 30 children, with few additional resources for any kind of activities. A Houston public official, who had observed after-school programs run by the schools, told an interviewer that "75 percent are just more classes. . . . In most cases just regular teachers who have been there all day already, and I'd say there's a degree of burnout" (WSACCP, 1985). Core (1978, p. 4) discussed one "well-meaning" urban principal who described "with some pride" an after-school program that kept "300 children seated in the cafeteria under the supervision of one teacher until parents came."

In the absence of formal initiatives, community organizations that wanted to start after-school programs often had to beg and borrow space, in former fire houses, basements, or school cafeterias. Those trying to work with schools to expand programming, especially YMCAs and YWCAs, found schools to be a difficult partner. Administrators worried about liability. Principals worried about wear and tear on the physical plant. Custodial staff were reluctant to work overtime. Teachers acted as though "you're using their living room" (Pullum, 1985). School districts, under financial pressure themselves, were reluctant to share costs (such as custodial overtime) or to rent space to after-school providers at lower rates than they charged other service providers. A quarter to a third of the budgets in some school-based programs went to rental. The director of a YMCA-operated after-school program in the Buffalo schools noted that his main problem was convincing school administrators that his program was not just another way for the school to earn some rental money, but a developmental support for children served by the school (WSACCP, 1985).

New Sources of Financing Run Into a Fiscal Crisis

Except for a brief period during World War II, after-school programs had always relied almost exclusively on private funding, from individual donors, corporate donors, community chests and United Ways. Most fees were purely symbolic. As noted earlier, the federal funding mechanisms and programs associated with the War on Poverty (supplemented in a few cities by foundation funding) had provided a small amount new funding. A modest amount of CETA (Community Employment Training Act) money continued to be used to fund positions in after-school programs. (CETA workers were a mixed blessing, since CETA sometimes sent unqualified or inappropriate people to after-school programs as staff, and the positions were unstable from year to year.) Title IV-A of the Social Security Act appears to have provided a small amount of funding for after-school programs. For example, in Portland, Oregon, the YMCA used Title IV-A funding to run 12 "latchkey" programs.

Beginning in 1974, Title XX of the Social Security Act, which was focused partly on helping low-income parents achieve self-sufficiency, provided a potentially more significant funding stream for after-school programs. Title XX funds enabled child care centers to provide more after-school care. (At the same time, school-age care funding usually came out of the same pot of money allotted to a city for preschool care, leading advocates to describe the process as "robbing three-year-old Peter to pay eight-year-old Paul" [Golden, 1981, p. 24].) Agencies licensed as child care providers, as well as selected other community agencies, were eligible also for funding from the Department of Agriculture's Child Care Food Program, initiated as a pilot program in 1968 and made permanent in 1978.

The promise of new funding for after-school programs was nonetheless undermined by fiscal crisis at all levels of government, combined with high inflation. Over the course of the 1980s, the real dollar value of Title XX funding declined by half. The percentage of city expenditures covered by federal aid fell from 22% to 6%, forcing cities to shift their own resources to basic services, which did not include after-school programs (Weir, 1993). In 1977 the San Francisco Recreation and Parks Department had 119 full-time recreation directors; 10 years later it had 55. Community Development and Social Service block grants provided some modest new funding, when after-school providers were able to fight their way onto local political agendas and wish lists. But this funding was sporadic and unevenly distributed. Private funders such as United Ways were also weakened by larger economic events, compounding after-school programs' funding difficulties.

Under sustained financial pressure for most of the decade, after-school providers were forced to raise fees and parent co-payments (and even then many ran operating deficits). They soon discovered that even modest fees kept children from participating, as low-income parents could not or would not pay for a service that they did not view as a necessity. A 1989 study of after-school programs in New York City found long waiting lists in free or nearly free programs, and no waiting lists (or empty places) in fee-based programs (Seligson & Marx, 1989). Erickson (1988, p. 91) cited one single parent who told her that "the only community after-school program available for her two youngest children, aged six and eight, would consume 39 percent of her take-home pay."

CHANGING IDEAS SHAPING AFTER-SCHOOL PRACTICE

After-school programs in the 1970s and 1980s were also buffeted by an unusual mixture of ideological crosscurrents. The feminist movement began to influence perceptions of what girls needed from after-school programs. The goal of preparation for domestic roles receded, replaced by the idea that girls could be and could do anything. A new emphasis on gender equity was defined at first as gender integration; separate activities for girls were discontinued in most programs, even though such activities historically had provided a valuable social space for girls. Support for and enrollment in all-female institutions was declining throughout society. Independent girls' clubs, which by 1974 included 134 local affiliates in 700 program sites, were losing members and struggling financially and came under pressure to merge with boys' clubs. Girls' clubs experimented with joint projects and programs with boys' clubs, with limited success. Boys' club leadership and staff reportedly were unable to take seriously girls' desire for an equal voice (Phelps, 1995). When older boys and girls were together, boys tended to monopolize activities.

The Renewal of Child-Centered Philosophy. Further, after-school programs were influenced by a movement to stem the institutionalization of childhood and to liberate children from adult intrusion and control over their lives. Winn (1981, p. 191) noted the "strange sort of affection" provided children in settings such as after-school programs. Suransky (1982) argued that adult-led institutions seemed to rob the child of his or her self, through appropriating and trying to shape and control the child's everyday life experience. In adult-led institutions the child had only the "illusion" of choice, the "freedom to take the right option but not the wrong one" (p. 72). The emphasis, moreover, was on "a denial of conflict in favor of a strong socialization toward order, structure and harmony" (p. 76). Children's rights advocates accused those who cared for children of ignoring their true developmental

needs "in favor of adult needs for manipulation, convenience, control and
. . . system maintenance" (Erickson, 1988, pp. 87, 88).

After-school providers themselves worried about the suppression of
children's agendas. Core (1978, p. 4) wrote that the danger of after-school
programs was that they would be a place where children were "kept, waiting for something to happen, a place where children are further institutionalized and isolated from the normal pursuits of childhood." She warned
against "confiscating" the after-school hours of children, even with the well-
meaning intention of protecting children during those hours. Another provider argued that children's after-school hours should not be seen as as "time
when children are simply vulnerable to the perils of non-supervision" and
"not simply [time] to cram more information into children's brains or even
to immerse them in a bath of special activities thought by adults to be culturally appropriate" (Fink, 1986, p. 11).

Children's rights themes were consonant with the philosophies of early
childhood providers, who were assuming a growing role in the after-school
field. As their forebearers in the play-school movement had done, providers
with early childhood backgrounds articulated a nurturant, child-centered and
play-oriented vision for after-school programs. Evidence of an early childhood orientation could be seen in programs organizing classrooms into interest areas, which included dramatic play and block play. Providers with
an early childhood background reiterated the Progressive notion that children loved to experiment and learned by doing, emphasized a balance between large-group and small-group or individualized activity, and argued
against sex-role stereotyping. They opposed "too much structure, which is
said to cause children to lose touch with the personal creativity through which
they work out emotional conflicts and develop intellectually" (Martin &
Ascher, 1994, p. 14).

Educational Agendas Intrude. The renewal of a child-centered (some called
it "development-centered") thrust in after-school programming, never dominant to begin with, was constrained almost as soon as it reappeared, by yet
another perceived crisis in public education. In 1983, the U.S. Department of
Education published *A Nation at Risk*, a commission report in which its authors
argued that the well-being and future of American society were threatened by
"a rising tide of mediocrity" in the public schools (U.S. Department of Education, 1983, p. 1). The authors noted that many children were not acquiring
literacy, achievement test scores were declining, and children were not spending enough time learning. If the reaction in the 1960s had been to decentralize
the schools, loosen up curriculum, trust children, and give some control to the
community, it was now the opposite—to tighten accountability and administrative control and to reemphasize basic skills and direct instruction.

After-school providers did not need a report by the U.S. Secretary of Education to know that the children they served were struggling with school. They observed the consequences every day during homework time, which was becoming ubiquitous, and witnessed it from year to year as children gradually disengaged from school and withdrew from educational tasks (Halpern, 1990). They observed the schools in their neighborhoods continue to deteriorate, under tremendous financial pressure. Class sizes were growing, and recess, gym, and the arts were disappearing from school schedules. As in the 1930s, there were sporadic calls for after-school programs to fill in activities deleted from school schedules. And as in the 1960s, there were calls for after-school programs to take on the problem of educational failure directly, by helping foster children's basic academic skills (see, e.g., Sheley, 1984). Yet this role sat uncomfortably with providers, who continued to believe their mission to be broader and who continued to define their programs as a complement to school. In describing the after-school program at the Center for Family Life, a community-based agency in Brooklyn's Sunset Park neighborhood, Ellowitch and colleagues (1991, p. 19) remarked that "while the program has addressed issues related to literacy and schooling throughout the years, the staff is quick to emphasize that they not view their program primarily as an educational one. . . . Rather they aim to provide an environment in which the whole child will be stimulated and nurtured. . . . The staff emphatically stresses that learning not be conceived in the narrow sense that schools, and often parents, take for granted."

CHILDREN WITH GROWING SUPPORT NEEDS, PROGRAMS WITH LIMITED CAPACITY

In addition to their struggle to find an appropriate role in meeting children's educational needs, after-school programs were increasingly serving children with a variety of vulnerabilities. The long-term process of social and economic disinvestment in inner-city neighborhoods, which had slowed modestly in the 1960s, accelerated again during the 1970s and 1980s. By the late 1980s, the neighborhood had become important in a very different way to low-income children. It had always defined whom children interacted with, whom they learned from, and how and what they played. Now it had become a "risk factor." Formal and informal sources of nurturance, supervision, and socialization for children were thinning out. A steadily higher percentage of children and families had difficulties, leading researchers to describe a new phenomenon that they labeled "concentration effects." Gangs increasingly provided one of the few coherent sources of support, structure, and identity for children.

In a study by this author of a network of inner-city after-school programs sponsored by the Chicago Youth Centers (CYC), staff reported that each year, the children served seemed to carry a greater load of worries and stresses, because of family problems, school conflict, neighborhood violence, and stressful life events (Halpern, 1990). Too many program participants were forced to fend for themselves and sometimes for younger siblings. This same study revealed a major transformation in the way children approached the world between the ages of 6 or 7 and 10 or 11, with enthusiasm and curiosity replaced by wariness, disdain, and competitiveness. Staff in the CYC programs felt compelled to assume nurturance and socialization functions previously assumed by parents and relatives. One staff member told the author that "no one is these kids' parents anymore" (p. 47). Another noted that, given how little some of the children had, even the little things the program did took on greater importance than in the past: "snacks in the afternoon, a trip to the museum, individual attention, positive role models, consistent adult behavior, a kind word from a group leader" (p. 16).

Yet it was also at this historical moment that after-school programs were in some ways at their weakest as institutions. Chronic financial pressures were leading programs to cut back on core staff and specialists, materials, even snacks and field trips. Daily practice in many programs serving low-income children was survival oriented, defined by routine, lack of thought, and the limits of staff skill in designing and carrying through engaging activities. Arts and crafts predominated. Frontline staff with little more than a high school education were required to construct their roles on their own, with little preparation or conscious guidance. By the time they had acquired some sense of their role, they often as not moved on to another job. Because staff in many programs were part-time, they had little time to plan, think, recover, work through issues, and even develop individual relationships with children (Halpern, 1990; Martin & Ascher, 1994).

CONCLUSION

In the turmoil experienced by "traditional" human services in the 1960s, after-school providers discovered that they were perceived as both old and new. As in other mainstream institutions, settlements, boys' clubs, and other community-based providers were attacked for being irrelevant, unresponsive, and part of an effort to maintain the existing social and economic order. Yet after-school programs were also seen by service reformers as an innovative, flexible way of reaching children and as an alternative to inflexible, bureaucratic public institutions (i.e., schools). Because their work was not primarily about defining poor people, or controlling access to resources, after-school providers never experienced the kind of attacks experienced by schools, the welfare system, or public housing authorities.

During this period, after-school programs became ensnared in the paradox of equal-educational opportunity in American society, and would not again escape it. As Marris and Rein (1973, p. 70) put it, "The schools cannot care equally for the education of every child, whatever his skills, unless the man he will become is equally valued, whatever he can contribute. And this no competitive economy can itself ensure. The fundamental obstacle lay in the structure of opportunities." After-school providers faced the task of reconciling their historic goals of giving children a sense of belonging, of validating their individuality, and of supporting their unique strengths, with the new, tougher goals of helping address the effects of economic inequality and social exclusion and of helping low-income children compete. On a daily basis, programs' struggle with academic purposes became most evident around homework. Providers felt caught between pressure from schools and parents, and what they perceived to be children's need for fun and enrichment. Moreover, most of the homework children received was poorly designed and uninteresting, typically dittos and worksheets.

The growing involvement of the early childhood community in afterschool programming created at least some counterweight to instrumental pressures, by renewing the emphasis on play and on the needs of children as children. Erickson (1988, p. 101) noted that, as a growing and unregulated service, after-school programs presented both "much potential for exploitation" of children and "tremendous opportunities to start over" with more creative, child-centered approaches. Yet persistent funding constraints prevented such opportunities from being realized. Lack of funding would, in fact, create perverse pressures on goals and philosophies in the 1990s, as the new funding that became available was increasingly tied to instrumental purposes.

4

After-School Programs Come Into Their Own

Contexts for learning exist wherever children spend their time.
　　　　—H. Villaruel and R. Lerner, *Promoting Community-Based*
　　　　　　　　　　Programs for Socialization and Learning

We are intent on improving academic performance. You don't do that
by having kids hanging on the monkey bars.
　　　　—Atlanta school superintendent Benjamin Canada, in D. Johnson,
　　　　　　　　"Many Schools Putting an End to Child's Play"

Interest in after-school programs grew steadily throughout the 1990s. Elected officials, police chiefs, school superintendents, and community leaders all called for expanded after-school programming. There were foundation initiatives, city-level initiatives, new federal programs, and efforts by scores of community groups around the country to create more after-school programming in their communities. In his January 5, 1998, inaugural address, for instance, Boston mayor Thomas Menino told the audience, "Today, I am announcing the Boston 2:00-to-6:00 Initiative. Its mission will be to offer quality, affordable after-school activity in every neighborhood to every child who wants it."

Why were after-school programs suddenly receiving so much attention, after residing at the margins of social provision for decades? In part, it was school-age children's turn to be a source of public attention and worry. There was also a sense that other child-rearing institutions and contexts were not providing the supports that these children needed. Academic and media reports pointed to an increase in risky and self-destructive behavior among older school-age children and young adolescents, as a result of the growth in numbers of children left home alone after-school and of dangerous neighborhood environments. Elected officials, particularly governors and business leaders, were virtually obsessed with the failure of schools to educate low-income children. After-school programs appeared to be a timely and fresh response to both social and educational problems. The author of a *Newsweek* article noted a "new awareness" among police, social service providers, and policy makers that "structured activity during out-of-school hours is absolutely critical to confronting many of the nation's most vexing social problems" (Alter, 1998, p. 29). A National Academy of Science report noted that "after-school programs have increasingly become the focus of solutions to practically every problem faced by children and adolescents" (Gootman, 2000, p. 5).

As interest in after-school programs grew, the characteristics of the after-school field as a whole, as well as the quality of individual programs, began to receive more attention from funders and policy makers. The field, as such, had certain strengths—diversity in sponsorship; lack of bureaucratic constraints; a relatively positive, modest, and flexible adult agenda for children; close ties to communities served; responsiveness to community needs and priorities; and respect for children's language and culture. Yet it was also marked by inadequate and insecure funding, isolation among individual providers, poorly paid staff with limited formal training, weak (and sometimes nonexistent) curricular planning, and lack of a supporting "infrastructure" for those working at the frontline. The decentralized and fragmented nature of the after-school field, combined with the marginal operating conditions of many programs, created challenges both to "system building" and to the capacity of providers to band together in negotiating new expectations and external demands.

In the early part of the decade, after-school programs were still largely "outside" public policy, though they finally had some opportunity for public funding through federal child care funding streams. Youth-serving organizations, settlements, and other community-based agencies made tentative efforts to redefine their after-school programs as child care, at least for a portion of children served. By mid-decade, the after-school field was beginning to be pulled into a tighter embrace by schools and school systems. Public and private initiatives created new funding opportunities, but much of the new funding was designed to enlist after-school programs in the effort to improve low-income children's academic achievement. After-school programs were caught up in calls for longer school days and school years, more learning time, and increased efforts to ensure that children met common learning standards. The specific mandates that accompanied new funding opportunities once again required providers to decide how flexible they wished to be. Providers found their historic tenets difficult to sustain, particularly the general idea of after-school time as fundamentally different from schooltime.

Public and policy interest also raised the stakes for after-school programs, as a result of the promises sought and made about outcomes. Funders (and even a few sponsors) began talking about "results-oriented" after-school programming. They asked evaluators to tell them if after-school programs "worked," whether such programs were effective in preventing a range of problems and in strengthening social skills and improving academic achievement and attitudes toward school. Funders wanted to know what "dosage" was required to achieve effects, which components of after-school programs were most effective, and whether benefits outweighed costs. These questions further heightened tensions about purpose, identity, and approach. After-school programs historically had tended to define their efforts in broad, diffuse terms and had tended to address children's struggles and support needs without measuring and labeling. These tendencies were now threatened. Moreover, there was a basic tension between the growing policy interest in, and evaluation pressures on, after-school programs and the marginal conditions under which most programs continued to operate.

ARGUING THE RATIONALE AND NEED FOR AFTER-SCHOOL PROGRAMS

In a general way, after-school programs became a focus of policy attention because politicians, law enforcement officials, helping professionals, foundation staff, and others decided that children's out-of-school time mattered. It was no longer to be treated as a family or community issue, but as a public one. The experiences children had in their communities during non-school hours were recognized as a "third leg" in the triangle of human development (along with family and school [Comer, 1992, p. 18]). The after-school hours were characterized as presenting both heightened risk and unusual opportunity for children (Hofferth, 1995). Mayors proclaimed the safety of children and the quality of children's after-school lives as an important dimension of the quality of life in their cities.

If out-of-school time mattered, it followed, at least according to those with a sudden interest in this daily time period, that it ought not be left just to existing after-school providers to decide how and why it mattered. The new proponents—politicians (and their staff), law enforcement officials, education officials, public policy "think tanks" and foundation staff—wanted a strong voice in shaping low-income children's out-of-school time. The problem was that the after-school community proved to have a surprisingly weak voice in the ensuing debate. It was not just funding-related dependence that silenced this community. There was no mechanism for converting a century of after-school practice and custom into a coherent argument for after-school programs as a distinctive child development institution, with certain inherent strengths worth protecting (as well as problems needing attention).

The outcome of debate about rationales was important, because it would shape the expectations and emphases of stakeholders. If out-of-school time mattered primarily because of specific social problems or issues—for instance, the need for school-age child care; failures of the schools or juvenile crime—that implied different objectives, day-to-day preoccupations, and ways of relating to children rather than because it was important to support children's normal developmental needs. The same children could be (and in fact were) thought to be a threat and to need protection themselves, to need compensatory and remedial experience, or to deserve access to developmentally enriching experiences (including time free from adult control). Various potential rationales and arguments for after-school programming created a complex mix. Although some overlapped or were complementary, others seemed mutually contradictory.

CHILD CARE AND SAFE SPACES AS KEY CONCERNS

The most basic rationale for more after-school programming continued to be children's need for supervision after school. Of the 10 million or so children ages 6 through 13 living in or near poverty (i.e., in families with incomes less than 150% of the federal poverty threshold), about 6 million lived in families in which both parents or the single parent worked. Children in these families were seen to face a variety of risks associated with self-care after school. These included too much television; too little exercise; feelings of boredom, loneliness, and worry; risks of accidents; stress associated with caring for younger siblings; and, among older children, susceptibility to the influence of "problematic" peers and to experimentation with drugs, sexual activity, and gangs (Dwyer et al., 1990; Pettit et al., 1997).

Although these risks had some basis in reality, especially for low-income children, they were also exaggerated. As noted in chapter 3, a number of situational factors, as well as individual differences between children, influenced the self-care experience and its effects. In reviewing the evidence from studies of self-care, Belle (1999, p. 35) stated, "Some studies report problems for unsupervised children, others find no differences between supervised and unsupervised children, and credible studies have reported poorer outcomes for children who spend after-school time with older siblings, babysitters, after-school teachers, and their own mothers, than for children who spend after-school time on their own" (p. 35). In her own research, Belle found that as children grew older, some (though by no means all) preferred self-care, seeking greater autonomy after school. In spite of such complexities, and in spite of contradictory research findings on the effects of self-care, statistics about the alarming extent of self-care were nonetheless used to suggest a major social problem.

A second, and related, argument for after-school programs held that low- and moderate-income children needed safe spaces for recreation in the after-school hours. Inner-city neighborhoods lacked secure public spaces for children to use, and street culture posed far greater risks to children than in the past. Local traditions of "collective parenting" had broken down, and neighborhood adults were transformed from protective figures to threats to children's safety. As a result of all these changes, parents felt compelled to restrict children's movements and forbid outdoor play. Attentive but restrictive parental strategies clashed with children's need for gradually increasing independence and autonomy. (Paradoxically, in trying to isolate their children from harmful community influences and dangers, parents sometimes saw a need to isolate them from all community institutions, even potentially positive ones [Brodsky, 1996; Jarrett, 1998].)

If many low-income children experienced too much restriction, others were too much on their own, not just physically but also psychologically. These children resided in families in which parents' best intentions of attending to their children's developmental needs were overwhelmed by personal difficulties or long working hours (and sometimes long commutes). Such parents did not have the capacity, or in the latter case, the time, to focus on their children's daily lives, to monitor their well-being, intervene when necessary with school authorities, provide important supports such as help with homework, or seek out and link their children to community resources (Herr & Halpern, 1993). Comer (1992) argued that while children and young adolescents needed more support and guidance than ever before, they seemed to be getting less of these things. He described a new phenomenon that he called the "no parent family."

Even when parents had the wherewithal to seek out resources for their children, such resources often were not available. Thus some proponents of after-school programming focused on the discrepancy between low-income children and their more economically advantaged peers in access to and opportunity to participate in arts, sports, and cultural activities. In a study by Littel and Wynn (1989), comparing an inner-city and a suburban community in the Chicago area, the authors found a greater number and variety of such resources in the wealthier community—no surprise. They also found that in the low-income community some available after-school activities were perceived as interventions, intended to prevent or address problems; in the advantaged community, most activities were designed to be fun and enriching, providing opportunities to explore interests, build skills, and experience success.

AFTER-SCHOOL HOURS, TIME USE, AND SCHOOLING

During the 1990s, the preoccupation with efficient and productive time use that defined adult life in American culture spread to childhood, and to the out-of-school hours. Two sets of concerns drove this new preoccupation.

The first, alluded to earlier, involved adults' worry about the waste and danger of idleness, or "doing nothing," during the after-school hours. Whether or not their parents worked, too many low- and moderate-income children were seen to be "adrift after school" (Larner, Zippiroli, & Behrman, 1999, p. 4). Unsupervised play was described as a lost opportunity. The sponsor of an after-school initiative in New York City argued that "children who spend after-school hours in unstructured, unsupervised activities are at increased risk for poor grades, truancy, substance abuse" (After-School Corporation, n.d., p. 5). The National Governors' Association undertook an initiative focused on the after-school hours whose slogan was to "make every minute meaningful." The new utilitarian proponents of after-school programming were arguing, in effect, that since children were not "utility maximizers," adults would fill this role for them.

The second part of the time use story involved continuing concern about the failure of schools to help low-income children acquire literacy and numeracy. Although this failure was acknowledged to have complex causes, the main one was thought to be lack of time during the school day for mastering basic skills and covering the curriculum. A 1993 report by the National Education Commission on Time and Learning reported that "unyielding and relentless, the time available in a uniform six-hour day and a 180-day year is the unacknowledged design flaw in American education" (Lofty, 2000, p. 204). By mid-decade there were repeated calls for longer school days (and school years), more time on task in school, fewer "frills" such as art and gym, and reduction or elimination of recess (Pellegrini & Bjorklund, 1996). In justifying the Atlanta school system's decision to end recess, Superintendent Benjamin Canada argued, "We are intent on improving academic performance. You don't do that by having kids hanging on the monkey bars" (Johnson, 1998, p. A1).

The two sets of concerns about time use converged on after-school programs, suggesting, first, that they had a role in assuring more productive use of the after-school hours and, second, that an obvious focus of that more productive time use could be to extend academic learning time, in effect to extend the school day. Over the course of the decade, the idea of after-school programs as an extension of schooling would steadily gain credence. The director of a citywide after-school initiative in Boston noted that, when it came to children's learning, "it's no longer enough to just have a school day" (cited in Wilgoren, 2000, p. A1). The authors of a report on the 21st Century Community Learning Centers, a federal initiative to support after-school programming in schools, noted that the centers gave students "more time to learn, improve their academics, and engage in other educational activities outside the structured school day" (U.S. Department of Education, 2001, p. 8). To further the aim of what came to be called extended learning opportunities, policy makers (and not a few academics) argued the need for continuity in children's learning experiences between the school hours and after-school hours.

As noted in Chapter 3, long-standing after-school providers were uncomfortable with the idea of their programs as an extension of the school day. They preferred to think of after-school experiences as at least somewhat discontinuous with school experiences and to think of after-school programs as a complement or even an alternative to school. Thus in the course of a research study on literacy activity in after-school programs, a staff member at Interfaith Neighbors in New York City told this author that they made literacy activities in their after-school programs different from school "because we can." And the coordinator of literacy activity for a network of small settlements asked rhetorically, "Why would you want to extend the goals and methods of a failed system into the after-school hours?"

Some education critics themselves argued that low- and moderate-income children's academic difficulties were caused not by lack of learning time but by the basic nature of schooling and by social-class differences in both school resources and in how children were treated by schools. If schools' formal work was about teaching and learning, their de facto work was about apportioning success and failure (Varenne & McDermott, 1998). As children advanced in grade, teacher styles became less nurturing. Teachers gave less positive reinforcement to children (Stipek, 1992). Especially in schools serving low-income children, there was a tendency to emphasize deficits rather than strengths; little willingness or capacity to deal with individual differences in learning speed, style, capacity, and motivation or with language difficulties; and generally little attention to how an individual child was faring (Jackson, 1997; Stipek, 1992). Curriculum was constructed differently for low- and moderate-income children from how it was structured for their wealthier peers (see, e.g., Anyon, 1980). For instance, the curriculum for the former provided less opportunity to explore, construct, problem solve, and create. Low-income children's voices were silenced in a variety of ways in school; that is, their own lives and experiences were made to seem irrelevant to the learning agenda, and their role in shaping that agenda was suppressed.

The alternative critiques of schooling implied that the potential of after-school programs was not to provide more time in school-like learning activity, but different kinds of learning experiences. These experiences would, for example, respect individual differences, attend to children's point of view, encourage their sense of "voice," incorporate their home and community culture, and put them in active roles as learners. As Resnick (1990, pp. 183–184) put it, in arguing for the importance of "other" institutions (such as after-school programs) in supporting children's literacy development, the idea was not to mimic school but rather to provide "truly alternative occasions for literacy practice." Still, the qualities that distinguished after-school programs as learning environments stood more as ideals than as reflections of prevailing practice in the field.

CONTINUITY AND CHANGE IN PROGRAM GOALS AND EMPHASES

The new pressures on and expectations of after-school programs took shape gradually. Through the early part of the decade, most programs continued to reflect providers' historic view of what children needed after school—some mixture of care and protection, enrichment, time for informal social interaction and play, and modest academic support. In one study, providers used such terms as "decompress, noncompetitive, peer control, teacher-facilitated, child-centered, choice and flexibility" to describe their work (Martin & Ascher, 1994, p. 14). As had the leaders of the play school movement, providers spoke of creating spaces where children could be themselves, where they felt safe to express hopes, fears, and ideas about the world.

Much of what after-school programs looked like and did was familiar. Programs had arts and crafts and table games, physical activity (including martial arts), weekly visual and expressive arts or cultural activity, and perhaps some tutoring, reading time, science activity, and/or computer time. Some programs continued to design longer-term projects organized around a particular theme, for example mapping the community (physically, institutionally, and socially) or exploring different cultural heritages or parts of the world. Most programs continued to divide children into younger and older age groups, allowing for the creation of distinct environments and schedules, suited to the needs and preferences of each. The room or space for the younger group typically resembled an early childhood classroom, with activity areas and plentiful games, books, and supplies. Conversely, that for the older group often resembled a casual living room, with some comfortable furniture but also materials for activities.

Some programs continued to use a club or class structure, particularly for older children, with the specific choices reflecting a mixture of staff skills, population served, and specialists recruited. Most clubs and classes were the same as those that had been provided for decades. New clubs reflected newer preoccupations and social goals. One New York City program offered such clubs as "African dance, jump rope, community service, math tutoring, debate, percussion, poetry, cheerleading, jazz dance, ice hockey, leadership training, literacy activities and outside play" (Reisner, 2001, p. 82). Erie Neighborhood House in Chicago provided, among other clubs, girls' flag football. A handful of programs taught children how to build Web sites or create online magazines. There was also an increase in the number of thematic programs, with an emphasis on one or more of the visual or performing arts. A program in Boston, for example, offered mask-making, dance, drumming, stilt-walking, puppetry, clay-making, theater, and silk screen, all taught by local artists (Halpern et al., 1999).

Community context continued to influence priorities. In one deteriorating neighborhood in Boston, the author was told by the director that his main goal was "to keep kids off the street and alive." The director of a program in a public housing development in Chicago emphasized that "we've always viewed our [program] buildings as sanctuaries within the environment. When kids come in . . . they're not just physically safe but emotionally safe" (Merry, n.d., p. 17). The renewed wave of immigration during the decade shaped after-school program activity in many neighborhoods. Programs serving children in immigrant families helped mediate between family and school, particularly when children were having academic or social problems. Immigrant groups sometimes had strong priorities for their children, which also shaped practice. For instance, Asian and Southeast Asian parents preferred academically oriented programs, complemented by components that helped children maintain their native language and culture. The director of a Boston program serving children from Chinese immigrant families commented that parents did not want children to have free time or downtime at the program. Rather, they wanted a focus on homework and on helping children learn English (Halpern et al., 1999).

By the mid-1990s, reading and homework time began to take a more prominent place in the daily life of after-school programs. As in past decades, it was common to see children curled up in a chair or on a sofa or sprawled on the floor, reading for pleasure. This was usually an individual choice. Homework was a different matter. Children were receiving more homework, and at younger ages. Whether working or not, parents were coming to depend on and expect after-school programs to be responsible for homework. After-school providers understood that it made some sense for them to take responsibility for homework. A Chicago director remarked that many of his children's homes lacked basic academic resources, adding, "We have encyclopedias here, dictionaries, rulers, everything you need to deal with your homework plus a quiet place to do it" (Spielberger & Halpern, 2002, p. 27). Homework help was a logical task for a growing army of volunteer tutors, among them college students, professionals, retirees, and high school students. Homework could also be a good "social literacy" experience, with children helping and teaching one another. Providers began to see the homework help they provided as the reason they were valued by the community.

At the same time, homework began to crowd out other activities and projects, including time to relax and play, to sit and have conversations. The evaluators of one initiative found that 40% of activity observed during one particular program year was academic (mostly homework), 20% was enrichment, and 20% was sports; of the remainder, only a fraction was informal, child-initiated fun (Walker et al., 2000). Shifting responsibility for homework to after-school programs exacerbated parents' disengagement from schooling and reinforced the idea that they had little role in ensuring their children's success in school. After-school staff were not only ambivalent about the time homework consumed, but also sometimes skeptical of the value of homework itself. The director of an after-school program in Brooklyn claimed, "It's always been a tradition that children don't want to do their homework. That's obvious. But at this particular historical stage, and in this community, there seems to be a real edge to it. . . . schools just aren't making the work interesting to children. . . . content has become increasingly work-book oriented. All the meaning has been bled out of the things that children are asked to read" (Ellowitch et al., 1991, p. 19).

Academic expectations of after-school programs seemed to grow year by year. By late in the decade, organizations such as the National Governors' Association and the Council of Chief State School Officers were arguing that after-school programs were an important element of the campaign to improve the standardized test scores of low-income, urban children. After-school programs that wished to participate in "Boston 2:00-to-6:00," the mayor's initiative, were required to tie their programs to the public schools' learning standards. Proposals to the federal government's 21st Century Community Learning Centers program, a major funding source, received extra points if they emphasized improving standardized test scores as a primary objective.

THE STRUCTURE OF THE FIELD

The after-school field had always been characterized by diverse sponsorship, with individual sponsors setting their own policies, priorities, and practices. This pattern continued into the 1990s. The largest providers to low- and moderate-income children were private, nonprofit social service agencies and, toward the end of the decade, schools. The former category was itself heterogeneous, including child care centers, settlement houses, other community and neighborhood centers, child and family service agencies, national youth-serving organizations, particularly Boys' and Girls' Clubs, YMCAs and on a smaller scale YWCAs, and local (or city-specific) youth-serving organizations.

In some cities, parks and recreation departments provided after-school programming in field houses and recreation centers, and as did PAL (Police

Athletic League) centers. Libraries emerged as a growing after-school base if not as formal providers, in response to an influx of children sent by parents looking for a safe after school space. A 1997 survey of Chicago's 88 branch libraries found children using them regularly after-school for homework and socializing. The numbers varied, from as few as 15 to as many as 175, with an average of about 60 children per library each day (Halpern et al., 1997). Churches (and sometimes networks of churches) provided some after-school programming, as did Catholic schools, ethnic mutual assistance associations (self-help organizations based in immigrant and refugee communities, often country- or region-specific, that provide a variety of supports to families in the early stages of acculturation), selected public housing authorities, a rapidly growing group of tutoring/mentoring organizations, and even a few community development corporations.

In the early part of the decade, youth-serving organizations (particularly Boys' and Girls' Clubs, and to a lesser extent park districts and PAL programs) maintained their historic open-enrollment philosophy, with children becoming members for a nominal fee and then dropping in whenever they wished during the year. By the late 1990s, many had moved toward a "closed enrollment model," with a fixed group of children coming in 3 to 5 days a week. The growing number of providers who viewed their primary purpose as offering child care had a more explicit agreement with parents with respect to responsibility for children during certain hours. Programs in agencies that operated from a recreation or youth-work tradition tended to have relatively large groups, high adult-child ratios, and a whole-group orientation in activities. Those that operated within an early childhood/child care tradition tended to have smaller groups, lower adult-child ratios, and a focus that was more on individual children. (YMCAs were distinct in that they operated out of both traditions, and their programs often had features of both.)

The proportion of programming provided by each type of institution varied from city to city, and neighborhood to neighborhood. In Boston, for example, the Boys' and Girls' Clubs were the largest single provider; in Los Angeles the schools were. In New York City the large network of historically sectarian (but now mostly nonsectarian) family service agencies played a distinctly important role; in that city and in Chicago, settlement houses also played a prominent role as providers. Churches and mutual assistance associations tended to have small, minimally funded and staffed programs and used as many volunteers as they could find. At the same time, they played a critical role in filling the many "micro-gaps" in after-school program coverage. The programs run by the latter also played a critical bridging role between immigrant families and mainstream institutions such as schools.

During the 1990s a variety of intermediary organizations emerged to support and extend direct services. Some, such as the Partnership for After-

School Education in New York City and the School's Out Consortium in Seattle, provided technical assistance and training to providers. Others, such as Arts in Progress in Boston, the Marwen Arts Foundation in Chicago, and Studio in a School in New York City, linked artists to after-school programs to provide instruction in the visual or performing arts or to help program staff strengthen their own arts activities. Cultural institutions such as museums and dance or theater companies also became more involved in supporting after-school programs, offering on-site activities and workshops, making their own resources available at minimal cost, or providing guest artists. Children's museums also provided some resources. Boston's Children's Museum, for instance, had a program called Expanding Youth Horizons, which offered training, technical assistance, and materials to after-school programs in literacy, math, and science. In Philadelphia an interdenominational network of churches, the Northwest Interfaith Movement, created the School-Age Ministry, to develop and support after-school programs in low- and moderate-income neighborhoods. In Chicago, the After School Action Program in Uptown-Edgewater served as a hub, support mechanism, and "broker" for a network of 30 small providers (primarily church congregations and ethnic mutual assistance associations, as well as a few public housing tenant associations). Its staff helped member programs to seek out funding, organize training, and link to other intermediaries that provide arts, science, tutoring, and other resources for the programs.

The Persistence of Nonprofessional Staffing

The great majority of after-school program staff continued to be non-professional and to work part-time, with few or no benefits. Most staff had either a high school diploma or, less commonly, an associate (AA) degree, and little or no formal preparation for work with children. The majority of (but by no means all) program coordinators and directors had at least a bachelor's degree. Salaries in the field averaged around $7 an hour for front-line staff and slightly more, $8–15 an hour, for coordinators and directors. Staff employed by public agencies—schools, park districts, and libraries—not surprisingly had higher hourly wages than those employed by private, nonprofit agencies.

The majority of programs continued to draw staff from the same racial and ethnic backgrounds (and sometimes the same neighborhoods) as the children served. In programs serving language-minority children, the majority of staff would typically be bilingual, and the language used in a program would flow easily back and forth between English and the language of children's home communities. Some after-school programs relied partly on college students. A Seattle program director noted that college students brought enthusiasm and a youthful way of interacting with children, but that it was also helpful to have older staff, who tended to be steadier and sometimes more committed (Halpern et al., 1999). A handful of programs sought to hire young artists, to deepen the skill available to teach specific arts.

As noted earlier, a growing number of after-school programs used volunteers, mostly from organized programs such as Big Brother and Big Sister, from college work study or service learning, and from national service programs, notably Americorps. Volunteers typically helped with homework, provided tutoring, and read to children. They also helped with such tasks as escorting children to and from programs. Although appreciating the contribution of volunteers, especially their role in ensuring more individual attention to children in a field that was too thinly staffed, providers worried that reliance on volunteers contributed to the misperception that after-school programs could be enlarged and strengthened through "volunteerism."

LACK OF ADEQUATE FINANCING

Historically, after-school programs serving low-income children had relied on a variety of private funding sources for the bulk of their revenue, and this pattern continued in the 1990s. Principle sources included the United Way, local foundations, individual donations, and in-kind contributions of space and time from volunteers. Parent fees continued to be a small and unreliable source of revenue for programs serving low-income children. Those parents needing child care after school felt they could forego it, and gamble with self-care, if the costs were too high. This pattern differed markedly from that of early childhood care, for which parents paid as much as a third of disposable income for whatever care they could find. In economic terms, parental demand for after-school programs was inelastic. When programs serving low-income children charged fees, such fees typically provided between 15% and 20% of revenue and were usually charged on a sliding scale, with the majority in a typical program paying $20 per week or less. (Halpern et al., 1999; data presented in this section comes from a study of the budgets and financing of 60 after-school programs in Boston, Chicago, and Seattle conducted by the author as part of the MOST—Making the Most of Out-of-School Time—evaluation.)

By the early 1990s, some public funding was finally finding its way to programs in low-income neighborhoods. Almost all that funding was embedded in categorical programs with other primary purposes—early childhood child care; compensatory or remedial education; juvenile delinquency, drug, and violence prevention; family support; and nutrition. Child care subsidies, for which children through age 12 were eligible, provided the largest source of public funding. Between 1992 and 1997 total federal funding for children birth through age 12, the bulk coming from the Child Care and Development Block Grant (CCDBG), grew from about $1 billion to about $3 billion annually. About 30% of all children subsidized through CCDBG were school-aged, and of these subsidies about two thirds went to after-school programs (the rest went to home-based care or kith-and-kin care). Child care subsidies were distributed unevenly across programs. Among the minority of programs that had revenue from such subsidies (either contracts or vouchers), those could constitute anywhere from 10% to 90% of total revenue. In general, children subsidized through child care funding constituted less than 10% of all low-income children who participated in after-school programs.

Other, smaller public sources of funding came from federal and state Departments of Education, the Department of Justice (Title V delinquency prevention funding), the Child and Adult Care Food Program (in neighborhoods where 50% or more of children in a program's service area were certified for free or reduced lunch), Social Service and Community Development Block Grants, Empowerment Zone funds, Department of Housing and Urban Development funds (some of which are directed to particular youth-serving organizations, such as the Boys' and Girls' Clubs), and "Tobacco Settlement" funds. In a handful of cities, including San Francisco and Seattle, and counties (for example, Florida's Pinellas), special tax levies for children's services also provided a modest funding stream. For instance, San Francisco's Proposition J, passed in 1991, set aside 2% of the revenue collected from property taxes for children's services, including after-school programs.

All told, public funding from different sources provided about 30% to 40% of total revenue for after-school programs serving low-income children. Public funding helped some programs to some degree, and many other programs not at all. The great majority of after-school programs struggled constantly to raise small amounts of money from different revenue sources, year after year. The majority of programs had three or four revenue sources, some as many as eight or nine. Both private and public funding sources were unreliable, leading to significant fluctuations in revenue from year to year. As the director of a Boston mayoral initiative noted, "What I see these poor community-based programs trying to do is a travesty. They have to go after these little pots of money from many, many different sources. . . . they have to beg and plead to survive" (S. Robb, personal communication, 11/17/98).

A GROWING ROLE FOR SCHOOLS
AND SCHOOL CONCERNS

By mid-decade, the after-school field began to be affected by the view of new proponents, including philanthropists and politicians and other government officials, that schools were the best base for after-school programs. They argued that children were already present (reducing transportation problems) and that schools had the necessary facilities, space, or both and therefore could accommodate large programs. Schools were seen to be a "respected" and a "core" community institution; parents were thought to feel safest with their children in the school building; and school-based programs were seen to provide greater potential to provide continuity in meeting children's academic needs. As a U.S. Department of Education report argued, by locating after-school programs "within public public schools we can see that students receive educational enrichment and academic assistance directly linked to their classroom needs" (2001, p. 14).

Principals and teachers were, as always, ambivalent about having after-school programs in their buildings and classrooms. Principals in school districts who were forced to cut back on arts, physical education, and other "frills" appreciated the potential of after-school programs to "backfill" these activities. Principals also viewed after-school programs as a draw in recruiting students. A New York City principal commented, "When people tour our school, I tell them the school day lasts from 8:30 a.m. until 6:00 p.m. This is helpful for recruitment" (Reisner, 2001, p. 42). Other principals and teachers saw mostly added risks, headaches, intrusion in classrooms, wear and tear on already deteriorated physical plants, and strain on already tight budgets. Practical concerns seemed to mask deeper worries about loss of control. Referring to the freedom of movement that children were perceived to have in after-school programs, one principal told an interviewer: "If kids sit on a desk the next thing you know they'll be standing on it. It's the same thing with running in the hall. . . . My concern is that it might spill over into the day time" (Walker et al., 2000, p. 49).

Growth in School Sponsorship

Such worries aside, the arguments for school-based after-school programming, and the money that followed, contributed to a steady growth in school systems as sponsors. A number of states and municipalities appropriated funds for school-based after-school programming. In some cases, schools ran their own programs. These might consist of little more than academic remediation, with snack and some recreation if there was time, or might be a more balanced program. School-run programs typically used teachers or classroom aides as staff, a practice that had mixed results. Some teachers loved the freedom to be more creative and to relate to children in a different way; others were too tired after-school to put energy into the after-school program. Participating children were sometimes impressed, sometimes perplexed, by changes in teacher demeanor after school. It was also not uncommon for large numbers of children to be placed in a cafeteria or auditorium, under the care of an aide who had few materials and little support in planning activities.

In a number of cities, including Boston, Dallas, Denver, Kansas City, and Seattle, school systems contracted or otherwise collaborated with community-based organizations or other public agencies, which ran programs in local schools. In Boston, for instance, schools provided the sites for more than 50 after-school programs run by other agencies. Dallas providers included the Parks and Recreation Department, the Scouts, Campfire Boys and Girls, churches, and child care agencies. In Seattle, 16 middle schools provided space for programs funded by the Parks and Recreation Department, which operated some programs itself (using public school teachers) and contracted with community agencies to run others. Also in Seattle, schools served as host sites for programs run by the YMCA, a partnership that would become increasingly common in other cities.

The growth in school-based sponsorship of after-school programs was spurred by a number of multisite or multicity after-school initiatives, most of which relied on a mixture of public and private funding. Some initiatives promoted one or more models, with certain goals, features, and requirements. Among the better-known initiatives were New York City's Beacons (eventually replicated in other cities), Los Angeles's L.A.'s BEST (Better Educated Students for Tomorrow), Extended Service Schools (or ESS, a multicity initiative that promoted four different models, including the Beacons), and New York City's The After-School Corporation (TASC).

Although all these initiatives were motivated by concern about low-income children's school difficulties, they varied in the extent to which they emphasized school-like activities. L.A.'s BEST, which began in 1988, and the Beacons, which began in 1991, predated the decade's preoccupation with school success. Local L.A.'s BEST programs tended to balance academic and nonacademic emphases. As of the mid-1990s, a typical program included such activities as homework help, a weekly science or math activity, arts and crafts, computer instruction, visual and performing arts, sports, and some site-specific activities such as dance and drill teams. The Beacons were originally conceived as a drug prevention and violence reduction initiative. The general idea was to create school-based "safe havens" and community centers, offering a wide range of social, health, and recreational services, to adults as well as children and adolescents. Each Beacon had an Advisory Council, mandated to include school principals, parents, youth, and community residents and usually including teachers and neighborhood-based providers. The after-school program emerged as the core activity in almost all Beacons, typically an activity-based program, with children signing up for specific clubs and classes, rather than coming every day.

Late in the decade, the number of new school-based initiatives multiplied rapidly. Some, such as Boston's 2:00-to-6:00 Initiative; Columbus, Ohio's CAP CITY KIDS; San Diego's "6 to 6"; and Seattle's Project Lift-Off, were mayoral initiatives. Others, for example, initiatives in Denver and St. Louis, were initiated by and based in the community education departments of local school districts. Almost without exception, these newer initiatives were motivated by a desire to improve children's academic achievement and school conduct and were guided by the idea of creating continuity in learning between the schoolday and after-school hours. While the writers of their program materials talked of creating safe, enriching, and supportive learning environments, they also urged the linking and "aligning" of after-school activity and the school district's curriculum or learning standards.

The major federal initiative of the era, the U.S. Department of Education's 21st Century Community Learning Centers, required schools themselves to run after-school programs, with community partners playing varied, modest roles. Federal funding began in 1998, at $40 million per year and by 2001 had grown to $800 million per year. Grants to individual schools ranged from $35,000 to $200,000 per year, averaging about $100,000, for up to 3 years. (School districts or consortia of schools sought and received larger grants, up to about $2 million per year.) About 25% of funding from this program found its way to nonschool institutions, although it is unclear how much of this went to community-based after-school providers. In late 2001, the initiative was folded into the reauthorized Elementary and Secondary Education Act and effectively handed over to the states as part of the act's block grant approach. This left the future of the initiative in the hands of state education departments and local school systems, both of which were facing growing funding constraints due to unexpected loss of tax revenues.

CHALLENGES FOR COMMUNITY-BASED AGENCIES IN WORKING WITH SCHOOLS

The majority of school-based after-school programs continued to be operated by community agencies, and as this number grew the implication of and challenges associated with working in schools became a major issue for the field. While community-based organizations saw in school sites an opportunity to expand their programming without having to build new facilities, they also saw their role as important community institutions threatened. They resented the argument that "schools are often not only the best, but also one of the only decent and safe places for children" (in this case made by the Fund for the City of New York, the sponsor of the Beacons [Cahill et al., 1993, p. 2]). Such statements seemed to minimize community-based organizations' historic and continuing role in children's lives. The children living near a particular community agency often literally grew up there, graduating from child care to Head Start or preschool, and then to the after-school program. Community-based organizations were deeply rooted in their neighborhoods, close to home physically, socially, and psychologically. Community-building advocates argued also that it was critical to sustain a variety of institutions in low-income neighborhoods. For instance, the many smaller agencies (including churches and MAAs [Mutual Assistance Associations]) in some neighborhoods filled numerous microgaps in after-school program coverage and played a critical role in meeting the distinct needs of different cultural and language groups.

Philosophical Tensions. As a practical matter, community-based agencies found it difficult to negotiate philosophy and goals with the schools in an equitable way. Principals in particular felt entitled to determine program priorities. There was some variability in their perspective. The principal of a Beacon school in New York City argued that "our kids go to school seven hours a day and it's intense learning. For them to go to an after-school class and do some tutoring is ridiculous. . . . These kids need to have fun" (Walker et al., 2000, p. 47). A New York City principal in a TASC school reportedly required teachers to limit the amount of homework they assigned "so students could finish homework during after-school hours and still take advantage of enrichment opportunities" (Feister, 2000, p. 27). The predominant view was closer to that expressed by one Boston principal: "We need to extend the school day. And how do you do that? This [new after-school program] is a superlative opportunity" (S. Robb, personal communication, November 19, 1998).

Community-based providers working in and with the schools felt "torn," as one New York City agency director told this author. They wanted better communication with teachers about how children were faring in school and about what kinds of struggles children may have been experiencing. They heard and saw that test preparation pressures were reducing time in school for interesting (or in some cases any) science or social science, for reading and writing for pleasure. They were acutely aware—indeed they saw every day during homework time and other activities—that growing numbers of children served were struggling to acquire literacy and numeracy. Dave Piel, longtime director of the Carole Robertson Center in Chicago, told a colleague of the author, "I've seen a decline in literacy levels. . . . I was going through some of the archives recently, and I noticed that some of the letters kids wrote back then were really logical and coherent and made sense. That kind of thing is hard to come by now" (J. Spielberger, personal communication, 5/28/88).

Yet, as noted earlier, they also sensed that they did not want to reproduce the schools' dominant approach to children's learning and literacy development—reliance on poorly written commercial textbooks, worksheets, and tests; a focus on searching for and correcting errors; and the use of standardized questions and assignments (Shannon, 1990). The director of school-age child care in the city of Seattle told this author and colleagues that "it's very important for us [the after-school community] not to change our global view of reaching and caring for the whole child. . . . you know . . . their [school officials'] idea . . . for an ideal after-school program is drill-and-practice, to fill the gap in what didn't happen between 9 a.m. and 3 p.m." (Spielberger, personal communication, 1998b).

More than a few program directors expressed the belief that their program had to counter the messages children received about themselves and their capacities in school. The director of the Carole Robertson Center in Chicago, which had a reputation of working closely over the years with two nearby "feeder" schools, told the author that "ideally [we] should be a complement and extension of the school day, if the schools were educating children the way that we know they can. But realistically, here in Chicago, I think we are sort of an antidote to school for kids" (Spielberger, personal communication, 1998a). The writing teacher in Arts and Literacy, a Brooklyn-based after-school program housed in two elementary schools, told the author and a colleague that his ways of working with children were "the opposite of conventional schooling in that there is no copying, no correct spelling, all the lessons are taught in both languages and are conducted in both languages. . . . I want the kids to have a sense of accomplishment" (Spielberger & Halpern, 2002, p. 67). The director of the Bicycle Action Project in Chicago (a program in which children and early adolescents learn to repair bikes) told an interviewer, "When kids walk in here, it is entirely different than when they walk into school. They're not expecting to fail. They open the door differently, their caps turned back on their heads, they're ready" (Merry et al., n.d., p. xx).

Community-based providers also struggled with an increasingly common expectation that they commit themselves to helping address school learning standards and to helping improve standardized test scores. As revealed in interviews with principals in schools sponsoring TASC programs in New York City, their first two priorities were "improving students' homework completion and quality" and "improving students' literacy and math problem solving on tests" (Feister et al., 2000, p. 12). As in Boston and Seattle, principals involved with the TASC initiative also wanted the community-based providers with whom they contracted to join the schools in ensuring that children met the citywide learning standards for elementary students. Providers working with Milwaukee's 21st Century Community Learning Center program were required to host a reading initiative (Lets Read) that used a scripted, structured "skill-building" approach that was derived from the school district's reading program.

Providers knew that children had other needs, and were not in a state of mind for academics after a day of school. They knew that children liked after-school programs precisely because their climate and approach to learning activities was very different than that in school. Providers thus bowed to pressure to express school-like goals in rhetoric (especially in proposals to funders), while in practice trying to maintain balanced programs. For example, the director of the Valentine Boys and Girls Club in Chicago told the author that they had become "an educational program with a recreational slant." Providers argued that in addition to homework help and reading time, activities as varied as drama, dance, music, ceramics, photography, film making, computer workshop, and cooking helped support one or another school learning standard. Providers argued that they would help schools by exploring academic subjects in more integrated, contextualized, applied, or experiential ways. In a different vein, they simply set some limits on academic tasks, starting with homework.

A more discrete, but nonetheless important, tension in school-based work revolved around the numbers of children to be served. In the larger school-based initiatives, there was both an emphasis on efficiency and a tendency to be preoccupied with scale: how many children could be reached and served per school. Contracts often required community-based agencies to operate on a larger scale from that to which they were accustomed, for example, serving 200, 300, or more children, rather than 40 or 50 or 60. (One TASC site, at PS 241 in Manhattan, was committed to serving 900 children, an almost unfathomable number for an after-school program.) The emphasis on serving large numbers of children made it difficult for providers to keep track of and respond to children's individuality, just the problem that schools themselves had always had. Agencies operating TASC programs sometimes found it difficult to sustain the intimacy and informality that had characteristically defined their own programs. The need for large numbers of new staff led in some cases to widespread use of college and even high school students and to significant new problems in supervision and training. (A TASC Initiative "Resource Brief" discussed, with no apparent irony, training sessions for "young" staff, including high school students, that focused on "working with depressed children, understanding child and adolescent development, working with parents to address [children's] personal problems" [The After-School Corporation, n.d.].)

Practical Challenges. As ever greater numbers of community-based organizations worked in and with schools, the historic logistical challenges faced in such situations became endemic to the field: access to space, janitorial schedules (for cleaning classrooms and cafeterias and for closing up the school), union rules, and gaining the trust of teachers and principals. In spite of the argument that schools had plentiful space, in some cities, schools in low-income neighborhoods were both overcrowded and heavily used after school, forcing community-based providers to have to fight constantly for space and to move from one space to another. Lack of access to space ironically conflicted with pressures to enroll significant numbers of children from a school population (Reisner, 2001).

The space given to community-based providers in schools was rarely dedicated to the after-school program. This meant having to pack away materials every day; severe limitations in carrying out long-term projects; an inability to display children's work and to post rules; and in some cases lack of a sense of safety, predictability, and ownership of space among children and lack of office space for staff (Walker et al., 2000). Borrowing a classroom meant working "on top of" a room full of equipment, materials, and student work that often could not be touched or moved. Classrooms also were not suited to children's need for physical activity. School staff, worried about damage, wear and tear, and the inability to clean the school on schedule, commonly put restrictions on what could be used and even how. In a number of TASC initiative sites in New York City, classroom teachers reportedly refused to permit the after-school program to use their classrooms (Reisner, 2001, p. 45). The typical alternative was to put several groups of children into the cafeteria, an often sterile setting and a difficult environment for quieter activities, requiring an intimate scale. In general, it proved difficult to redesign and reshape school space, to alter what one writer described as the "fanatical impoverished regularities" of most school environments (Kennedy, 1991, p. 38). In other words, it proved difficult to create a rich material environment to provide an alternative to the more restricted environments of school and (for some children) home as well.

When the relationship between a community-based organization and a school worked, one could see why it was deemed to have potential. In Seattle, where there is a history of community-based organizations running programs in schools, after-school directors occasionally noted that teachers would talk to after-school staff about homework or tutoring support needs. Teachers and after-school staff shared information about children's interests and talents and family issues or worries. The after-school program at a particular school might be described in the school's Web site, featured in the newsletter, included in schoolwide events, and be part of the parents' night at the beginning of the year. In one of the Extended Service Schools, a principal relied on staff from the community agency to seek out children's views on what kind of after-school program they wanted. As Yost (2000) noted, "A partnership [between schools and community-based organizations] provides a mechanism for having a conversation about the needs of all children" (p. 3).

Yet in spite of such specifics, the administrator of the City of Seattle's school-age child care program expressed frustration that too often the schools did not view after-school providers as a partner and resource: "[There is] this sense of a system, and even a building, that's under siege, that has so many demands on it, yet at the same time . . . is not conscious of the resources that are truly right next door, or even within the same building." She noted as well that principals appeared to not understand how community-based organizations operated: "Principals simultaneously want to keep their expenses down, and even perhaps earn a little rent, and don't understand that community-based agencies have no magical public source of funds to be able to provide after-school programs; they have to generate revenue through fees, subsidies, etc." (J. Spielberger, personal communication, 5/20/88).

Studies found that in school-based programs run by nonschool organizations, the support (or lack of support) of the principal was critical in determining how well the program succeeded (Halpern et al., 1999; Feister et al., 2000; Walker et al., 2000). Developing and maintaining good relationships with principals was one more time-consuming task for program coordinators that already had too many such tasks. After-school providers learned to work with teachers and school staff who were supportive and to avoid others. In general, it took 2 years (or program cycles) for trust and mutual understanding to develop, at which point a program might start gaining access to more space and material resources Yet high rates of principal and teacher turnover could put the task of building a trusting relationship back to square one. More than a quarter of the New York City Beacons, for instance, experienced "moderate to severe leadership instability" (Warren, 1999, p. 7). The evaluators of the Extended Service Schools initiative reported, "Because principal turnover in the schools was quite high, trust levels [between school and community-based organization] did not always increase over time. When a new principal came into a school, program staff had to build new relationships and sometimes lost access they had once enjoyed" (Walker et al., 2000, p. 51).

Interviews by the author and colleagues with a wide range of program directors, trainers, and others over the course of a decade elicited far more frustration than satisfaction with the schools. The director of Parents United for Child Care, a Boston organization that worked with community-based organizations to set up after-school programs in schools, noted that it was difficult to get school administrators "to think beyond concrete, logistical issues—custodians, space, lights, liability—to what kinds of programs ought to happen, what the experience should be like for kids." One longtime after-school provider in Chicago likened working with schools to wading in a river: "One comes upon warm currents, then cold, then warm again, then cold again" (J. Spielberger, personal communication, 5/12/88).

PROGRAM QUALITY EMERGES AS AN ISSUE

Beginning in the early 1980s, a few organizations had begun to write and speak about the attributes of good after-school programs. Most notable was Michele Seligson and her colleagues, at the Wellesley School-Age Child Care Project, who undertook a series of "action research" projects, surveying and visiting model programs around the country. They published program case studies and, though they were primarily interested in school-age child care as a social movement, articulated principles of good practice (see, e.g., Baden et al., 1982; Seligson, 1983; Seligson & Allenson, 1993). The conceptualization of quality in these years drew heavily on work from the early childhood care and education field and focused on such attributes as staff-child ratios; group size; amount and use of space; arrangements for safety, health and hygiene; and provision of learning and play materials.

By the late 1980s, traditional youth-serving organizations, spurred by funders such as the United Way, were focusing more on quality. A few undertook organizational assessments, began to work on standards to guide local programs, or established in-service training programs. As more providers focused on quality, the diversity of the after-school field and its lack of central, guiding organizations was found to complicate the task of finding a common definition of good programming. A handful of reports and studies nonetheless began, incidentally, to build a common profile (Halpern, 1990; McLaughlin, Irby, & Langman, 1994; Vandell, Shumow, & Posner, 1997).

This emergent profile included staff qualities, such as warmth and flexibility, skill in observing children and recognizing support needs, and adequate understanding of children's developmental needs at different ages. It included aspects of program scheduling and curriculum, notably a flexible and relaxed schedule, time and opportunity for children to explore interests, long-term projects and activities sufficiently demanding to be absorbing and to pose a feeling of challenge, opportunity for children to create and construct, and to put things together in their own way, exposure for children to both their own heritage and the larger culture and time and space for privacy and opportunity for unstructured play. And it included such basic structural features as adequate and protected space, an adequate number of staff to ensure individualized attention to children, nutritious snacks, and a safe and predictable environment for children (and for staff as well).

As researchers began to use specific sets of attributes as a frame for examining prevailing practice in the after-school field, they found a mixed and in some cases troubling picture. A study by this author of eight inner-city programs in Chicago found that staff lacked time, and in some cases skill and inclination, to design and carry out interesting, challenging activities and projects or to develop individual relationships with children. This study also revealed variability in the quality of homework help, due in part to limitations in staff members' own literacy skills (Halpern, 1990). A study by Vandell and colleagues found wide variability in the emotional climate of after-school programs—from warm, informal, nurturing, and homelike, to restrictive, regimented, and institutional; in the skills of staff in understanding and responding appropriately to children; and in the quality, choice, and range of program activities. Of one program, the authors commented that "in general, materials were limited and many of the projects initiated by staff were uncreative and repetitive"; of another that "its activities were very similar to those the children were required to do in school. . . . children were restricted to their seats and prohibited from talking" (Vandell et al., 1997, pp. 15, 16). In a study of children's out-of-school lives that included after-school programs, Belle (1999) found that supervision of children was sometimes erratic and staff were sometimes arbitrary. She also found that some children were removed by their parents from after-school programs "because they encountered repeated violence from other children, harsh punishments or inattention from after-school teachers, intolerable levels of noise or a dearth of engaging activities" (p. 160).

Studies conducted during the 1990s also began to focus on the causes of quality problems. In addition to staffing limitations, program design, and scheduling-related issues, these included lack of a supportive infrastructure in the after-school field, limited agency capacity to use what external support existed, and lack of quality assurance mechanisms in the field. Inadequate funding—for individual programs and for the field as a whole—underlay many of the other problems of after-school programs. A study by the author and colleagues found that after-school programs in low-income communities typically received enough revenue to cover only two thirds of costs, forcing them to cope in a variety of ways that undermined quality. For instance, programs reduced staff hours to a minimum, refrained from filling staff vacancies, limited their purchase of supplies and materials, hired fewer specialists than they needed, and so forth (Halpern et al., 1999).

As I describe in the following two chapters, particularly chapter 6, the challenge of improving program quality became linked to that of strengthening after-school "systems" and the field as a whole. There were calls, and sporadic efforts, to professionalize the field, to develop college course sequences and certificates for after-school providers. Efforts were begun to promote a national accreditation system similar to that used in the early childhood field. A small number of training and technical assistance organizations emerged to provide program improvement support. Not least, a handful of initiatives strove to bring the fragmented provider community together for joint planning, mutual support and learning, and advocacy.

CONCLUSION

At the beginning of the 1990s, the phrase *after-school programs* was hardly heard in debates about how to better meet the developmental and support needs of low- and moderate-income children. By the end of the decade, after-school programs had come to be viewed as one of the most promising responses to the challenges facing such children. Stresses within families, the loss of outdoor play space, and growing questions about schools gave new valence to long-standing purposes for after-school programs—supervision and protection; opportunity to test interests, nurture talents, and express oneself through arts and sports; exposure to both one's own and the larger culture; and suggested new purposes—an extra measure of adult attention and care; a physically safe space to play; a setting providing additional help with homework; time to explore alternative purposes and uses of literacy; and not least an alternative setting in which to observe different standards of behavior, try on different selves without risk of ridicule, and experience success.

The new interest in after-school programs was, nonetheless, largely instrumental, creating dilemmas for long-standing providers and for the field as a whole. One was the need to contend with and balance diverse expectations from diverse stakeholders, while trying to keep a space in which children could be children. In New York City's TASC initiative, for instance, site coordinators noted that they had to constantly adjust their rhetoric and balance their actual emphases "according to the stakeholders involved. . . . parents attached great importance to homework completion. . . . the principal's priority was improving test scores, [while their own agencies] focused on providing a safe environment during the after-school hours" (Feister et al., 2000, p. 13).

A related challenge was that of coping with heightened, and largely inappropriate, expectations. New political friends and funders were asking after-school programs to do everything from boost children's standardized test scores to reduce juvenile delinquency, teen pregnancy, and drug use (see, e.g., Whitaker et al., 1998). And they were asking programs that were already resource starved to accomplish these purposes cheaply. The major funding initiatives of the era, such as TASC and the 21st Century Community Learning Centers, calculated that children could be adequately served for $1,200 to $1,500 per year, far below what even the most basic program with few or no specialists actually cost.

The strengthened case for and list of potential tasks for after-school programs heightened the importance of reflecting on their appropriate roles and on reasonable expectations of them. Although a handful of proponents argued that low-income children deserved access to the same kinds of developmentally enriching activities as those purchased by wealthier families for their children, no one would or could make the argument that after-school programs should be viewed as a normative developmental support, available to any low-income child who was interested and shaped by children's preferences. First of all, too many low-income children had one or another pressing support or intervention need. Second, this was a decade for practical, utilitarian social action. As the evaluators of a large initiative put it, "Most people . . . believe that an ideal after-school program should be a place for youth to engage in a range of productive activities" (Walker et al., 2000, p. 46).

In some respects, the major question facing the after-school field during the decade was how after-school experiences should relate to school experiences. After-school providers wanted, as always, to be useful, for example, helping children with homework, but not at the cost of losing their distinct identity. As the director of the after-school program at Erie Neighborhood House in Chicago put it, they did not want to become "homework programs." After-school programs had always prided themselves on being institutions in which children could have a broader range of experiences from what they had in school. They had created space and time for developmental needs that schools had ignored or addressed intermittently. They had focused on the "whole child," accommodating individual differences in learning style, interests, and capabilities. One reason that after-school programs were now receiving more attention was that schooling was perceived as problematic, and they were perceived as different than school. Yet, as schools became a growing base for after-school programming and school-related funding a growing funding source, after-school programs were also being asked to support, and extend, the mission and work of schools, including inculcating basic skills (and remediating skills deficits) and, by implication, apportioning success and failure.

In urging continuity and close coordination between after-school programs and schools, some new proponents argued that there would be a two-way stream of influence. For instance, schools would learn and absorb after-school programs' philosophy of active and integrated approaches to learning. Yet schools had rarely managed to create another part of themselves to meet children's other needs. This reality was a major reason that many providers were ambivalent about how closely they wanted to integrate their work with that of the schools. As one experienced program director argued, "An after-school education program can have its own identity, rooted in and responsive to the community it serves. It need not follow the agenda of the schools in order to provide real growth and learning opportunities" (Shevin & Young, 2000, p. 51).

At the turn of the century, the after-school field seemed to be at a critical juncture. It was identifiable and yet heterogeneous, vibrant and yet still fragile, a protected space for play and exploration yet increasingly burdened with compensatory tasks. Although coming to be viewed as an important child development institution, after-school programs still had no dedicated funding stream of their own, at the federal, state, or local levels. (Some described the after-school field as a "stepchild.") The one significant new source of funding, in education, appeared to threaten the community-rootedness, diversity of sponsorship, and broad (if diffuse) philosophy that most providers valued and that served diverse populations of children well.

5

The Mixed Qualities of After-School Programs

The children all seemed to like "M," and when they arrived they hugged her and told her about their day. [Yet] while she and the other staff seemed warm and caring, they were incredibly directive. And they did most stuff for the kids except play for them. . . . They told the kids what to do and when to do it all the time.
Evaluation of the MOST (Making the Most of Out of School Time)
Initiative: Final Report, R. Halpern, J. Spielberger, and S. Robb

Among the historic and emergent challenges facing the after-school field, one stands out, and in fact organizes the others: to broaden the base of programs providing good experiences for children. Addressing that challenge will require that stakeholders in the field attend to a number of tasks. The first two, largely conceptual, will be to clarify the role of after-school programs in meeting low-income children's developmental needs, and from that to develop a more specific picture of the types (and qualities) of experiences children should have in after-school programs. Subsequent tasks include identifying the program attributes that lead to good experiences for children, the domains in which programs most need assistance, and the types of supports most likely to be helpful to programs. Finally, it will be necessary to figure out how to organize and offer support to programs.

In this chapter and the one that follows, I begin the process of mapping after-school programs on to the developmental tasks of middle childhood; provide a closer look at the qualities of and challenges facing after-school programs, and describe the supports that will be needed to strengthen the after-school field in the coming years. I draw heavily on in-depth program observations and interviews undertaken in the course of two recent studies (Halpern et al., 1999; Spielberger & Halpern, 2002).

THE ROLE OF AFTER-SCHOOL PROGRAMS IN MEETING
LOW-INCOME CHILDREN'S DEVELOPMENTAL NEEDS

Consideration of the role of after-school programs begins with reiteration of the developmental tasks of middle childhood. This age period, roughly the elementary and middle school years, covers a great deal of developmental ground. During middle childhood, children acquire (or fail to acquire) the knowledge, skills, and dispositions necessary for effective participation in their society (Collins, 1984; Erikson, 1950). In American society, that has meant acquiring literacy and numeracy; gaining basic knowledge of literature, the sciences, and social sciences; acquiring such habits as persistence in abstract tasks, punctuality, and time discipline; and learning to accept a growing variety of (sometimes arbitrary) rules. Yet during middle childhood children also turn their imagination and creativity toward culturally valued activities in the arts, sports, and other areas. They explore interests and discover talents. They acquire a more complex understanding, or view, of themselves, and begin to forge a distinct identity, including a sense of competence; a motivational structure; a sense of where they, their family, and community fit in the larger society; and an idea of what their occupational options might be (Cook et al., 1996). Children continue the gradual process of separation from their parents, becoming more "at home in the world" (Suransky, 1982, p. 21). They learn to initiate and sustain their own social relationships. Older children learn to "self-regulate from moment to moment"—to get homework done and make decisions about how to spend time and with whom (Belle, Norell, & Lewis, 1997). And they develop a more complex moral compass.

As they engage these tasks, school-age children continue to need many of the same psychological supports as their younger peers, notably love and protection, approval, and sustained attention from significant adults (Cottle, 1993; Nightingale, 1993). More than younger children, they need opportunities to explore interests and to test and nurture special abilities. They need formal instruction, modeling by "experts," and practice in different symbolic systems and disciplines; and exposure to the broader cultural world. School-age children need opportunity for initiative and "practical hints on how challenges might be addressed" (Csikszentmihali, 1993, p. 43). They need opportunities to feel assured of their own skills for self-care and that they can depend on others (Buchholz, 1997, p. 160); safe physical spaces free from direct adult supervision; and adults close enough by to offer a measure of security. And they need time and space—to develop their own thoughts, daydream and reflect, do nothing if they wish, be bored, try on and rehearse different roles and identities, learn friendship and how to handle interpersonal conflict, rest and be quiet, and not least have fun and take risks of their own design and choosing.

It can be argued that after-school programs are well-suited to provide many of the supports and experiences that children need as they engage the developmental tasks of middle childhood. At their best, after-school programs respond to children's individuality, attend to children's point of view, and encourage their sense of "voice." They are responsive to children's interests and put children in active roles as learners (regarding focus and content, pace, approach, goals, etc.). They are good settings for apprenticeship experiences in arts, sports, and literacy. Because their agenda is not so full, after-school programs theoretically afford time to pursue activities in depth. Children need not feel pressure to master new learning challenges quickly. After-school programs are good settings in which to explore links between "a society's cultural heritage and [children's] personal experience" (Damon, 1990, p. 48). They can encourage children to use their own histories and experiences as a "springboard" for creative work (Hill, Townsend, Lawrence, Shevin, & Ingalls, 1995). At the same time, they have, at least in theory, time and resources to contribute to low-income children's store of cultural capital.

After-school programs are supportive of the social dimensions of children's learning. Their activities are full of children sharing, collaborating, helping one another, and working and playing together. Adults play supportive, rather than directive, roles, and they are nonjudgmental. As a result, children usually feel safe psychologically as well as physically, and there is a relatively low risk of failure. Finally, after-school programs can afford to provide children the social space they need, for spontaneity, physicality, and unrestricted movement, as well as a measure of privacy. Of all formal institutions, after-school programs can most afford to be nonutilitarian about childhood, to respond to children's individuality, to create interesting and manipulable material environments, to provide opportunities for children "to seek out experience for its own sake" (Moore, 1986, p. 231).

Taken together, these attributes make after-school programs a compelling institution—at least in ideal terms. This inherent attractiveness is reinforced by the sense that low- and moderate-income children are not getting developmental needs met in other settings. As noted in chapter 4, parents in low-income families may be too busy coping and trying to meet basic family needs to spend time talking with and attending closely to their children. They may not have the language or literacy skills to help with school-related tasks. Chin and Newman (2002) recently studied the conflict between welfare reform, which has sent large numbers of poor mothers, many of them single parents, back to work for often long hours, and growing demands by urban school authorities that parents play a more active role in supporting their children's school progress. Of one mother, they note that "Debra simply does not have the energy to check homework or to read to them [her children] like she used to. She knows how important monitoring is; she believes it is her responsibility; but she can only do so much" (p. 36). Another child in this study had only been doing his homework 2 days a week—the days that he went to an after-school program (p. 39).

School itself has been found to be a steadily more unwelcoming place for low-income children as they advance in grade. Teachers' styles often become less nurturing; for example, teachers give less positive reinforcement to children and spend less time conversing with them and listening to what they have to say (Calkins, 2001, p. 21). There is less willingness to accept and deal with individual differences in learning speed, style, capacity, and motivation, or with language difficulties; and there is generally less attention to how an individual child is faring (Stipek, 1992). There is less room for the knowledge and experience children bring from their home communities. In some urban schools and school systems, these inherent attributes of schooling increasingly are complemented by military-style discipline; hours spent on rote drilling designed to strengthen basic skills; lack of recess, arts, and physical education (Brooks-Gunn, Roth, Linver, & Hofferth, 2002); and the constant fear of being held back or singled out for summer school or after-school remediation.

On a day-to-day basis, observers have noted increased school-related stress, frustration, and mental exhaustion among low-income children (Wilgoren, 2000). Speaking of a particular child whom she was worried about, the coordinator of a Chicago Park District program remarked, "I can tell if he's had a bad day in school, you know. . . . It's terrible, he has been throwing things, his temperament's just been crazy" (Halpern et al., 1999). Over the long term, research finds a gradual disengagement from school among low-income children; a decline in feelings of self-efficacy; and a growing belief that reading, writing, and learning in general are senseless, unpleasant, even painful activities (Voelkl, 1997). Among older children, observers note a foreclosure in a sense of possible later identities, what MacLeod (1987) has described as "leveled aspirations."

Observing such family and school patterns in the lives of children they serve, after-school providers sometimes feel compelled to try to do and be everything. An after-school program director in California claimed, "Sometimes I feel we understand children more than the classroom teacher. We wear many hats. We are asked to do it all, and we do" (California Department of Education, 1996, p. 19). A Boston program coordinator commented, "You know, I don't know where to start with them, because they don't get it at school" (Halpern et al., 1999). The internal pressures that after-school providers feel are exacerbated by the inordinate expectations of funders, initiative sponsors, and other new "friends" of the after-school field.

Yet realistically, after-school programs cannot and should not be asked to take on too much. For one thing, it is their modest adult agenda, and the fact that they are socially oriented as well as task oriented, that allows them to be a comfortable setting for many children. Key attributes of good after-school programs—such as time and opportunity to explore talents, interests, and possible identities without risk of failure or ridicule; emphasis on experience for its own sake and on process rather than product; and the idea of adults spending time with children that is focused on children's lives and agenda—turn sour when linked to narrowly instrumental aims and societal worries. For another, the large majority of after-school programs currently operate at a minimal level. While a handful of programs reflect the attributes enumerated earlier, most simply lack the wherewithal to do so.

A CLOSER LOOK AT THE QUALITIES
OF AFTER-SCHOOL PROGRAMS

Two recent studies by the author and colleagues, involving detailed observations and interviews in 20 after-school programs in a variety of communities, provided a detailed picture of the qualities of after-school programs and pointed to key program improvement tasks within the field (Halpern et al., 1999; Spielberger & Halpern, 2002). Not surprisingly, we found a field with some strengths and a number of problems. While most programs in our two studies were reasonably comfortable places for children, two distinct sets of constraints were observed across a range of programs and came to embody the quality of challenges facing the field. The first concerned staff structure, skill, and patterns of relating to and interacting with children. The second concerned the activity structure of most programs.

SAFE PLACES

The principal strength of the after-school programs that were studied was the fact that children typically saw them as safe contexts, free from pressures experienced elsewhere and also as places where they could be "themselves." This was no small thing. Feeling and being safe—not just physically but psychologically safe—are prerequisites for taking the risks entailed in learning and trying new activities. In addition, program staff recognized and respected children's family and community culture and language. Conversation, for example, flowed informally and easily between children's non-English native language and English. Most programs strove to create a relaxed atmosphere, and about half were flexible in structuring participation in activities. Most programs provided a reasonably good context for children to do homework. Many programs afforded a weekly opportunity to participate in dance or theater or art, opportunities that probably would not have been available otherwise to participating children. The cross-age grouping in some programs provided opportunities for children to help one another.

STAFFING-RELATED CONSTRAINTS

From a structural perspective, many programs were too thinly staffed: There were not enough staff members and most or all staff other than the coordinator were part-time. (Among smaller sponsors, for example, a church or mutual assistance association, there might be only one paid staff member for an after-school program serving 30 to 50 children.) This had a range of negative consequences: Staff were sometimes too busy managing the larger group of children to learn about individual children's interests or attend to their support needs. Staff typically had little or no time to plan their daily and weekly work, or reflect on that work, and not infrequently planned and prepared activities while children were already present, for example, during homework or snack time. When a staff member was sick there was often no one to available to substitute, leading to cancellation of activities or combined groups.

Inadequate numbers were compounded by high rates of turnover, which could reach 40% a year. Turnover occurred at any time during the year, often unexpectedly; and it was not uncommon for programs to have staff vacancies for long periods (i.e., a month or more). Turnover limited children's sense of continuity and stability. It put added stress and demands on program directors, reducing the time they had available for planning and supervision. A program director in Boston described how "the day before we opened in September a group leader quit for a higher-paying job outside the child care field and 3 weeks later another group leader quit for higher-paying full-time employment." The director herself had to work in the classroom for a number of weeks until she could find replacement staff. The unpredictable timing of turnover not only multiplied the stress on remaining staff (already stretched thin), but sometimes forced programs to hire people who would not ordinarily be selected. Turnover also limited the effectiveness of staff development efforts. A Chicago program director said, "It's like starting over when you lose your really strong, really solid staff" (Halpern et al., 1999).

The Effects of Limited Skills. With respect to knowledge and skills, staff did not always know how to gauge children's interests (a task that is difficult in any case) or how to plan and facilitate children's engagement in activities. And program coordinators spent too little time helping frontline staff learn how to design interesting activities (especially across a wide age range), discern and stimulate children's interests, or organize resources to support child-initiated projects. Staff with little or no formal preparation for work with children tended, naturally, to focus on activities with which they felt comfortable (and moderately competent), such as homework help, supervision of recreation and games, and arts and crafts.

Observations and discussions with staff suggested that many were uncomfortable about their identity and strengths as readers and writers, and this also emerged as a problem. (While it is clearly unreasonable to expect frontline [i.e., direct care] staff in after-school programs to be expert visual or peforming artists or skilled in teaching particular sports, it does seem reasonable to expect an adequate level of literacy.) Lack of literacy skills, even among those who were college students, constrained some staff members' ability to help with homework and the likelihood that they would serve as models or mentors for children around literacy. For instance, we rarely observed staff reading or writing or discussing reading and writing. Lack of staff conviction around literacy was sometimes apparent in lack of follow-through—starting to read a story and then not finishing it, beginning a writing project and then not responding to the writing or doing anything with the products. It was also difficult for after-school staff to attend to that part of their role that called for building children's confidence as readers and writers. For example, it sometimes appeared hard for staff to respond primarily as an interested audience for a child's writing and refrain from correcting a spelling or grammatical mistake.

When after-school staff were insecure about literacy-related activity, or did not receive training or information or support, they tended to imitate the worst literacy practices of schools instead of the best ones: using dittos and worksheets, tracing letters, drilling children. Such practices were made even more inappropriate by the fact that children were required to do school-like drilling without any surrounding conceptual framework—assignments were not part of a carefully sequenced program, there was little or no feedback, and they were completed haphazardly.

As after-school programs have come to use more volunteers for homework help, tutoring, reading to children, and so forth, the literacy skills of these auxiliary staff have come to be an issue. In our two studies, high school youth proved to be particularly variable in these roles. We observed instances in which they were patient, persistent, and good at explaining concepts, and other instances in which they showed little skill. The staff member in charge of homework help at an East Harlem program told us that some high school tutors had trouble reading deeply for comprehension themselves, and so could not really help younger children learn to read more deeply in turn. Increasingly, college students also have variable literacy skills. One New York City settlement that relies on college students for staff feels compelled to test them on basic skills before hiring them, in order to be sure they have adequate literacy and numeracy skills to help children with homework.

The Mixed Quality of Staff-Child Interaction. Staff behavior in the programs we observed often had a mixed quality, in a few senses. It was typically strict but warm. We observed many hugs and even a few kisses. Staff typically seemed to like the children and enjoyed being with them. Some, nonetheless, could be quite strict at times, and there seemed little rhyme or reason to staff intervention. Random episodes of discipline were mixed with warmth and caring. We occasionally observed harsh or belittling behavior. Staff energy levels varied widely. Staff also were not particularly attentive to individual children who were quiet or unengaged. We occasionally observed staff to be tired or disinterested.

In most programs, individually focused interactions tended to be more effective, sensitive, and supportive than group-focused ones. During the latter, staff tended to be unduly strict or regimented, issuing directives or insisting on silence and order. In some programs, for example, snack time was fairly regimented: All children had to be seated at their tables in groups and be quiet before anyone received snack. In one program, whichever table was quiet first received snack first. (This was a problem for slow eaters whose table was picked last, since they hardly had a chance to take a bite before the food was cleaned up.) The transition from snack to activities involved lining up quietly and waiting for the go-ahead. Transitions often invoked excessive order. The director of the Chicago's park district after-school programs explained that she had struggled with frontline staff at different sites over the issue of lining children up to go from one room to another, a practice she thought they imitated from schools: "They line them up, they take 20 minutes to line them and they move them. And I say, 'You're only going from here to there. . . . couldn't you just walk with your group and talk [while you are walking]?'"

Staff with little understanding of the reasons for children's behavior, or formal knowledge of how to relate to children, tended to draw (consciously or not) on the behavior of authority figures in their own lives, and especially on the more punitive behavior of such figures. For instance, when staff were in a teaching situation, they often displayed the worst qualities of teachers (i.e., those involving gratuitous or excessive group control), rather than the best. As noted earlier, they tried to re-create what they believed was a school-like atmosphere, and in particular the strict demeanor of teachers and the regimented quality of schools. In one program, children spent the majority of time in their seats, being quizzed and drilled on spelling, sentence construction (through dictation), and math problems. Children were required to stay in their seats and remain silent unless called upon during the provider's academic lessons. Although she was able to maintain the attention of, if not engage, the majority of children, some were distracted, restless, or tired.

It was not uncommon for programs in our studies to have both strong and very weak staff. In one, for example, the group worker for the oldest group was quiet and calm in her interactions with children. The group worker for the middle group was very strict and rule-oriented. She insisted on quiet, order, and obedience. She controlled and motivated the group with a point system. Children earned points by behaving obediently, helping out, and guessing the correct answer on quizzes. They received demerits for behavior she did not like. Her intentions seemed positive—to strengthen children's basic academic skills. She praised children for their mastery of academic material. At the same time, she was also observed to be negative (e.g., frequently saying what she didn't like about the children's behavior), harsh, and occasionally demeaning with children. The group worker for the youngest group was basically warm and empathic, attuned to individual children's needs and feelings, but at times did not recognize the impact of her words and behavior on her charges.

ACTIVITY STRUCTURE: ROUTINIZED AND FRAGMENTED

The after-school programs in our studies tended to rely heavily on the routine created by an unvarying daily and weekly schedule. Activities were divided into small time segments (e.g., 30 to 40 minutes), making it difficult to plan and carry out in-depth or long-term projects. (This problem was compounded by some programs' reliance on shared or borrowed space, which also reduced the opportunity for sustained work and long-term projects.) Activities and projects were usually short-term, meant to be completed that day; often seemed designed with relatively little thought; and tended not to create opportunities for children to express their own intentions and creativity, or to work gradually toward mastery. The bulk of time not devoted to homework was occupied by "routine activities" such as board games, arts and crafts, group games (e.g., bingo), and open gym/recreation.

On a daily basis, children typically did not have much choice of activity, although they could sometimes choose not to participate in the planned activity. A few programs were closely bound to their schedules, moving children from one segment of the afternoon to the next in rigid, prescribed steps. Others were best described as laissez-faire. And still others had posted schedules, which seemed not to be adhered to. Both scheduling and implementation of schedules was complicated by the fact that in some programs, participating children came from different schools and arrived throughout the afternoon.

Children were often half-engaged and slightly bored. Of one program we noted: "After homework was done children hung out with peers, drew pictures, and played board games. The day ended in the gym, with the children playing ball, jumping rope, or running around, while the staff stood aside talking to each other. There was little in the way of planned activity during the three observations." Of another: "The atmosphere in this program was very relaxed, but there was also a distinctly aimless quality to it. Both children and staff appeared bored and seemed to be marking time. With one exception, staff did not engage the children, but rather supervised them loosely. Two staff members spent much of one visit talking to each other. At one point they actually left the building for 10 minutes to go to a store to buy food and smoke a cigarette." And of a third:

> Children drifted from area to area within the program space, not settling on an activity. Some went to the pool to swim. Some children migrated to the gym, where they played for a while on their own. At one point a staff member tried to organize a game, to be chosen by the children, but the game proved too difficult for some of the participants. Confusion ensued, and after 10 minutes the game ended. . . . The schedule of activities as laid out seemed clear, but it would have been impossible to deduce this from watching what happened: There didn't really seem to be a plan and the staff didn't seem clear on what was supposed to occur.

In almost all programs in our study, homework was coming, or had already come, to take a central place in shaping the program day. The emphasis on homework-first reportedly was driven by parental expectations, and children sometimes continued doing homework well into activity time. The climate observed during homework time varied enormously. In the majority of programs it was relaxed and informal, yet purposeful:

> Children worked on their homework alone or in pairs. Staff and volunteers circulated and sat with children going over unfamiliar words, hard-to-follow instructions, or difficult math problems, talking through the steps to solutions. When children finished their homework, a staff member or volunteer would ask to see it, provide feedback and point out errors to be corrected. Children left their seats, wandered around and socialized; although if they became too animated a staff member intervened.

Yet a strict, school-like climate was not uncommon, nor, occasionally, was a noisy and chaotic one:

> The children were required to be quiet and remain in their seats, and they had to raise their hands if they had questions or needed assistance.

Children who had no homework or finished it quickly were given dittos to work on. Homework assistance was given in both English and Chinese. The majority of the children were compliant and worked quietly; a few appeared to chafe at the structure. . . . Some children appeared to be day-dreaming, a few apparently looking out the window for friends to come by.

The principal problem with homework time, from a structural perspective, was that it crowded out other activities. Children were reported—and observed—to receive more and more homework each year, with an hour or more not uncommon for children as early as third grade. Homework time clearly benefited children whose parents were not able to help because of language difficulties. Yet more often than not—especially given the dubious quality of some homework assignments—it eliminated or severely reduced the opportunity to carry out potentially more enriching activities.

EXCEPTIONS THAT PROVED THE RULE

It was not always clear why some after-school programs worked while others did not. For example, we came to know one program with both typical staffing constraints and a characteristic activity structure that nonetheless worked on almost all levels. The schedule included a first hour (2:30–3:30 p.m.) characterized as "rap, lap, nap and snack," basically free time and a snack; homework and reading from 3:30 to 4:30 p.m.; a different scheduled activity each day from 4:30 to 5:15 p.m.; and free time again from 5:15 to 5:30 p.m., or whenever children were picked up. The scheduled activities on different days included circle time, discussion, or both; science/health/nutrition; large-motor activity; and arts and crafts. The schedule was implemented very flexibly, and transitions were informal and low key. Children arrived, settled in, found a spot for homework, and when done with homework were free to shift to an activity. Younger children with no homework were free to go right to an activity area to play. As the day proceeded, children were free to choose activities.

One key to this program was a warm, relaxed, family-like atmosphere. Staff had strong relationships with the children, who seemed to genuinely like them. The children were active and used the relatively rich material environment with confidence. When it was necessary to intervene, staff did so in a firm but not harsh manner. (At the same time, it did not appear that any long-term projects were under way.) Both children and staff in this program were at once engaged and relaxed. Children were lively, sometimes noisy, and displayed a sense of ownership of the classroom environment. Staff set limits, and were firm when necessary, but in a calm manner and in the service of safety and keeping interactions on a positive plane. While they let children play and sometimes get into and resolve conflict on their own, the staff also seemed attuned to what was occurring and were always close at hand.

THE PROMISE REALIZED: PROGRAMS THAT REFLECT IDEALS FOR THE FIELD

One goal of our research was in fact to identify after-school programs thought to be doing interesting work with children, describe their approaches and activities, and derive some tentative principles of potential use to the larger field. The programs we identified were diverse in many ways. They were sponsored by settlements, churches, boys' and girls' clubs, and public housing developments. They served children from a variety of ethnic and racial groups. They had distinct emphases. Yet they also shared certain general characteristics. For instance, directors were able to articulate clear goals and guiding philosophies. Most programs were able to socialize new staff into a shared understanding of the work. Directors and staff were concerned about the details of implementation and attentive to the importance of regularity and consistency. Almost all programs structured time for staff to meet, plan, and discuss the daily work with children. These meetings served as occasions for directors to reiterate core principles and practices.

I have selected two of the programs from the larger group of exemplars, to give the reader a sense of how their elements worked together to create exceptional experiences for children.

An Arts and Literacy Program Serving Latino Children

This program, sponsored by a community-based social service agency, served a largely Latino neighborhood. The actual programming took place in local schools, in borrowed space—classrooms or cafeteria. The staff were almost all young artists in fields such as photography, video, dance, cartooning, instrumental music, creative writing and drama. (The director was herself a sculptor.) Staff worked about 20 hours a week, and reportedly started at $15 an hour. The program used the arts as a vehicle for promoting literacy as well as a variety of other traits and abilities. These included skill in specific art forms, creativity, love of learning, connecting to (and critiquing) culture, and less directly, learning to work as part of a group, reacquiring good work habits, achieving self-assessment, and learning to pay attention to details. Behind these was the goal of affirming for participating children that their thoughts, wishes, and perspectives were valuable and that they had something of value to communicate and share.

The basic program model was built on monthlong projects designed by the staff, with input from children. The projects were shaped by a common, defined process, both before work with children was begun, and then with the children. There was a general plan that included the basic concepts to be conveyed (for example, in one photography project it was "understanding composition" and "color as mood"), learning and skill development goals, the steps in carrying out the project (described as breaking the product of a project and its activities down into component parts), and the "vocabulary" involved. The scope and length of the projects seemed intended to give children a visceral sense of what it took to work through an idea, from planning, to the trial and error of implementation, to review and revision.

When a project was completed, staff and children sat down to review it. Children critiqued their own work and also learned to critique one another's work. In reviewing a completed project with a staff member they revealed the vocabulary and concepts they had learned, which in turn became part of each child's portfolio. For example, one photography project included such vocabulary as composition, focus, documentary, and perspective, as well as aperture and shutter. At the end of the project the photography teacher sat down with particular children and reviewed their understanding of key concepts, asking, for example, the word for something "when it is not blurry" (i.e., focused).

Most projects observed by or described to the author involved more than one symbol system. The drama teacher had children write monologues using specific objects as an inspiration and then perform them. The "cartooning" teacher had children write about the characters (i.e., who they were) before drawing them. The children also learned how to use a story board to plan a narrative. The photography teacher had children give titles to their compositions. In one music project the children worked in groups to write lyrics, learning about verse and chorus, constructing a story around a theme (people, place, emotion). During one observation, the writing teacher led an exercise in which children wrote short stories and then drew pictures representing scenes in the story that were put on a "picture wheel," which rotated as the story progressed. In another activity, the other writing teacher had children create "noise poems," corresponding to sounds they were familiar with. (Children went out into the streets, identified neighborhood sounds, and converted them to poetry, including made-up words.). The dance teacher used words to explore movement, for example, asking kids to think of movement/ action words that begin with s—*swinging, stretching, standing*—and then demonstrate those words. She also created a dance out of the pictures and story in a picture book about a particular Puerto Rican myth.

In addition to working across symbol systems, a number of other key ideas shaped the work of this program. One was that children had different preferred ways of learning and expressing themselves and that having projects in a range of arts allowed children to find their expressive and creative niche. Another was that each of the arts had its own concepts, structure, and vocabulary, and relatedly that a particular artistic product was the result of a large number of identifiable technical and creative skills. A related idea was that artistic skills were built by breaking down the creative process into discrete steps and smaller elements for children to master. The staff discussed with the children what it takes to make, what must be considered in making, a painting or photograph or poem or dance composition.

Some activities were deliberately designed to raise children's awareness of the key concepts of a discipline. On one occasion, the author observed a poetry-writing class, in which the children were writing poems using the vertical and right-to-left structure of Chinese calligraphy poems. The writing teacher said that he was trying to get the children to understand the structure and conventions underlying different kinds of writing. On another occasion, the photography teacher pressed a group of children on what was behind a picture. He told an observer that he wanted to help children develop what he called "a visual language," by which he meant the ability to use a variety of concepts—foreground-background, perspective, shape, silhouette, isolating, and framing—to create a visual composition. The dance teacher worked with children to understand how dance used physical space and time. She also talked of "movement vocabulary," with individual movements the equivalent of words that are combined to create movement sentences, a group of movements that when combined convey a complete thought, and then compositions.

Staff also shared a commitment to helping children create artistic products that broke free of the stereotyped images from popular culture that saturated their lives. One of the creative writing teachers told an observer that he tried to get the children "to work toward originality and away from simply repeating stories they have heard or using the same characters from cartoons and games." Yet staff also realized that they could use popular culture to achieve their aims. Thus, for example, one photography project involved creating a CD cover (which involved creating a pretend rock group, giving it a personality and a name, etc.).

Not least, the staff seemed especially attuned to the interpersonal dimensions of their roles and of an after-school program, talking about wanting children to feel safe, to have a sense of continuity and familiarity and the opportunity to explore who they are. One of the writing teachers noted that it was through his relationship with the children, and his efforts to "affirm who they are . . . that they would start to take chances." This teacher, himself a poet and Latino, focused strongly on encouraging children to overcome what he noted as an aversion to writing, and to seeing themselves as writers.

It was also clear from his feedback that he was giving children reasons to be proud of their writing. Children were eager to share their writing with him, and other children would gather round as he read a child's piece of writing.

This program reflected what seems a delicate balance between process and product. Staff recognized the important role of performance and product as part of the creative process, and for affirming for children that they did have something to contribute, to say, while also recognizing why some children were reluctant to take risks associated with creativity. In music, children performed the songs they had written for family and friends. The program staff published an annual anthology of children's work, mostly poetry, also including a play and some minibiography. They organized an annual street festival, in which children performed some of the work they had produced during the year.

A YOUTH AGENCY WITH ROOTS IN SOCIAL GROUP WORK

This program, founded in the mid-1950s to reach out alienated youth in a rapidly changing low-income community, served primarily older school-age children (10–14 years of age), in three sites: a "main" site, a site for an all-girl's program, and a site at a local elementary school. The program was characterized by the use of literacy activities, especially writing, for self-exploration, self-definition, and personal expression ("expressing one's life"); to provide opportunities for children to share their voices with others, both peers in the program and a wider audience; and to help children better understand and grapple with the "social realities" they faced.

The activities at each site were somewhat different, but shared a set of underlying assumptions and a common philosophy. These included the importance of creating a safe, predictable environment for children (and for staff as well); the importance of trusting relationships as the key to other work; and the need to deliberately build and continuously nurture a sense of community. Staff also seemed attuned to a need to counter children's feelings that they could not be successful—at school in general, and with particular reading and writing tasks. Putting these elements together, the overarching goal was to create settings in which children felt safe and valued, but were also challenged to think and question.

The program had a strong social work perspective, a legacy of its origins as well as of the current director, a social worker. Staff were a mixture of social workers and educators/artists. Children were given a psychosocial assessment (including an academic assessment) upon enrollment. They were then assigned to staff who acted loosely as "case managers." Staff paid special attention to the role of groups, and received some training in social group work theory and principles (e.g., group development, group dynamics, the evolving role of the leader). Group-building and -maintenance activities could be seen throughout the program. For example, rituals played an important role in activities. At the main site on one occasion, children were gathered at the beginning of the day to "check in/check out." Each had a chance to share something about his or her day—an event, thought, or feeling. On another occasion a staff member used a "talking stick" to wrap up an activity, passing the stick from child to child, offering each a chance to share his or her thoughts.

The main site was closest in structure to a typical after-school program. It emphasized homework help and tutoring and ran an extended "adventures in learning" program, exploring specific topics in depth. (During the year of observations, the focus was on the history of African American music in the United States—children read books, did research on jazz and blues, listened to and discussed music, developed an illustrated time line, and prepared biographical material on key figures.) Behind these specific activities was the idea of providing a safe space where children could choose either to hang out or be actively engaged in projects. During one visit, the main room was observed to be rich with the products of children's activities—artwork and writing on the walls, a mobile hanging from the ceiling—and full of social life, as small groups of older children talked to one another, played board games, and talked with staff.

The main site used high school students for the bulk of homework help, and this was observed to work well—the children really liked the relationships with older youth, and the high school students seemed familiar with some of the homework assignments. On one occasion a high school student was observed to work with a young girl for almost an hour and a half, helping her memorize a poem by writing it with her, going over words the girl did not understand, discussing the meaning of the poem, and sharing associations.

Some children at the main site received weekly tutoring, focused on either homework or a school topic or assignment the child did not understand. Dialogue journals were used as organizers for tutoring. Children wrote out their assistance needs and goals for tutoring, did some autobiographical writing, wrote in response to specific questions posed by tutors and staff (for instance, about books children were reading), and engaged in ongoing dialogue with tutors about a range of personal topics. Dialogue journals seemed to be used in a variety of ways by children and tutors; for instance, some contained math problems, others poems that a child or tutor liked, others discussion of politics, trips, feelings and moods, needs or worries, and long-term goals.

The program at the separate site for girls included rap groups, visual and performing arts activities, academic tutoring, creative writing, a Spanish club, career exploration, and training to mentor younger children. These activities focused on girls' loss of confidence and sense of self as they entered the early adolescent years, both with respect to school success and with respect to "what they know"—about the world, relationships, themselves, their feelings, and so forth. Tutoring was an important activity, and the tutors who worked with the girls were all female, mostly professional women. As at the main site, tutoring was organized around use of a dialogue journal. Most of the girls were noted to be way behind their grade levels in school. There was a weekly writing group whose main goals were to help girls overcome their fear of and anxiety about writing and to give them a concrete sense that "there are reasons to read and write." Writing activities included autobiography (with individual assignments driven by particular questions), individual and group poems, and pop songs. (The writing group leader used other art forms, especially music, as a lead in to writing.) As groups solidified over time, girls were encouraged to share their writing and give each other feedback. Girls also read literature selected to generate discussion about their lives and experiences, or about writing itself.

CONCLUSION

Some of the less thoughtful practices and less positive adult-child interactions seen in after-school programs appear to be easily altered, others less so, being tied to deeply rooted constraints faced by most programs. Stronger programs reflect a mixture of more easily transferable practices and more ineffable traits. As described earlier, even the somewhat weaker programs discussed in this chapter had positive elements. Thus even when staff seemed a bit abrupt, or did not appear to really observe and listen to children, they were generally affectionate, and staff-child relationships were comfortable. Yet more deeply interesting and engaging activities occupy a small part of the life of most programs. Beyond limitations in staff skills, the reasons for this pattern probably include the simple power—in effect the gravity—of routine, and the time and work it takes to plan. Broad spatial, temporal, and curricular regularities among after-school programs also create certain leveling effects with respect to children's experience. One can, nonetheless, see in the case studies why and how specific qualities can make observable differences in those experiences.

In the two case study programs, as in other exemplars not described in this chapter, one sees a distinctive sense of purpose, of thoughtfulness about the program as a whole, about what that program was trying to do and to accomplish, accompanied by distinctive adult roles. Staff conveyed excitement about program activities, and often employed an apprenticeship model of teaching and learning, making visible to children the invisible skills underlying expertise in an activity. (This meant that while not all the adults in a particular program had to be deeply skilled in one or more performing or visual arts or literacy or sports, at least a few were.) These programs afforded children plentiful opportunity for practice, performance, and feedback, with the adult (as well as peers) providing an audience for children's demonstration of mastery. Staff created occasions for "festival," in which the broader community could come together in seeing and celebrating the accomplishments of children.

Staff in these programs made an effort to connect activities to children's lives. For instance, a mural might use historical figures that were important to children's ethnic or racial group. There was recognition that children seem to have different preferred ways of learning and expressing themselves. Staff created settings in which children felt safe and valued and yet could also explore who they were and where they fit. The programs focused on relationships as well as tasks, making time for conversation about life as well as for talk about the work at hand. As the writing teacher in one case study program noted, it was through his relationship with the children and his efforts to "affirm who they are . . . that they would start to take chances." The program directors spoke explicitly of their programs as places where children and adults have time to talk, to seek and get explanations.

One sensed in these programs that staff took children seriously, on the one hand respecting their intentions and point of view, on the other realistically appraising their skills and recognizing that some children had not had opportunities to explore and develop their abilities. Staff recognized the importance of affirming for children that they had something to contribute, to say, while also recognizing why some children were reluctant to take risks associated with creativity and engagement itself. Staff recognized children's developmental struggles and actively provided support, without either labeling or making too much of those struggles.

Finally, the exemplary programs we studied point to the importance of balance in many aspects of program life. These include, for instance, a strong sense of purposefulness, but room for children's own agenda (put differently, adult responsibility for structuring engaging activity, yet opportunities for children to make the program theirs); a sense of seriousness but room for playfulness; and clarity about rules and expectations, with room for children to make their own rules. They point to the value of a relaxed view of time; of room for talk; of accommodating children who needed to move, to work, at different speeds, to finish an activity, when practicable, without being stopped because "it's time for something else."

6

Supporting and Strengthening After-School Programs

Professional views of what children need seem utopian given the straits in which school-age child care centers currently operate.
L. Martin and C. Ascher, *Developing Math and Science Materials for School-Age Child Care Programs*

The basic concerns about program quality described in the previous chapter suggest a number of basic foci for program improvement efforts: how time is organized, the characteristics of engaging activities and projects, how staff think about and relate to children, how much choice and control children have over activities, and how space is used. With respect to activity structure (and overroutinization), programs could be urged, for instance, to set aside 2 or 3 full afternoons every week for long-term projects. On those days, parents would know that children were not doing homework at the after-school program. There ought to be many more skilled artists and other specialists working part-time in after-school programs, to work with staff to design and lead engaging activities. Time use can be reconfigured to create more opportunity for "metatalk," talk about things—school, grades, family, community, friends, worries, books, music, life; and to afford greater flexibility for children who need and want to move at different speeds. Space can be reconfigured to afford children a measure of privacy and some freedom to reshape the setting, to convince them that "the world is not a finished product" (Kennedy, 1991, pp. 2, 44).

Over time, program improvement efforts would, logically, turn to the more subtle attributes discussed at the end of chapter 5: helping program staff think through a guiding philosophy, sense of purpose, and role; considering what kind of staff configuration is needed; gradually building a climate balancing a range of elements, including deeply engaging projects; providing opportunities for children to explore identity, opportunity for self-expression in different symbolic systems, and some time away from adult-led activity.

What kinds (and combinations) of supports will help after-school programs more fully incorporate the basic and then more subtle attributes of good practice? And how should these be organized, in a heterogenous, decentralized field with thousands of small, sometimes isolated programs? To the present, there have been only a handful of efforts to test different program improvement strategies, and even fewer to figure out and begin to build an infrastructure of people and organizations to provide those supports found to be most helpful. The MOST Initiative, discussed in previous chapters, was one such effort. Another ongoing initiative is the Baltimore After-School Strategy, part of the broader Safe and Sound Campaign. Underlying any effort to support and strengthen after-school programming is funding, and later in the chapter I examine the prospects for expanded funding in the after-school field.

APPROACHES TO PROGRAM SUPPORT AND IMPROVEMENT

Program improvement strategies in the after-school field fall into a few categories. Some focus on strengthening programs as a whole: licensing, development of program standards, accreditation (linked to standards), and long-term technical assistance. Some are aimed specifically at strengthening core staff, for example, short-term training and workshops, specialized postsecondary courses and course sequences, and assorted incentives and other strategies to reduce staff turnover. Some are intended to strengthen or enrich program "curriculum." These include efforts to link specialists, usually visual or performing artists, to after-school programs, or, in the case of museums, to help programs develop specialized activities or projects; development of "packaged" curricula in specific content areas; and development of resource libraries. Small facilities and equipment improvement funds have been created for after-school programs in a handful of cities. There are, finally, strategies not focused specifically or solely on program improvement. Examples include the creation of provider networks; efforts to promote parent involvement in different dimensions of program life; and grants to support inclusion of children with special needs.

Although one can find examples of these strategies in many cities, implementing them in a coherent and sustained way will require greater attention to system-building in the after-school field and a significant expansion of funding. Mechanisms will have to be developed to focus on such citywide tasks as information gathering, assessing program support needs (neighborhood by neighborhood and program by program), planning and priority-setting, seeking new resources and rationalizing use of existing resources, linking institutions with specific curricular resources to others who need those resources, and assessing effectiveness of program improvement investments, among other tasks. This in turn will create a framework for addressing funding questions, including how much new funding is needed, where it might come from, and how it might be structured.

STRENGTHENING PROGRAMS AS A WHOLE

Licensing, Standards, and Accreditation. Licensing, typically by the state agency responsible for child care (and focused on the same types of program attributes), plays a modest role in the after-school field. It has been helpful for establishing minimum standards in such areas as space and light, fire-escape plans, hygiene, and staff-child ratios and, in some states, for requiring programs to screen potential staff for histories that would make them unfit to work with children. But it has had little influence on many factors that underlie program quality. Many after-school programs are exempt because of their structure, purposes, or auspices. The child care framework that guides most states' licensing standards also does not fit some after-school programs well. For instance, physical facilities often do not fit child care licensing standards. Licensing rules are silent on the question of what kinds of enrichment experiences children ought to have in after-school programs and actually prohibit some kinds of activities.

Development of standards and program accreditation are related strategies, borrowed from other human service fields. They have proven modestly promising as program improvement strategies, although used thus far on a very limited scale. The National School-Age Care Alliance (NSACA), a membership organization, has published a set of "quality" standards, linked to a structured self-assessment process involving staff, parents, children themselves, and other stakeholders. Together, the standards and accompanying process are meant to serve as a framework for accreditation in this field. The standards focus on such categories as human relations, indoor and outdoor environment, structure of activities, safety, and nutrition. They say little about the substance of after-school program activities (nor do they address the types of attributes described at the end of Chapter 5). Large provider organizations such as boys' clubs and YMCAs have developed their own standards for local programs to use, as have some public agencies (such as park districts), a few citywide after-school initiatives, and a handful of cities. In the majority of cases, these alternative standards are similar to or actually model themselves on the NSACA standards.

One pilot effort to use the NSACA standards and self-assessment process, with accreditation as a goal, had mixed results (Halpern et al., 1998). Using an external framework to reflect on one's own program provided "a place to start" and could prove "eye opening," as one program director put it. It gave staff permission to step back from day-to-day pressures and some-times led staff to rethink how they were relating to children and how they were designing activities or using space. A number of programs had never sought or received feedback from parents or children before (one child wished that the staff would stop screaming all the time). Parents both offered spe-cific recommendations for changes in practice, for example, more feedback from staff on how their children were faring, and affirmed the work staff were doing. One parent stated, "I just expected my children to have fun and socialize, and I didn't really expect them to build relationships; which is great, a good part of it" (p. 51). Preparing for a potential accreditation site visit gave a few programs leverage within their agency to argue for more resources, including space and facilities improvements. The process led some programs to develop program improvement plans.

At the same time, the majority of programs in this pilot had such limited resources and were at such a minimal level of functioning that they could not carry out the activities that were part of the self-assessment process. They also could not make use of the technical assistance available to help with the whole experience. Program staff sometimes did not know how to convert feedback into "actionable" plans. Staff turnover in a number of programs, especially at the coordinator level, limited the continuity needed to make the lengthy self-assessment and goal-setting process work. Staff turnover, fund-ing instability, and agency-level change also led to deterioration and rever-sals in gains made by programs in various domains.

In its ongoing After-School Strategy, Baltimore is using both the NSACA standards and a complementary set of substantive standards to guide program improvement efforts. The latter are organized as "cognitive development, recreation, workforce development, artistic development, civic development, and open time" (Marzke & White, 2001, p. iii). A portion of the funding going to individual after-school programs is set aside for quality improve-ment. Programs are required to include quality improvement plans, with an attendant funding request, in their annual grant applications (although it is not clear who is responsible for helping them implement these plans). The general and substantive standards (noted earlier) are used to guide quality improvement foci. Presumably, each subsequent year's grant application will then include discussion of activities and progress in relation to the past year's quality improvement plan. First year plans focused on such issues as staff training and support, safety, indoor space, staff qualifications, and inter-actions between children (p. 16).

Long- or Short-Term Technical Assistance. Long-term technical assistance to programs (sometimes linked to standards, less commonly to preparation for accreditation) is a potentially important, but as yet largely untested, program improvement strategy. (The MOST Initiative, again, offered modest experience with this strategy.) A long-term time frame, for example, a year, affords the technical assistance provider time to develop a specific profile of the strengths and weaknesses of a program and its staff; to build relationships and gain trust; to develop a coherent, progressive program improvement plan with an adequate time frame; to continually reinforce ideas and messages; and to review new practices after staff have had some experience with them. One obvious drawback to long-term technical assistance is the fact that a handful of programs can use up most of the technical assistance resources available in a city, leaving scores of equally deserving programs with no support. It is also not easy to know which programs to choose for technical assistance, those that are most vulnerable but thereby also have limited capacity to use support, or those that are less vulnerable but could probably make better use of assistance.

Focused or short-term technical assistance is more common, though still not widespread, in the after-school field. It is sometimes focused in the area of expertise of a particular technical assistance provider, for example, space use, creation of a library or literacy center, or designing literacy or art activities. It can also be focused on issues raised by program staff, for example, how to make homework time more effective, finding ways for older children to help younger ones, or examining and refining the program schedule. For many programs, focused or short-term technical assistance is easier to manage and assimilate. It is often linked to programs' professional development efforts for staff. At the same time, it logically has more discreet effects on overall program functioning.

Short- and long-term technical assistance will not be practical strategies until the after-school field has many more experienced technical assistance providers. School's Out Consortium in Seattle, a longtime training and technical assistance provider, has developed an interesting model for addressing this problem. Called the Trainers Apprenticeship Program, it uses its own experienced technical assistance staff to provide 40 hours of individually tailored mentoring, coaching, guided training, instruction in adult learning and "quality standards," and actual site work, over a 9-month period, to experienced program coordinators and staff. Participants are paid for the time they commit to the program (NIOST, 2001, p. 6). The After-School Corporation (TASC), the New York City initiative described in chapter 4, has developed an *On-site Training Services Catalogue*. In the catalogue, each of 37 "approved" trainers/technical assistance providers describes the types of workshops or other activities it can offer, the number of sessions and hours per session, and costs and availability of follow-up services. Some providers on the list offer training in specific substantive domains such as arts, literacy, technology, or environmental education; others in general areas such as classroom management, curriculum or activity planning, space use, basic orientation to after-school work, working with volunteers, creating "community," and so forth.

STRENGTHENING STAFFING

Leaders in the after-school field have argued repeatedly that it will not be possible to significantly improve children's experiences in after-school programs until staff are better prepared to work with children, such problems as staff turnover are addressed, and a viable career path is created in the field. It has been argued that staff development has to become an "intrinsic part" of the life of sponsoring agencies. Just as they might use structured self-assessment to examine their program for children, providers should assess their current approach to supporting and nurturing staff (Hill et al., 1995). Some argue also that the after-school field itself will not be taken seriously until staffing is professionalized (California Department of Education, 1996).

In-Service Training. Preservice training is virtually nonexistent in the after-school field. Most new staff are simply thrown into the work and are required to figure out their roles for themselves. By default, occasional in-service training has become the central staff development strategy in most programs. In-service training, which can last from a few hours to a day or 2, is sometimes provided by an agency for its own staff, perhaps using outside presenters, and more commonly provided in workshops or conferences sponsored by the few intermediary organizations that exist in the field. These include the Partnership for After-School Education (PASE) in New York City, Schools' Out Consortium in Seattle and the After-School Institute in Baltimore. PASE, for instance, has sponsored an annual conference for all the city's after-school providers since the mid-1990s. The conference offers a wide range of hour-and-a-half workshops in specific curricular areas, such as the arts and literacy, staff development and training, fund-raising, working with schools, program planning, and so forth. Conferences seem helpful for giving staff a sense that they are part of a larger field, and for strengthening providers' sense of purpose or motivation.

Arts and cultural organizations, which may have their own activities for children, are beginning to provide in-service training to after-school programs, either through grants received for that specific purpose or as a fee-based service. Program coordinators in specific neighborhoods have occasionally worked together to develop in-service plans for a program year, and then taken turns hosting and leading in-service sessions. Frontline staff enjoy visiting other programs. On occasion, large sponsors such as Boys' and Girls'

Clubs and YMCAs have had "open training," inviting other providers to send staff. Citywide child care resource and referral agencies, which often provide extensive workshops for child care providers, have also begun to provide some training for after-school staff.

The content of in-service training has tended to be about basic issues—development in middle childhood, room arrangement, scheduling, homework help, interesting arts and crafts projects, snacks, and classroom management. (When asked, frontline staff, struggling with control of children, often request training in conflict resolution, behavior management, discipline, and so forth. These staff do not understand, and those who offer training usually don't help frontline staff see, that behavior problems would largely disappear if children were more engaged by program activities.) Anecdotal reports suggest that even the most basic information is helpful. A frontline worker at Erie Neighborhood House in Chicago claimed that a session on school-age children helped her look at them differently: "Before I would just say 'no, no, no, I'm in charge,' but I learned you can't do that, especially with the older kids. . . . you have to give the 10 to 12 year olds a little leeway" (Halpern et al., 1999).

Training approaches that have been found to be relatively more effective in the after-school field have been practical and concrete, have concentrated on a few basic messages or ideas, and have included follow-up activity by the coordinator. Too often when staff have brought ideas back from a workshop or conference, they have found it difficult to implement them, because a coordinator was not supportive, there was no mechanism for discussing program changes, or other program concerns had a higher priority. Groundwork has to be laid to free up frontline staff to participate in training experiences outside their agency. Substitutes have to be found, and the coordinator has to make it clear that participation in a particular event is important and valued. Ideally, staff should be reimbursed for time spent in professional development activities.

Although in-service training has tended to focus on frontline staff, there is growing recognition that training experiences for coordinators are both more critical and have more enduring benefits than those for frontline staff. Coordinators are more likely to be professional—most have bachelors' degrees; many have majored or taken course work in fields relevant to after-school programming; and a sizable minority are committed to after-school work as a career. Coordinators also have a greater responsibility to shape their programs and, at least in theory, have primary responsibility for training frontline staff.

Staff Meetings. Staff meetings provide a de facto training and staff socialization experience. At their best, they provide time to discuss and process what is happening in a program every day, to describe the achievements of and discuss concerns about individual children, to reaffirm the value of and express doubts about the work being done. They offer the coordinator an opportunity to articulate program goals and philosophy and provide more experienced staff an opportunity to model activity and project planning for newer ones. The director of a Bronx program noted, "We held weekly [staff] meetings during which we examined teaching techniques such as journal-writing, creating flip books, using measuring and other math skills in the context of science experiments. . . . We offered curriculum brainstorming meetings in which the staff collaborated on turning project ideas and research into actual lesson plans for their work" (Shevin & Young, 2000, p. 50). A handful of programs around the country bring staff together before children arrive each day, to get them focused and organized, or less commonly at the end of the day, to talk about what occurred and plan for the next day.

Observation of Frontline Staff. Observation of and feedback to frontline staff by program coordinators would seem to be a simple, straightforward staff development approach. Frontline staff report that they want feedback on their daily work (as well as on coordinators' expectations for their role performance), in order to improve their skills (Halpern, 1990). But such feedback is more the exception than the rule, in part because coordinators typically do not feel confident about this aspect of their role, in part because they have many other daily responsibilities. As a result, the majority of frontline providers in the after-school field, while sensing that they are meeting children's needs in some ways, report not feeling sure about whether they are doing a good job (Halpern, 1990).

Professionalizing the After-School Workforce. Leaders in the after-school field have long assumed that a more professional workforce would lead to higher quality programs. This assumption derives largely from studies in the early childhood field, which have found that more highly educated staff provided more sensitive, responsive, consistent, and stimulating care to young children (see, e.g., Helburn et al., 1995). By implication, a concerted effort would have to be made at some point to draw 2- and 4-year colleges into the work of preparing after-school providers and engaging with the world of after-school programs. Colleges and universities have been reluctant to develop courses, course sequences, and specializations in after-school programming because it has not been clear that a distinct and sizable after-school profession is emerging. Frontline or supervisory staff wishing course work are left to seek it out in early childhood education, group work, or leisure and recreation. While modestly helpful, courses in these disciplines do not provide information in critical areas, such as development during the middle childhood years, the purposes and assumptions behind after-school programming, or design of activities and programs suitable to school-age children of widely varying ages.

When they have offered courses and course sequences specific to after-school programming, higher education institutions have found that demand was less than anticipated. A professor at Bunker Hill Community College said, "We have too many start ups here with innovative plans and then no students show up" (Halpern et al., 1999, p. 206). The completion rate among participants in course sequences in two MOST-supported initiatives, among community colleges in Boston and Seattle, was about 25%. In some instances, even partial or full tuition subsidies were not enough to lure prospective or existing staff to enroll (Halpern et al., 1999). Existing staff saw little financial gain in taking postsecondary courses, given the low wages in the after-school field and lack of any obvious career path to higher wages. Staff in most programs received no salary increments for courses taken and usually were not paid for any hours spent in class. Some lacked time to take courses, whether because they were already college students and could not handle more course work or because they had other part-time work. Some lacked confidence in their academic skills. Some staff did not intend to work in the after-schoool field for more than 2 or 3 years. An instructor at Seattle Central Community College, which for a while offered an associate of arts degree with a specialization in school-age care, noted that

> the [after-school] field really struggles with commitment on the part of staff to this as a profession. It's been seen more as a semi-profession. . . . You know, its the whole gamut—they're underpaid, they do split-shift work. A lot of them are doing this to gain experience working with children, which is fine. You know they're moving on to elementary education degrees or special needs, something like that. . . . we'll get people excited and [enrolled] in the classes, and then half disappear or they're off to another job. (Halpern et al., 1999, p. 174)

Factors that moderately increase staff interest in pursuing coursework include strong and persistent encouragement from supervisors, having an agency pay tuition up front, rather than reimbursing staff after completion of a course, and arranging for course credits to count toward a degree (or toward requirements for certification in a neighboring field). There is some very tentative evidence that staff are more likely to attend "neighborhood-based" classes, but these only work when they are heavily subsidized and there are enough local programs to attract a community college (Halpern et al., 1999).

More broadly, the elaboration of professional preparation and professional development structures for the after-school field, in particular college courses and credentialing, await the further definition of the field itself and the creation of a coherent applied knowledge base from the constituent elements of child care, education, recreation, social group work, and expressive arts, as well as delineation of the most relevant child development knowledge. While the daily work of after-school providers and the small literature on best practice suggest the kinds of knowledge and "competencies" after-school providers need, it is not clear who needs what knowledge.

Addressing Turnover. Reducing staff turnover is as much a program improvement goal as a strategy. It would, obviously, improve continuity in staff-child relationships, build a critical mass of experienced providers, and increase the return on investment in staff training. I am personally skeptical that there is much progress to be made on this problem; rather, program improvement strategies have to be built around it. (Many after-school programs, for example, deliberately hire college students as staff, knowing they will leave in a year or 2.) Nonetheless, a few strategies for reducing turnover, mostly still proposals, are worth noting. One involves creating full-time jobs of which after-school work is a part. For example, in a community-based agency an after-school staff member might work in the morning in a Head Start or prekindergarten program or as a family support specialist; in a school-based program he or she might work as a classroom, cafeteria, or recess aide. This offers the advantage of rounding out after-school work with related types of work. It does not, however, address the fact that, as noted earlier, many people such as college students choose after-school work precisely because it is part-time. Another strategy for reducing turnover has been to seek ways to offer benefits, particularly health insurance. One idea here is bring a number of small programs together to create an insurance pool that would lower costs. More discreet strategies include giving staff specific roles, such as homework help coordinator, to foster a greater sense of ownership of the program, and creating individualized plans for development of specific skills and competencies, which would give staff some sense of progression, if not a career path.

Differentiated Staffing. In spite of rhetoric about professionalizing the field, after-school programs are likely to remain paraprofessionally staffed for the forseeable future. Staffing will be strengthened not by professionalizing primary care staff but by incorporating artists and other specialists to work alongside them, in an approach that can be called differentiated staffing (an approach that can also be viewed, obviously, as a curriculum improvement strategy). After-school programs have always subcontracted with specialists to lead and teach activities, especially in the arts. But most programs have understood these specialists as occasional supplements, not as as core staff. The idea behind differentiated staffing is to hire specialists, for example, young artists, and integrate them into the daily life of an after-school program. They could assume some current primary care responsibilities, providing the less specific relational supports children need, or work in roles complementary to nonspecialists, who would formally be considered primary care staff.

STRENGTHENING CURRICULUM

Strengthening curriculum is a potentially powerful program improvement strategy. By *curriculum*, I mean (1) objectives for and assumptions about children's experiences in a program in specific content areas (e.g., arts, literacy, social/cultural studies, natural sciences, math) and around specific developmental tasks (e.g. exploring identity, feeling and being productive, exercising imagination); (2) planned activities, projects, materials, and learning experiences in relation to these content areas and developmental tasks; and (3) specification of the role and approach of primary-care staff or specialists in guiding and otherwise structuring children's experiences. Curriculum can derive from a set of material resources, or can be implicit in a project or set of activities planned by a skilled specialist.

With respect to written or material curricular resources, a majority of after-school programs have resource notebooks with individual activity ideas (accumulated idiosyncratically over a period of years) and have at least a handful of published books and manuals with activity ideas. Few programs have coherent curricula in specific domains or content areas, as outlined earlier. Staff typically use available materials in a fragmented, nonsystematic way (Halpern et al., 1999; Spielberger & Halpern, 2002). It is not clear why after-school programs do not seek out and use written curricular resources more fully. The early childhood background of some coordinators may contribute to an emphasis on child-centered rather than content-centered programs. After-school providers may not know where or how to find relevant curricular resources, know how to evaluate them, nor have money in their budgets to purchase such resources.

It can be argued that the first task in strengthening curriculum actually begins before the location and purchase of useful materials. It is to think through (and write out) program philosophy and goals, both in general and for particular kinds of activities and experiences. (That is in part why a good curriculum also serves a staff development function, helping strengthen staff capacity to think and act as "instructional leaders" and as shapers of the physical and social environment.) For example, as described in chapter 5, Interfaith Neighbors in New York City has a clearly articulated philosophy that includes creating a safe, predictable environment for children (and for staff); the importance of relationships as the key to other work; and the need to build and nurture a sense of community (Lyons, 2000). Its stated goals include the use of reading and writing for self-exploration, self-definition, and personal expression; the provision of opportunities for children to share their voices with others; and activities that help children better understand and grapple with the social realities they face. As another example, Chicago's Erie House has developed a clear program philosophy regarding homework: to provide some homework help, but to make clear to parents that theirs is not "a homework program." Other experiences are important for children after school, and children will not be required to do homework while at the program.

Material Curricular Resources. Building on this basic "identity" work, strengthening curriculum might involve four kinds of resources. The first, as noted above, is guides, books, manuals, and so forth, some organized around units, some by age. There are literally hundreds of such guides, mostly developed for the education field, but potentially adaptable to after-school programs, in every field: art, music, literacy, social studies, natural sciences, math, and so forth. These often contain ideas and approaches that require some skill to translate into fully designed activities and projects. They are nonetheless useful in nudging staff to try more serious and thoughtful projects. Some programs have used these as a resource to develop their own curriculum, with lesson plans. For example, programs have given staff with expertise or experience in particular curricular domains time to develop a set of lesson plans for other staff to use. Staff with art backgrounds at the after-school program of Forest Hills Community House in New York City developed an Arts Curriculum consisting of lesson plans for such projects as developing family crests, puppet-making, making vases using ancient and modern symbols, and doing chalk drawings on sidewalks. Each lesson plan includes activities spanning a few sessions and includes purpose, technique, vocabulary, discussion questions, materials, and a step-by-step outline of the actual activity.

A related type of curricular resource is a somewhat fully designed curriculum that leaves room for adaptation. These also exist in many forms. One example is a curriculum called KidzLit, a book discussion curriculum developed for after-school programs by the Developmental Studies Center of Oakland, California. Each participating program receives booklists, for children of different ages and for different types of issues of concern to children; facilitators' guides, with "big ideas" from the books; questions and themes to guide book discussion; vocabulary lists; and ideas for writing, drama, and art activities to accompany book discussion. KidzLit involves book reading by a staff member, book discussion and other supplementary writing, and drama and art activities. (Ideally, children would have the choice to read along, but most programs can only afford, or choose to purchase, one copy of the 10 to 15 books that might be used over the course of the year.) Another example is Science in Our Communities, developed by Boston's Museum of Science, a 5-week curriculum kit that includes materials, lesson plans, and background information for implementing staff.

Institutional and Civic Resources. A third type of resource is located outside the program. More potential than actual, it encompasses the cultural, natural, arts, literacy, civic, and economic resources in the neighborhood and around the city: museums (e.g., science, natural history, art, children's, ethnic, etc.), libraries, parks, arboretums, gardens, waterways, theaters, sports venues, outdoor markets, stores, manufacturing plants, and so forth. Program staff often are unfamiliar with the range of potential resources in their city, and even when familiar with them often need help in understanding exactly what they offer and how they might be experienced, explored, and used. A staff member of Boston's Museum of Science stated that "for the majority of staff of after-school programs, museums aren't part of their life, so they don't consider them a resource, or even a fun place to be" (Halpern et al., 1999, p. 119).

Bringing in Specialists. As alluded to earlier, strengthening curricular resources can be accomplished less directly by hiring staff with specialized expertise, both to work with children and to help with curriculum development. More commonly, programs subcontract with or otherwise host specialists (who may work for specialized intermediary organizations) to lead activities in specific content areas. In some cities, performing and visual arts groups, and more selectively organizations that focus on creative writing, are now subsidized by local foundations to bring the arts into community institutions such as after-school programs. While these organizations usually send out specialists to work directly with children, some also train after-school staff to carry out activities in specific art forms. They tend to employ young artists or arts students, who use this work as a means of being able to continue their own creative work. A typical offering might involve a once- or twice-weekly session, for an hour to an hour and a half, for 4 to 6 weeks. Participation is sometimes voluntary, sometimes mandatory. The artist might spend a few weeks introducing children to the basics of a particular art form and then have children work individually or as groups on a project, perhaps culminating in a public display of the product or in a performance. There is occasional follow-up, but it is usually up to program staff to follow up with children who decide they would like to pursue an art form after the visiting artist has left.

Arts intermediaries (and cultural organizations such as museums) have varying degrees of knowledge about after-school programs and may themselves need help in understanding what will be required to develop a useful role. In Boston, for example, the staff of Arts in Progress, funded by the MOST Initiative to enrich the curricula of after-school programs, were surprised by the modest level of functioning of many programs, and had to significantly reduce their own expectations of the partnership. (The same proved true with other curricular resource partners, for example, the Museum of Science.) Resource organizations, and after-school programs themselves, have also tended to underestimate the amount of preparation and commitment involved in introducing outside resources into programs. It entails more than just setting aside an hour or 2 each week for specialists to come in, run their activity, and leave. Artists working with programs in the MOST cities complained of lack of space and materials, arriving at a program site unexpected in spite of careful planning, and lack of interest in and ownership of their activities among program staff. Program staff in turn complained of artists who lacked understanding of the children they served.

Linking Programs to External Resources. A missing piece of the curricular enrichment puzzle is one or more organizations in a city that can identify and keep track of individuals and organizations with expertise in particular areas and an interest in working with after-school programs. The Partnership for After-School Education (PASE), a training and technical assistance intermediary in New York City, has provided this function informally for a number of years, in part because it runs an annual conference with workshops by a wide range of specialists. PASE has recently developed a directory of resource providers, that should prove useful if kept up to date. A staff member of the the Baltimore Community Foundation is overseeing an initiative, called A-Teams, that has identified and is funding curricular resource organization to work with after-school programs. This staff member helps make the linkages to local programs (when necessary) and monitors the relationships between its grantees and local after-school programs. Examples of those funded include Baltimore Clayworks, which has a yearlong clay arts program in two community centers; Chemical People, which runs West African drum and dance in after-school programs; and the Parks and People Foundation, which sponsors girls' volleyball leagues.

STRENGTHENING FACILITIES AND EQUIPMENT

Providing grants for facilities and equipment improvement has proven to be moderately helpful, especially when tied to technical assistance to programs in space use. Grants of as little as $500 to $3,000 can be very useful to resource-starved programs, because such programs almost never have funds for capital purchases (e.g., purchase of nondisposable equipment rather than supplies), let alone capital improvement. In the MOST Initiative, such grants were used, among many other ways, to build cubbies for children; purchase books and bookshelves; upgrade wiring for computer use; install an intercom system; purchase musical instruments; purchase art, photography, printmaking, science (e.g., microscopes) or similar equipment; create new activity areas; purchase book and equipment carts; install air conditioning; improve outdoor play areas; and make space more accessible to disabled children. Larger MOST grants of $5,000 to $15,000 were given competitively, based on space improvement plans created with the help of designers and architects paid by MOST to act as space use consultants. These consultants worked to help staff see that how they organized their rooms and where they placed materials affected children's opportunity for choice and self-direction, and their ability to work on sustained activities. In Chicago, MOST sponsored a workshop in which after-school providers could observe space consultants from the Illinois Facilities Fund provide "makeovers" to actual programs with space problems (e.g., one located in a school lunchroom, one in an old and poorly lit basement space).

New equipment and reconfigured space were particularly helpful in making rooms less institutional and more intimate, in creating additional usable space, and in creating better defined functional areas within rooms. One program built a reading loft. Another, located in a large, square classroom, purchased some small area rugs and two couches, and these changed the way children used the room. The area rugs brought children down to the floor to work and play, also creating more flexible spaces. The couches became a base for reading, conversation, and just sitting back for a few minutes. Another program purchased small tables to replace large institutional-looking ones, which encouraged children to cluster in small groups for homework and other activities. This program also used new storage containers and shelving to section off small areas for particular kinds of activities, and purchased bulletin boards to display children's writing and art work. Providers who benefited from MOST facilities and equipment grants noted that they had never thought they could justify seeking capital improvement funds in their budgets, but now felt more comfortable arguing for the importance of such funds.

The program library is one aspect of the material environment in after-school programs that has been largely neglected. Many after-school programs have accumulated decent collections of children's books, through donations and purchases over a period of years. Yet they often have little idea how to organize and display books to generate interest and help children choose appropriate material, for example, rotating highlighted titles, using book cards for quick reviews of books, labeling books for degree of difficulty, and generally making the collection accessible and appealing to children. Here it would seem that professional children's librarians from local public librar-ies would be a useful resource.

STRENGTHENING CITYWIDE SYSTEMS

While it is possible to strengthen individual after-school programs with-out strengthening the local systems in which they are embedded—that is how most program improvement effort has been undertaken up to the present—it is not the most sensible way to proceed. In a field facing many practical challenges, with limited resources, a growing role and expectations, and continuing questions about identity and boundaries, it is critical to be stra-tegic. Rational and equitable distribution of resources, efforts to strengthen programs, efforts to increase the amount of after-school programming—all require a systemic lens. The city level makes sense for such a lens, for a num-ber of reasons. Different stakeholders—regulators, providers, resource or-ganizations, parents, and to a lesser extent funders—interact most regularly within the boundaries of a city. Cities tend to have high concentrations of low- and moderate-income families. And each city has a distinct after-school history, political and institutional culture, and neighborhood structure.

Currently, in most cities, the universe of after-school programs, resource and support organizations, funders, and regulatory agencies cannot be con-sidered a "system," in the sense of a variety of individual elements working together to form a unity or common whole. To start with, because the after-school field exists at the margins of (or even outside) public policies and public service systems, it has no formal, or at least no universally accepted, gov-ernance mechanisms at the city level. There are no commonly determined decision-making structures or procedures. There is also little or no trans-parency in the decision making that does occur. To the extent that it is iden-tifiable, leadership is diffuse and informal. With one or two exceptions, there are no mechanisms for citywide information collection, planning, and priority-setting, nor, for example, mechanisms for identifying obstacles faced by children and families in gaining access to after-school programs (i.e., money, information, transportation, scheduling), and for developing strate-gies to address those obstacles. In most cities, no institution has or takes re-sponsibility for identifying and maintaining a registry of individuals or local groups who can provide training and curriculum support in specific areas.

In other words, there are no mechanisms for marshaling resources or determining how to use them, or for agreeing upon principles to guide the use of new resources. Resource deployment is idiosyncratic at best. Some low-income neighborhoods are well served by after-school programs; others have few or no programs. Some providers are recognized and valued, and others are not. Families are sometimes not aware of programs that might suit their children. Providers are forced to rationalize the system as best they can at the program level, for example, integrating funding from multiple sources with different aims, priorities, and expectations. Many programs needing resource supports have insufficient information about what might be available, while many resource organizations are unable to reach programs most needing their resources.

At present, there is little sense of a field with a history and tradition upon which to draw. Everything seems new, even when it is not. Some individual providers and provider organizations view themselves as part of a common enterprise; others do not. Individual funders typically pursue their own goals, without considering what other funders are doing, let alone how their goals fit with those of long-standing after-school programs. New initiatives spring up and head off in their own direction, often with little heed to what has gone before or what else is currently happening. Such initiatives sometimes ignore years of prior work on a particular systemic problem. Individual funders and initiatives set their own standards of accountability and expectations, often without consulting those who actually work with children day in and day out.

Systemic challenges have taken a new turn, as schools have come to play a wider role in the after-school field. The schools' involvement has heightened an already pressing need for settings in which stakeholders can discuss what low-income children's experiences in after-school programs should be like, and what those experiences should be about. In addition to heightening the need for dialogue about philosophy, the growing involvement of schools has heightened dilemmas of power and control. As noted in Chapter 4, community-based providers have often found that such terms as *partnership, collaboration,* and *shared accountability* mask a very unequal relationship, when it comes to philosophy and goals, rights to space, control (if not supervision) of after-school staff, assuring security, and locus of accountability.

Although attention to system building is an imperative for the after-school field, the system-building process will, like program improvement itself, be a difficult one. MOST, the only city level system-building initiative during the 1990s, yielded a number of lessons on why and how this is so (Halpern et al., 1999). The idea guiding MOST was to create reasons, opportunities, and structures to bring after-school stakeholders within Boston, Chicago, and Seattle together to share information, coordinate activities, forge new links, do joint planning, and generally develop citywide strategies for addressing key problems facing the after-school field in their city. MOST relied on a carefully selected lead agency, volunteer committees, and working groups, one for governance or oversight and a few in

specific domains, staffed by the lead agency, and enough funding to presumably serve a leverage function and to pay for plans and strategies developed by the volunteer committees.

This system-building strategy proved to have strengths and limitations.
The resources provided by the funder, the Wallace–Readers Digest Fund,
about $1.4 million over 3 years for each city, were helpful to a resource-
starved field. Yet they proved much too modest either to alter the priorities
and behavior of many key stakeholders or to seriously support the program
improvement strategies developed. New working relationships emerged in
each city, sometimes through the committees, sometimes brokered by the lead
agency (for example, local directors' networks), sometimes stimulated by
MOST grants (e.g., a series of grants to link curricular intermediaries to
programs). It proved helpful to bring different segments of the after-school
community together on a periodic, sustained basis. Mutual understanding
improved. The likelihood of coordinated action increased. The head of child
care and school-age care programs for the Chicago Housing Authority commented that her role on the MOST governance committee was helpful because "I know we're going to see each other once a month, that alone. Do
you know what it would take just to coordinate the effort to bring us [pro-
gram and agency heads] in proximity to each other?"

At the same time, building consensus on a range of issues among a diverse group of stakeholders was time consuming and sometimes exhausting,
especially for already busy people volunteering their time. Planning, priority
setting, communicating, coordinating, collecting and analyzing information,
decision making, and distributing and monitoring the use of new resources
proved too burdensome a task for voluntary committees. Many lost energy
and participants over time. Long-range planning proved difficult in an unstable, shifting field. A new mayoral initiative could undo months or years
of efforts to build a democratic governance structure, as happened in Seattle.
It was difficult to engage scores of small programs and agencies in broad
system-building tasks. The directors of large-provider organizations and
smaller community-based programs recognized the need for greater coordination, yet also expressed some concern about loss of control and about the
potential for "oversight" by some who did not understand the after-school
field. They were also worried that new policies and standards would not be
not accompanied by the resources to make them achievable.

Since the conclusion of the MOST Initiative there has been little deliber-
ate citywide system-building effort (with the exception of Baltimore's After-
School Strategy, which is ongoing). Systemic developments have been shaped
primarily by initiatives coming out mayors' offices and by large-scale foundation initiatives, both of which have paid either incidental or very selective
attention to system building. Such attention has meant, for example, bring-

ing stakeholders together to develop citywide standards, or trying to gather information on where providers are located. Most current initiatives—Baltimore being one prominent exception—have simply assumed that the schools should be the base and the heart of any after-school "system," and have paid little attention to interests and support needs of the scores of small, isolated community-based providers critical to the after-school fabric in every city.

ENSURING MORE ADEQUATE, STABLE, AND FLEXIBLY STRUCTURED FINANCING

Inadequate and erratic funding underlies many of the quality problems in the after-school field, including building the infrastructure needed to support programs. To illustrate both the magnitude of the challenge and the effects of inadequate funds I summarize here a study that I conducted, linked to the MOST evaluation, collecting and analyzing information on costs, revenues, and expenditures from a sample of close to 60 programs in community-based agencies in Boston, Chicago, and Seattle. The full cost of a year-round, fully staffed, 5-day-a-week after-school program was found to average about $80 a week (or $4,000 a year) per child, including contributions of administrative and volunteer time and subsidized space; or about $60 a week ($2,500–$3,000 a year) without counting such contributions. These costs were based on prevailing frontline worker salaries of $7 per hour. When programs used specialists for arts or sports activities, costs increased accordingly. In contrast to costs, revenues in the programs that were sampled, though varying enormously from program to program, averaged about $40 a week per child (or $2,000 a year). In other words, revenues typically covered about two thirds of costs.

Agencies studied used a variety of strategies to cope with revenue shortfalls. Programs made most positions part-time, paying barely more than minimum wage, with few or no benefits. This meant that staff had little or no time for planning or reflecting on their work. When turnover occurred—itself caused in part by low wages and lack of benefits—programs would let staff vacancies run or simply increase the number of children served by a staff member. Programs reduced or eliminated field trips. They were unable to purchase adequate supplies and materials to create a rich classroom environment. They were unable to hire or provide logistical support for specialists, notably in the arts. When Arts in Progress, a Boston intermediary, tried to use the federal work-study program to place visual and performing arts students in after-school programs, it found that some programs could not even afford the modest contribution they were required to make to the students' stipends. Inadequate funding led to lack of resources for such management functions as fund-raising for a program, as well as program planning and supervision of frontline staff. It limited other agency supports for frontline practice, such as substitutes to free staff for professional development. It led to lack of resources for capital investment and improvements, for facilities and equipment.

THE MAGNITUDE OF THE FUNDING EFFORT NEEDED

Clearly, implementing the program improvement strategies described in this chapter will require a significant, sustained funding effort, both for support of direct services and for strengthening the infrastructure of the field. At the program level, for instance, funding is urgently needed to address a host of basic needs—to create daily and weekly planning time, to increase use of specialists, to improve space and purchase equipment and materials, to provide resources for field trips, and so forth. Whether or not higher hourly wages and improved benefits would attract more highly qualified frontline staff, it is unconscionable to pay those who work with children minimum-wage salaries. It is worth reiterating as well that, in a resource-starved field, even small amounts of money—for purchasing equipment and materials, releasing staff time, subsidizing the costs of preparing for accreditation—can have sizable effects on the quality of life of programs.

The first step in directing more funding to program improvement is to put this need in the broader context of needed public and private funding for the after-school field. No one knows the total federal, state, and local public funding for after-school programs. As noted in chapter 4, the principal sources of funding are the Child Care and Development Fund (CCDF), supplemented in some states by unused TANF (Temporary Assistance to Needy Families) funds designated for child care and school-age care, social service and community development block grants, and whatever funding is earmarked for after-school programs in the new education block grants under the reauthorized Elementary and Secondary Education Act (the No Child Left Behind Act).

While CCDF resources have been increasing in recent years, because of the contribution from unused TANF money, the current (late 2001–early 2002) recession is reducing that contribution. Currently, somewhat less than $1 billion of CCDF money may be available for after-school programming. About $1 billion has been theoretically appropriated for after-school programming in the new education block grants, but it is not clear what will happen to or with that money. All other current public sources of funds for after-school programming, including state initiatives, pale in relation to these two now uncertain sources. For example, Title V of the Juvenile Justice and Delinquency Prevention Act receives a total of $95 million in funding, only a small portion of which is used for after-school programs. By this author's rough calculations, including scores of small (and variable) state and local funding sources, total public funding for after-school programs may be at most $4 billion annually, and is probably closer to $3 billion. United Way and foundation funding probably contribute another $100 million or so.

American society spends about $250 billion annually on public education, perhaps half of which—say $125 billion—is spent serving low- and moderate-income children. Assuming that after-school programs will mostly serve this population of children, and bearing in mind that the "after-school day," from 3 p.m. to 6 p.m., is about half as long as the school day (although after-school programs often run all day on school holidays and during the summer months), a fully publicly funded after-school system might reasonably claim $40 billion to $50 billion a year in total public funding. Cutting that figure in half because the full amount sounds unrealistic would still leave a claim of $20 billion to $25 billion a year, more than seven times what is currently spent. In something of an understatement, a program officer at the Boston Community Foundation noted that, while foundations could help out, "in the end the public is going to have to make a fairly substantial contribution to the operating cost of after-school programs" (Halpern et al., 1999).

Until the public funding picture improves, the basic condition of the after-school field is not going to change significantly. In fact, the current funding base for the field appears to be eroding in the face of weak state revenues. In the past few years there has also been a trend toward reduction in per-child funding for direct services. This trend has been driven by the perceived need to reach more low-income children and by the business mentality of many new stakeholders. About 20% to 25% of low- and moderate-income children, aged 6 to 14, participate in after-school programs on a more or less regular basis. Given the need to create slots for hundreds of thousands more children in after-school programs, some argue that it is critical to find the least expensive way to provide services (one reason behind the push for schools as sites). Even though current per-child allocations, now averaging about $2,000–2,500 per year (for a 50-week year), have been demonstrated by this author and others to cover only about two thirds of the cost of providing modest quality services, sponsors of some new initiatives are trying to "get to scale" by using annual per-child allocations of $1,000 or less. This will lead predictably to even more fragile, unstable programs than now define the field, and will further reduce already grossly inadequate resources for program improvement.

Although data are scarce, it appears that only a tiny percentage of current public funding for after-school programs is devoted to program improvement efforts (especially strengthening the infrastructure of the field), and almost none to system building. The Child Care and Development Fund requires a minimum 4% "quality set-aside." The bulk of that set-aside is used for early childhood programs, but the mechanism exists to support program improvement for after-school programs. New Jersey, for example, uses CCDF resources to fund a modest School-Age Child Care Training and Technical Grant, and California to support development and dissemination of curricular materials and activity guides, by the California School-Age Consortium and California State University (Deich, Bryant, & Wright, 2001). A 5% set-aside for program improvement should be required of all public funding for after-school programs, including funding through federal block grants.

DIRECTING ANY NEW FUNDING

Given the perceived need to increase supply as well as strengthen programs, it will be important for states and cities to develop clear rationales to direct the use of funding and to consider different roles for different funding sources. Program improvement, and support for system-building efforts, seem to be especially appropriate investment tasks for foundations. National foundations might focus on the broader research and conceptual work desperately needed to clarify how such efforts ought to proceed. Local and regional foundations, whose staff are familiar with their communities, would then focus primarily on more practical investments.

As much as possible, funding should be structured to allow for some flexibility at the city, community, and program levels. That implies creating mechanisms for pooling funds from different sources and for linking that funding to a collaborative planning- and priority-setting process. Baltimore is one city currently trying to accomplish this through its After-School Strategy. The Baltimore Family League, a public agency created in the early 1990s to manage funding for human service reform, has assumed that same role for after-school funding. The league has become the common repository for different public and private funding streams and has designed a common contracting and contract monitoring process, used across those streams. The structure of and priorities embodied in the contracting process were developed by committees of stakeholders in the local after-school system. As noted earlier in this chapter, a percentage of every direct service contract with local after-school programs is set aside for program improvement activity. The programs themselves choose where and how to use program improvement funds.

CONCLUSION

Even if a concerted effort is made by licensing and regulatory authorities, institutions of higher education, funders, and sponsoring agencies themselves, the work of supporting and strengthening after-school programs will be slow and uncertain. The very fact that so many after-school programs are operating at a survival level poses problems for program improvement efforts, since the programs most in need of support often have the least capacity to use it. Most programs do not have the capacity to cope with more than one or two program improvement activities at a time. Improvements sometimes do not stick, because of the paradoxical combination of instability in many after-school programs (in staffing and funding) and gravity— the persistence of certain program cultures and the pull back to the level at which a program was operating in the past.

The fact that most after-school programs have only modest capacity to absorb and constructively use support creates a paradox. Although described separately on these pages, individual program improvement strategies not surprisingly worked more effectively when conceptualized and employed together with others. Still, affording a program the opportunity to get involved in a program improvement activity of whatever kind often stimulated self-reflection. For example, the very process of preparing for eventual accreditation, applying for a grant for facilities and equipment, and deciding about the content of training or new curricular elements led program coordinators to think more closely about their program, where it was and where they wanted to take it. It also led coordinators to talk with their staff about program needs, often for the first time. Some discrete changes in programs, such as more thoughtful schedules and better room arrangement and space use also appeared to have disproportionate effects. Involvement in program improvement activity often began to strengthen the identity of programs, to boost their energy and reduce the sense of barely getting through each day, each week, and each year.

Finally, at both the program and the system levels, program improvement strategies are more effective when they are explained and carried out in the context of a larger vision of what a good after-school program is all about. That larger vision gives the incremental program improvement process meaning, and provides a touchstone for providers in the face of the shifting ideological currents that increasingly define the after-school field.

7

A Different Kind of Child Development Institution?

Children interpret the world differently from adults, not because they have not yet learned to see the world "properly," but because they are viewing it on their own terms.
—B. Davies, *Life in the Classroom and Playground*

Non-school hours need not be fraught with peril or aimlessness.
—Carnegie Corporation, *A Matter of Time: Risk and Opportunity in Non-school Hours*

The history of after-school programs points to both the potential and the difficulties of constructing normative supports—as opposed to preventive or compensatory or remedial interventions—for low-income children in American society. From the start, after-school providers found themselves in a balancing act, with children's preferences on one side and their own, often ambivalent, instincts on the other. Providers wanted to, but did not fully, trust the children they served. They believed that their mission was largely positive—about protection, fun, exploration, enrichment, the "making of lives." Providers wanted the children they served to feel valued, and to have a place in their lives free from outside pressures. Children had the opportunity to provide input into programs. Yet providers also had no doubt that children's out-of-school time ought to be organized and supervised by adults, that, to grow up correctly, children needed the practical and vocational skills, guidance, and direction that they were not getting from home or school. After-school providers resisted the tendency of psychologists and social workers to pathologize childhood. Yet after-school programs were part of a broader movement to socialize immigrant children and institutionalize working-class childhood.

Like other human services, after-school programs did not evolve in a vacuum. Their rationales and goals, and to a lesser extent activities, were

shaped by major historical events and circumstances; prevailing social preoccupations; continuity and change in ideas about childhood and low-income
children; and developments in other institutions and settings, especially families, schools, and neighborhoods. Being undefined, the after-school hours were
a Rorshach image onto which social reformers and child-rearing experts
projected their anxieties about children and about broad social trends. After-
school programs assumed a modest role in addressing such concerns as urban
disorder, assimilation of immigrants, ideological threats to democracy, moral
decline, and mobilization for war, as well as such child-specific problems as
juvenile delinquency.

After-school programs' game rooms and gyms, clubs and classes, created
a distinctive developmental setting, at once socially and task oriented, peer and
adult oriented, somewhat free and somewhat restrictive. After-school programs
were far tamer than streets, playlots, and playgrounds, but children also re-
created elements of their own play culture. Because participation was voluntary, after-school programs tried to make themselves attractive to children.
Boys' Clubs, for instance, had an open-door policy, giving children some control over when and how they used club resources. Some children were drawn
to the athletic or artistic or vocational resources of after-school programs. Many
others preferred the streets, which were "theirs in a way that home, school
and settlement house could never be" (Nasaw, 1985, p. ii). Children played
street games and sports, observed others, hung out and talked, fought and teased
one another. Children's street culture was a "free-form escape from the onus
of coordinated time, compartmentalized space and rigid social relationships
. . . an opportunity for children to evolve their own forms of organization, to
honor their own imagination, and to explore the social terrain of the community" (Goodman, 1979, p. 24). There were, nonetheless, gender differences in
this pattern. Girls were not drawn to the streets as strongly as were boys, and
in that sense girls found after-school programs more hospitable.

The development of the after-school field took a turn beginning in the
mid-1950s, as both the nature of urban poverty and the ethnic and racial
composition of inner-city neighborhoods changed. Providers could no longer
avoid the issue of race by excluding minority children or by segregating them
in separate clubs. The neighborhoods in which after-school providers worked
were becoming more socially and economically isolated from the larger life
of the city, intensifying providers' sense of being a critical bridging institution for children, but also further straining inadequate resources. With the
War on Poverty in the 1960s, new community institutions emerged to challenge established ones, and long-standing providers had to fight for a role
and a place in their communities. As compensatory and remedial education
became a focus of poverty-fighting efforts, after-school programs were asked
to help with this new social objective.

After-school providers adjusted and adapted to the crosscurrents of the 1970s and 1980s—expanding rights movements, societal withdrawal from poverty-fighting efforts, accelerating deterioration in inner-city neighborhoods (reducing children's access to outdoor play spaces), and almost 2 decades of fiscal crisis in many older cities. During much of the latter decade, after-school programs seemed on the verge of national consciousness. They received media attention, children's advocacy groups fought for them, and politicians took note of them. The child care function of after-school programs was highlighted, as more mothers entered the labor force. Small amounts of public funding emerged. Yet throughout the period, after-school programming remained largely a community issue.

THE STAKES ARE RAISED

Over the past decade, low-income children's out-of-school time has become a significant public concern. Presidents, governors, mayors, legislators, justice and education officials, and business executives have all become proponents of after-school programming and have given this still marginal child-rearing institution much greater visibility. After-school programming has a place in the recently reauthorized Elementary and Secondary Education Act. Numerous states have established after-school task forces, with the mandate of creating statewide plans. As of this writing (mid-2002), there are some two dozen notable city-level initiatives underway.

The heightened societal interest in after-school programs should have been a boon to the field, generating new resources for chronically underfunded providers, fostering debate and research on the most important goals for children's out-of-school time and on the effects of particular kinds of out-of-school experiences. And it still theoretically could be. However, this new interest has coincided with two other trends that have dampened discussion about out-of-school time. One is an increasingly instrumental view of childhood, particularly low-income childhood, among elected and appointed public officials. As Kozol (2000a, p. 18) puts it, "The first ten, twelve or fifteen years are excavated of inherent moral worth in order to accommodate a regimen of basic training for the adult years." The second, and related, trend is a loss of faith in public education for low-income children, a perception that the schools have failed their mission. This has led public officials, foundations, and others to turn to after-school time, and therefore after-school programs, to help with school-related agendas.

Not all proponents are happy with the narrow, instrumental rationales behind current investment in the after-school field. A program officer at the Boston Community Foundation noted that "those kinds of arguments . . .

contribute to peoples' prejudices, especially about cities and minorities. You know—'you've got to fund after-school programs because otherwise they [the kids] are going to run wild in the streets and tear up your property'" (Halpern et al., 1999). Yet in a society in which children are viewed as the vehicle for social progress, and in which low-income children are viewed as vulnerable and vaguely threatening, it is difficult not to cast after-school programs in an instrumental role, and difficult not to give them a remedial agenda. After-school providers themselves have been unwilling or unable to articulate an alternative view of either childhood (especially low-income childhood) or of their role in children's lives. In fact they have appeared anxious to demonstrate their commitment to the current narrow agenda for children. To cite just one example, the Boys and Girls' Club of America is basing its new Project Learn initiative on "high yield" activities.

To be fair, the question of what after-school programs should be about is an inherently ambiguous one. There has never been consensus about how much adult intervention outside school is necessary for children to grow in a healthy way. Left sometimes to their own devices after school, most children do not "risk their own correct development into adult citizens" (Ennew, 1994, p. 136; see also Belle, 1999). Children live in both the present and the future. As Davies (1982, p. 165) describes it, "They know they will eventually be adults and adopt adult templates, adult scripts. At the same time, not yet being adults they have obligations [to] childhood." Most children neither want nor expect complete autonomy, just some space and some control. They want to have their own communities and also to feel a part of adult communities and institutions. Children want and need to play and yet, as they get older, to acquire the cultural capital and skills that are valued by their family, community, and society. Children do not automatically discover their own interests; some need an observant, discerning adult to help make connections. Many children struggle at some point with particular developmental tasks, and some need adult support with those struggles.

Children also differ in how they experience particular developmental settings and in what they need, want, and get from different settings. Former participants in after-school programs, not surprisingly, identify different aspects of their experience as central: one learning to debate, another hanging out in the game room, another the library, and still another discovering a love of theater (Berrol, 1995; Graff, 1995). As in the past, some children today like an organized schedule after school, while others do not; some need time alone, and others neither need nor want that. Some children want to get homework done and over with, whereas others are "saturated" with school work and want a break from it (Raphael & Chaplin, 2001, p. 22). The boundaries of even a well-equipped room can seem confining after a day at school, and for some children participating in an after-school program simply makes for a very long day. Belle (1999) found children's after-school program experiences to be "mixed," a result of the interaction of child characteristics and program characteristics. Some children found a new group of friends, found activities they liked, and engaged right away; others never connected with other children in the program and found the activities restrictive or boring.

THE LOSS OF PLAY

The central danger in the current instrumental and remedial climate surrounding low-income children is loss of balance in out-of-school experience, with, in particular, further reduction in opportunities for unstructured time and unsupervised play. Such time and play increasingly are perceived not as developmental necessities but as risk factors. Many low-income parents themselves, especially minority parents, believe that their children are "crying out for more structure, not less" (Johnson, 1998, p. A16). Yet low-income children, like all children, need at least some unstructured time, to decompress, "to figure things out," and to make mistakes and try to correct them (Buchholz, 1997, p. 239). Postman (1986) may be right when he claims that Americans of all ages are "amusing ourselves to death." At the same time, doing nothing or feeling bored are not necessarily negative states; they can recharge the mind and sometimes provide the mental foundation for other pursuits. Sutton-Smith (1990, pp. 2, 5) and Middlebrooks (1998, p. 16) describe a long list of things that children are doing when they are "just playing": legislating differences, experimenting with authority and power, clarifying meaning (of rules, etc.), changing meaning, redefining situations, distinguishing pretend from real, changing roles, exploring and developing relationships, dealing with conflict, coping with exclusion, finding refuge, and learning about space, boundaries, and territoriality.

After-school programs are, fundamentally, adult-controlled institutional settings, and some have asked whether such settings can provide the necessary conditions for play to thrive (Kennedy, 1991; Rivlin & Wolfe, 1985; Suransky, 1982). These conditions include the physical and social space for spontaneity, unrestricted movement, a measure of privacy, a lack of formal temporal structure (or schedule), the freedom to manipulate and alter the material environment, and at least a measure of unpredictability. (Jacobs, 1961, went even further, arguing that children's play requires "unspecialized" places, i.e., those not designed specifically for children.) The dilemma is that noninstitutional environments no longer provide these conditions either. The streets have long since lost their role as the counterworld that immigrants, particularly immigrant children, created to cope with a harsh, strange new society. Until recent decades, children were able to pursue freedom from adult authority because they knew deep down that they were not on their own. Children can no longer claim that powerful certainty.

The reality is that more children are now in after-school programs, and it can be argued that of all formal institutions, after-school programs can most afford to be nonutilitarian about childhood, to respond to children's individuality, to respect their desire for self-determination, to afford a measure of privacy, to be flexible about time, to create interesting and manipulable material environments, and to provide opportunity for children "to seek out experience for its own sake" (Moore, 1986, p. 231). After-school programs certainly contribute to adult encroachment on low-income children's already limited ownership of their lives. Yet at their best, after-school programs are relatively sensitive adult institutions, in which the adult agenda is relatively modest.

As the historical account suggests, after-school program providers have struggled, although not always successfully, to respect the importance of the peer group to school-age children, and to take children's point of view seriously. They have been cognizant of differences in children's interests. After-school program staff have attended to children's developmental struggles, without labeling or defining children by those struggles. They have tried to create a space for play among their activities and have always had an informal underlife. More than 50 years ago Lambert (1944, p. 58) wrote that the good after-school programs she worked with allowed children to "move freely and play with other children in small groups or alone." A half century later, in describing a Wisconsin program at which they observed, Vandell, Shumow, and Posner (1997, p. 15) report that one of its strengths was "the unstructured time in which children played together privately and in groups, taking advantage of the very substantial space available."

New Friends, New Challenges

Although after-school programs can afford to be nonutilitarian about childhood, it will not be easy to be so. The new friends of the field, especially those from the political and business communities, do not appear to understand—or at least do not appear interested in—the qualities that make after-school programs distinctive as child development institutions. While most of these new friends give lip service to the idea that after-school time should be different from schooltime, should provide a broader array of experiences for children, and should be at least partly shaped by children's preferences, their actual policies and mandates contradict their words. Even the rhetoric surrounding after-school programming is increasingly that of maximized time use, coordination between schools and after-school programs, and alignment and continuity between school and after-school agendas (see, e.g., Landberg, 1999).

To an extent, after-school time cannot help but be considered in relation to schooltime. Children do not have one set of developmental needs in one setting, another set in another setting. The influence of different child-rearing settings is commingled in terms of developmental effects (Condry, 1993). Different institutions should support one another to the greatest extent possible. But ironically, it does not follow that there should be continuity in goals and experiences between different developmental settings. Children appear to want and need boundaries between different types of experiences (Sutton-Smith, 1997). School, in particular, "has come to be such a particular, specialized institution, with its own particular brand of learning, that it does seem useful to set it in opposition to other institutions and different contexts for learning" (Hull & Schultz, 2002, p. 5). We would not want the attributes that lead children to come to feel discouraged in school—fragmented and disembedded learning, a preoccupation with compliance and obedience, lack of explanation for demands, the constant experience of being judged and ranked and with that the all too often accompanying experience of failure, the lack of time for processing and for simple respite—to filter into after-school programs. As the literacy coordinator for a network of small settlement houses in New York City asked, "Why would you want to extend the goals and approaches of a failed system into the after-school hours[?]" (Spielberger & Halpern, 2002).

Some proponents of closer relationships between schools and after-school programs argue that the presence of the latter in school buildings will serve as a stimulus for school staff to view and work with children differently (i.e. in a broader, more integrated, more positive way). This belief ignores a century of evidence indicating that such philosophical contagion—from after-school program to school program—is extremely unlikely. The few remnants of attention to children's nonacademic experience—recess, arts, and physical education—are being steadily squeezed out of the school day. Moreover, the current rhetoric of influential actors within the educational community consistently points to a desire to bring after-school programs into the orbit of schools. In a recent issue of a national bulletin that serves as a forum for principals, the writer of the lead article argued, "Given the higher standards for students' knowledge and abilities, coupled with the growing use of high stakes tests for decision-making regarding students' school placement and progress, there is heightened demand for quality after-school programs to help under-achieving students" (Butty, LaPoint, Thomas, & Thompson, 2001, p. 1).

It is conceivable that the pressure on after-school programs to help with narrow academic agendas can be turned aside through a deemphasis on the amount of formal learning time and a reemphasis on the idea that children acquire literacy, numeracy, and knowledge of disciplines through many routes, informal as well as formal. The press for continuity could lead educators to reconsider children's days as a whole, asking how the pieces ought to complement one another. There are precedents worth examining. During the 1960s and 1970s, some primary schools in England and the United States experimented with updated versions of progressive education. Under the rubrics of "integrated days" and "open education," their programs were characterized by a flexible temporal structure; cooperative, child-driven learning activity; a rich material and social environment; and a deemphasis on the distinction between formal and informal learning, schoolwork, and other kinds of activity. The result was that "the natural flow of activity, imagination, language, thought and learning . . . is not interrupted by artificial breaks such as the conventional playtime or subject barriers" (Brown & Precious, 1968, p. 13). More recently, schools in a few municipalities in France have experimented with a break for recreation and play for children during the early afternoon hours, with school resuming at 3:30 p.m. for 2 or 3 hours. The idea is to create a day that mixes formal learning, informal learning, and play in a way that more naturally follows children's inclinations and biological rhythms (Petrie, 1996).

The most that can be said is that it is not certain how the relationship between after-school programs and schools (as both institutions and structured experiences) will play out. For example, within the 21st Century Community Learning Centers, the major federal school-based and operated after-school initiative, there has been a gradual shift away from school-like emphases, in response to negative reactions from children and, to a lesser extent, parents and staff. After-school providers are also beginning to question the practice of spending so much time on homework, in part because the quality of that homework is so low. A handful of school administrators are becoming worried that they have an asset that could easily be spoiled. What is likely is that the dilemmas inherent in the relationship between schools and school-based after-school programs will be worked through on a case-by-case basis.

THE CHALLENGE OF STRENGTHENING AFTER-SCHOOL PROGRAMS

Assuming that the after-school field can retain its balance in the face of pressures to join those seeking a more utilitarian role for after-school programs, it still faces the problem of quality improvement. It is important to reiterate that, even with the current variability among programs, many, though by no means all, children instinctively like after-school programs and become attached to them over time. Some variability among programs is appropriate, given differences in community values and priorities and in the philosophies and priorities of sponsors. Yet as a whole, there is an unsettling discrepancy between after-school programs' capacity to create physically and (for the most part) psychologically safe places for children and their potential to create rich, sustaining relational and learning environments and interesting contexts for play and the pursuit of interests. Even the more transparent benefits of after-school programs depend on a variety of resources, program supports, and staff skills that too many programs in low-income neighborhoods are hard put to provide.

The field-building tasks seem enormous—developing an infrastructure of resource institutions, figuring out the staffing conundrum, securing more adequate space for after-school programs, linking hundreds of isolated local programs to curricular resources, engaging the higher education community, and securing funding for all these purposes. The organizational diversity and decentralization of the after-school field is in most ways a strength and hallmark. Yet it presents a continuing challenge to those seeking levers for quality improvement. As noted in chapter 6, some tasks are less daunting. There are straightforward fixes for a host of common problems, from schedules that are too rigid and routinized, to lack of day-to-day support and engagement of frontline staff by coordinators. The growing use of skilled specialists, especially in the arts, is a notably promising development in the field. Yet it too will require thoughtful strategy.

A basic, unresolved question concerns the locus (and by implication the governance) of the after-school field in the coming years. Decentralization and diversity of sponsorship have had many positive consequences for this field. Decentralization has limited bureaucracy and increased flexibility. Diverse sponsors bring different and complementary strengths to the work. Each local community has its own most trusted local institutions. Diversity of sponsorship increases parents' and children's choices. And it increases the chances that some local institution will step forward to fill local gaps in service. At the same, these attributes have complicated the tasks of locating responsibility and accountability and of creating a clear identity for the after-school field. Some providers view themselves as part of a common enterprise; others do not.

Some proponents see one or another public system, usually schools, as the logical locus for the field. Such a development is unlikely (and probably undesirable—for the reasons I have argued). In addition to the critical role of private, nonprofit agencies as providers, the growing role of a diverse array of supporting institutions (including arts, cultural, and civic institutions with other purposes that nonetheless want to contribute to children's experiences) suggests that models for after-school systems will have to be flexible ones. Stakeholders will have to view the task of building and maintaining working relationships as an ongoing cost of doing business in the after-school field. Funders will have to support this process; in other words, they will have to work with a loosely coupled enterprise, with no central point, and a shifting array of stakeholders.

CONCLUSION

In the larger fabric of children's lives, the after-school hours have always had an evocative, even a slightly magical quality. Reflecting on his experience growing up in the 1950s, Fink (1986, p. 9) writes that "we got something more sustaining than mere supervision. We got a total environment in which we felt connected to each other, to the physical resources of the neighborhood, and to the adults in the neighborhood." Dargan and Zeitlin (1990, p. 170) note that street play and street games "contributed to a neighborhood life which made growing up and living in the city memorable." These comments reflect a particular time and place. Yet they also reveal the power and resonance of the after-school hours. We are reminded that if something is being lost to children (and to their communities) when they are led indoors into after-school programs, memories are still being created that will shape and become part of their lives.

Perhaps as important, the context of low-income children's lives has changed in ways that change the role and valence of after-school programming. At one level those lives continue to be shaped, and buffeted, by the same deeply rooted societal preoccupations that have always shaped them. Yet low-income children also face distinct pressures today. Paths to adulthood have narrowed. The stakes seem higher for children, as do the costs of mistakes. One veteran fourth-grade teacher in New York City, explaining her decision to move to another grade level to avoid test preparation pressures, declared, "It hits them [the children] like a bomb the minute they walk into fourth grade. It's way too early to put this amount of pressure on them. I don't want to play a part in it anymore" (Goodnough, 2001, p. A29). Children appear to have a greater burden of care and worry—not just about school, but also about family, their own safety, and often that of siblings and about the future—and to have to bear that burden with less support.

How, then, ought the role and expectations of after-school programs be defined? The task for proponents is to construct a policy-and-practice framework that does three things. The first is to balance attention to the common developmental needs that all children share, with attention to the distinct needs resulting from the distinct circumstances of low-income children's lives. The second is to balance different adults' (including parents') agendas with an effort to imagine and accommodate what children themselves may want. The third is to be sensitive to the shifting role of a variety of institutions in low-income children's lives, while respecting the qualities that makes after-school programs distinct as a developmental institution. For providers, the parallel task is to design institutional settings that are not too institutional, settings in which children are neither too little nor too much on their own, in which they feel and are safe, yet in which they can experience a bit of risk and unpredictability; settings that keep a place for the informal and inter-personal—the spontaneous conversation among children at a table during snacks, a child's conversation with a group worker about family or school—while attending to the richness and seriousness of formal activity.

Such tasks for proponents and providers are difficult enough. They will be made impossible if after-school programs face too much pressure to serve purposes for which they are not well suited, and to address every child-related social problem produced by American society. After-school programs can work as a resource for children only to the extent that they are allowed to work from a modest and reasonable story line, one focused principally on their role as a normative support for children. However obscure to adults, children do have their own agendas. After-school programs may have to struggle to respect and support those agendas, but they should be encouraged and supported in engaging in that struggle.

References

KEY TO ARCHIVAL MATERIAL CITED IN TEXT

BWR: Boys' Workers Roundtable (located at Boys' Club of America, Atlanta)

CBC: Chicago Boys' Clubs (located at the Chicago Historical Society)

CC: Chicago Commons (located at the Chicago Historical Society)

CC/NB: Chicago Commons Materials at Newberry Library

GH: Grosvenor House (located at the Columbia University Library)

NUS: Northwestern University Settlement (located at the Northwestern University Library)

OCC: Olivet Center Collection (located at the Chicago Historical Society)

UNH: United Neighborhood Houses (located at the National Social Welfare History Archives, University of Minnesota Libraries)

WWB: Work With Boys (predecessor to Boys' Workers Roundtable, located at Boys' Club of America, Atlanta)

Abraham Lincoln Center. (1916). *Program notes and annual report.* Chicago: Author.

Abraham Lincoln Center. (1930). *Annual report.* Chicago: Author.

Addams, J. (1925). *Twenty years at Hull House.* New York: Macmillan.

Addams, J. (1972). *The spirit of youth and the city streets.* Urbana: University of Illinois Press. (Work originally published 1909)

The After-School Corporation (n.d.). *3:00 p.m.: Time for after school.* New York: Author.

All Souls Church. (1897–1902). *Chicago reports.* Chicago: Abraham Lincoln Center.

Alter, J. (1998, April 27). It's 4 p.m. Do you know where your children are? *Newsweek,* pp. 29–33.

American, S. (1898, August). The movement for small playgrounds. *American Journal of Sociology, 4,* 159–170.

Anyon, J. (1980). Social class and the hidden curriculum of work. *Journal of Education, 162,* 67–92.

Aronowitz, S. (1979). Foreward. In C. Goodman, *Changing sides.* New York: Schocken.

Beatty, B. (1995). *Preschool education in America.* New Haven: Yale University Press.

Baden, R. et al. (1982). *School-age child care: An action manual.* Boston: Auburn House.

Ballard, R. (1947). *Report by the director.* Chicago: Hull House Association.

Bellamy, G. (1912). The settlement movement and its possibilities. *Work With Boys, 13*(5), 288–295.

Belle, D. (1999). *The after-school lives of children.* New Jersey: Lawrence Earlbaum

Belle, D., Norell, S., & Lewis, A. (1997). Becoming unsupervised: Children's transition from adult care to self-care. In I. Gottlieb & B. Wheaton (Eds.), *Stress and adversity over the life course.* New York: Cambridge University Press.

Bernstein, S. (Ed.). (1976). *Explorations in group work.* Boston: Charles River Books.

Berrol, S. (1995). *Growing up American.* New York: Twayne.

Biber, B. (1942). *Child life in school: A study of a seven year old group.* New York: Dutton.

Boocock, S. (1981). The life space of children. In S. Keller (Ed.), *Building for women.* Lexington, MA: Lexington Books.

Borris, E. (1992). The settlement movement revisited: Social control with a conscience. *Reviews in American History, 20,* 216–221.

Borris, E., & Daniels, C. (1989). *Homework: Historical and contemporary perspectives on paid labor at home.* Urbana: University of Illinois Press.

Bowles, S., & Gintis, H. (1976). *Schooling in capitalist America.* New York: Basic Books.

Bowman, L. (1929). The play world of the city child. *Child Study, 7*(3), 67–69.

Bowman, L. (1933). The urge to belong. *Child Study, 10*(8), 219–221.

Boys' club visitor series no. 1, the Boys' club of the city of New York. (1918). *Boys' Workers Roundtable, 1*(1), 9.

Boys' work—the new profession. (1923). *Boys' Workers Roundtable, 3*(4), 23–25.

Brenzel, B., Roberts-Gersch, C., & Wittner, J. (1985). Becoming social: School girls and their culture between the two world wars. *Journal of Early Adolescence, 5*(4), 479–488.

Brodsky, A. (1996). Resilient single mothers in risky neighborhoods: Negative psychological sense of community. *Journal of Community Psychology, 24*(4), 347–363.

Brooks-Gunn, J., Roth, J., Linver, M., & Hofferth, S. (2002, Summer). What happens during the school day? Time diaries from a national sample of elementary school teachers. *Teachers College Record* [Online]. Available: http://www.tcrecord.org.

Brown, C. (1999). The role of schools when school is out. *The Future of Children, 9*(2), 139–142.

Brown, M., & Precious, N. (1968). *The integrated day in the primary school.* London: Agathon Press.

Buchholz, E. (1997). *The call of solitude.* New York: Simon & Schuster.

Butcher, W. (1920). Boys' club plans and program reports. *Boys Workers Roundtable, 1*(4), 20–23.

Butty, J., LaPoint, V., Thomas, V., & Thompson, D. (2001). The changing face of after-school programs. *Bulletin of the National Association of Elementary School Principals, 85,* 626, 1–4.

Cahill, M., Perry, J., Wright, M., & Rice, A. (1993). *A documentation report on the New York City Beacons initiative.* New York: Youth Development Institute, Fund for the City of New York.

Calhoun, D. (1969). The city as teacher. *History of Education Quarterly, 9,* 312–325.

California Department of Education. (1996). *School-age care in California: Addressing the needs of children, families and society*. Sacramento. (Prepared by the Department of Education, University of California at Irvine)

Calkins, L. (2001). *The art of teaching reading*. New York: Longman.

Capizzano, J., Tout, K., & Adams, G. (2000). *Child care patterns of school-age children with employed mothers*. Washington, DC: Urban Insitute.

Carnegie Corporation. (1992). *A matter of time: Risk and opportunity in non-school hours*. New York: Author.

Carson, M. (1990). *Settlement folk*. Chicago: University of Chicago Press.

Cavallo, D. (1981). *Muscles and morals: Organized playgrounds and urban reform, 1880–1920*. Philadelphia: University of Pennsylvania Press.

Chew, T. (1911). The streets as playgrounds. *Work With Boys, 11*(2), 1–7.

Chew, T. (1913). Twenty years experience in a mass boys' club. *Work With Boys, 12*(2), 336–339.

Chicago Commons. (1909). *Chicago commons newsletter*. Chicago: Chicago Historical Society Archives.

Chicago Commons. (1910). *Chicago commons newsletter*. Chicago: Chicago Historical Society.

Children's Advocate. (1987). *Libraries minding the children*. Berkeley: Author.

Chin, M., & Newman, K. (2002). *High stakes: Time poverty, testing and the children of the working poor*. New York: Foundation for Child Development.

Christopher House. (1914). *Christopher House yearbook*. Chicago: Chicago Historical Society Archives.

Clark, J. (1985). The stoop as the world. In R. Hiner & J. Hawes (Eds.), *Growing up in America: Children in historical perspective*. Urbana: University of Illinois Press.

Clement, P. (1997). *Child care in the industrial age, 1850–1890*. New York: Twayne.

Clendenen, R., & Beaser, H. (1955, February 5). The shame of America. *Saturday Evening Post*, pp. 30, 90–94.

Cloward, R., & Ohlin, L. (1960). *Delinquency and opportunity: A theory of delinquent gangs*. Glencoe, IL: Free Press.

Clusen, C. (1981, November 30). Schools experiment with extended day as a response to child care needs of working families. *Education Times*, p. 7.

Cohen, S. (1999). *Challenging orthodoxies*. New York: Peter Lang.

Coleman, J. (1966). *Equality of educational opportunity*. Washington, DC: U.S. Government Printing Office.

Collins, A. (Ed.). (1984). *Development during middle childhood: The years from six to twelve*. Washington, DC: National Academy Press.

Comer, J. (1992). A growing crisis in youth development. In J. Quinn (Ed.), *A matter of time*. New York: Carnegie Corporation.

Condry, J. (1993). Thief of time, unfaithful servant: Television and the American child. *Daedalus, 122*(1), 259–278.

Cook, T., et al. (1996). The development of occupational aspirations and expectations among inner-city boys. *Child Development, 67*, 3368–3385.

Core, M. (1978, December). When school's out and nobody's home. *The Record*, 2–6.

Cottle, T. (1993). Witness of joy. *Daedalus, 122*(1), 123–150.

Coyle, G. (1948). *Group work with American youth.* New York: Harper Brothers.

Crocker, R. (1992). *Social work and social order.* Urbana: University of Illinois Press.

Crosby, S. (1999, September 27). L.A. district extends after-school program. *Daily News*, pp. 1, 16.

Csikszentmihali, M. (1993). Contexts of optimal growth in childhood. *Daedalus, 122*(1), 31–56.

Cuomo, M. (1983, January). Message to the Legislature. Executive Chamber, Albany, NY.

Damon, W. (1990). Reconciling the literacies of generations. *Daedalus, 119*(2), 33–54.

Dargan, A., & Zeitlin, S. (1990). *City play.* New Brunswick, NJ: Rutgers University Press.

Davies, B. (1982). *Life in the classroom and playground.* London: Routledge & Kegan Paul.

Deich, S., Bryant, E., & Wright, E. (2001). *Using CCDF to finance out-of-school-time and community school initiatives.* Washington, DC: Finance Project.

Dewey, J. (1915). *Schools of tomorrow.* New York: Dutton.

Dillick, S. (1953). *Community organization for neighborhood development.* New York: William Morrow.

Dwyer, K., Richardson, J., Danley, K., Hansen, W., Sussman, S., Brannon, B., Dent, C., Johnson, C., & Flay, B. (1990). Characteristics of eighth-grade students who initiate self-care in elementary and junior high school. *Pediatrics, 86*, 448–454.

[Editorial introducing the first issue]. (1918). *Boys' Workers Roundtable, 1*(1), p. 1.

Elliot, J. (1921). The beginning of the Hudson Guild. *Boys' Workers Roundtable, 2*(1), 17.

Ellowitch, A., et al. (1991). *Portraits of youth programs: Education after-school.* New York: Institute for Literacy Studies, Lehman College, City University of New York.

Ennew, J. (1994). Time for children or time for adults. In J. Qvortrup et al. (Eds.), *Childhood matters.* Aldershot, Eng.: Avebury.

Erickson, J. (1988). Real American children: The challege for after-school programs. *Child and Youth Care Quarterly, 17*(2), 86–103.

Erikson, E. (1950). *Childhood and society.* New York: Norton.

Feister, L. (2000). *Beating the odds from 3 to 6 p.m.: Evaluation results from the TASC after-school program's first year.* Washington, DC: Policy Study Associates.

Fink, D. (1986). School-age child care: Where the spirit of neighborhood lives. *Children's Environments Quarterly, 3*(2), 9–12.

Finkelstein, B. (Ed.). (1979). *Regulated children/liberated children: Education in psychohistorical perspective.* New York: Psychohistory Press.

Finkelstein, B. (1987). Historical perspectives on children's play in school. In J. Block & N. King (Eds.), *School play: A source book.* New York: Garland.

Ford, B. (1977, April/May). The extended school day: Privilege, not punishment. *Childhood Education*, 297–301.

Ford Foundation. (1967). *Uniting two Americas.* New York: Author.

Franklin, A., & Benedict, A. (1943). *Play centers for school children: A guide to their establishment and operation.* New York: William Morrow.

Fredericksen, H. (1943). The program for day care of children of employed mothers. *Social Service Review, 17,* 159–169.

Fromerson, A. (1904). *Abstract from the Jewish Daily Forward:* In Years of immigrant adjustment. *Proceedings of the National Conference of Jewish Charities, 3,* 120–121.

Gilbert, J. (1986). *A cycle of outrage: America's reaction to the juvenile delinquent in the 1950s.* New York: Oxford University Press.

Gill, B., & Schlossman, S. (1996). A sin against childhood: Progressive education and the crusade to abolish homework. *American Journal of Education, 105*(1), 27–66.

Golden, D. (1981, October 11). Doors that open to latch key kids. *Boston Sunday Globe,* 21, 24.

Goodman, C. (1979). *Choosing sides: Playground and street life on the Lower East Side.* New York: Schocken.

Goodnough, A. (2001, June 14). High stakes fourth grade tests are driving off fourth grade teachers. *New York Times,* pp. A1, A29.

Gootman, J. (2000). *After-school programs to promote child and adolescent development* [Summary of a workshop]. Washington, DC: National Academy Press.

Graff, H. (1995). *Conflicting paths: Growing up in America.* Cambridge: Harvard University Press.

Gray, W. (n.d.). *History of school-age child care, 1890–1970.* Wellesley, MA: School-Age Child Care Project.

Greenberg, P. (1990). *The devil has slippery shoes.* Washington, DC: Youth Policy Institute. (Original work published 1969)

Guckert, E. (1935, April). A recreational council gets results. *Community Planning Bulletin No. 81,* 71–78.

Hall, H. (1971). *Unfinished business.* New York: Macmillan.

Halpern, R. (1990). *The role of after-school programs in the lives of inner-city children: A case study of the Chicago Youth Centers after-school programs.* Chicago: Chapin Hall Center for Children, University of Chicago.

Halpern, R. (1995). *Rebuilding the inner-city: A history of neighborhood initiatives to address poverty in the United States.* New York: Columbia University Press.

Halpern, R. (1999). *Fragile families, fragile solutions: A history of supportive services for families in poverty.* New York: Columbia University Press.

Halpern, R. (2000). The promise of after-school programs for low-income children. *Early Childhood Research Quarterly, 15*(2), 185–214.

Halpern, R., Spielberger, J., & Robb, S. (1999). *Evaluation of the MOST (Making the Most of Out of School Time) Initiative: Final report.* Chicago: Chapin Hall Center for Children, University of Chicago.

Hardy, S. (1982). *How Boston played: Sports, recreation, and community, 1865–1915.* Boston: Northeastern University Press.

Hardy, S., & Ingham, A. (1983, Winter). Games, structure, and agency: Historians on the American play movement. *Journal of Social History, 17,* 285–302.

Hart, R. (1979). *Children's experience of place*. New York: Irvington.

Hawes, J. (1991). *The children's rights movement*. Boston: Twayne.

Hawes, J. (1997). *Children between the wars: American childhood, 1920–1940*. New York: Twayne.

Heath, S. (1999). Rethinking youth transitions. *Human Development, 42*(6), 376–382.

Hedin, D., Hannes, K., Saito, R., Goldman, A., & Knich, D. (1986). *Summary of the family's view of after-school time*. Minneapolis: Center for Youth Development and Research, University of Minnesota.

Helburn, S. (1995). *Cost, quality, and child outcomes in child care centers*. Denver: University of Colorado.

Herr, T., & Halpern, R. (1993, January). *Kids Match: Addressing the challenges of linking inner-city children to activities supporting healthy development*. Chicago: Project Match, Erikson Institute.

Hill, S., Townsend, L., Lawrence, A., Shevin, S., & Ingalls, S. (1995). *Supporting community learning*. New York: Institute for Literacy Studies, Lehman College.

Hofferth, S. (1995). Out-of-school time: Risk and opportunity. In T. Swartz & K. Wright (Eds.), *America's working poor*. South Bend: Notre Dame University Press.

Holmes, W. (1929). Homework is school work out of place. *American Childhood, 15*(2), 5–7.

Hoyt, F. (1927). Old homes for new. *American Childhood, 12*(7), 5–6.

Hull House. (1957). *A social settlement in times of neighborhood change: A Hull House report*. Chicago: Hull House Association.

Hull, G., & Schultz, K. (Eds.) (2002). *Bridging out-of-school literacies with classroom practice*. New York: Teachers College Press.

Interfaith Neighbors. (n.d.). *Papers on the history of Interfaith Neighbors*. New York: Author.

Illich, I. (1970). *Deschooling society*. New York: Harper & Row.

Isaacs, S. (1932). *The children we teach: Seven to eleven years*. London: University of London Press.

Jacobs, J. (1961). *The death and life of great American cities*. New York: Vintage.

Jackson, J. (1997). *Primary grade schooling: A risk factor for African-American children?* Invited paper presented in the Lawrence Frank Symposium "Communities as Ecologies of Risk and Opportunity," Society for Research in Child Development, April 4, Washington, DC.

Jackson, S. (2000). *Lines of activity: Performance, historiography, Hull House history*. Ann Arbor: University of Michigan Press.

Jarrett, R. (1998, June). *Indicators of family strengths and resilience that influence positive child and youth outcomes in urban neighborhoods: A review of qualitative and ethnographic studies*. Review paper prepared for the Annie E. Casey Foundation, Baltimore, Maryland.

Johnson, D. (1998, April 7). Many schools putting an end to child's play. *New York Times*, pp. A1, p. A16.

Jones, E. (1943). Education to diminish delinquency. *Teachers College Record, 45*(2), 84–90.

Kadzielski, M. (1977). As a flower needs sunshine: The origins of organized children's recreation in Philadelphia, 1886–1911. *Journal of Sport History, 4*(2), 169–188.

Karger, H. (1987). *The sentinels of order: A study of social control and the Minneapolis settlement house movement, 1915–1950.* Lanham, MD: University Press of America.

Keller, S. (1963). The social world of the urban slum child. *American Journal of Orthopsychiatry, 33,* 823–831.

Kennedy, D. (1991). The young child's experience of space and child care center design: a practical meditation. *Children's Environments Quarterly, 8*(1), 37–48.

Kirk, R. (1994). *Earning their stripes: The mobilization of American children in the Second World War.* New York: Peter Lang.

Kirkland, W., & Johnson, M. (1989). *The many faces of Hull House.* Urbana: University of Illinois Press.

Kozol, J. (2000a, April 22). The details of life. *The Nation,* pp. 15–20.

Kozol, J. (2000b). *Ordinary resurrections.* New York: Crown Books.

Lambert, C. (1944). *School's out: Child care through play schools.* New York: Harper & Brothers.

Landberg, E. (1999). *A strategy paper: Aligning and linking out-of-school time programs with the Washington, D.C. public schools academic reform agenda.* Washington, D.C.: D.C. Agenda.

Larner, M., Zippiroli, L., & Behrman, R. (1999). When school is out: Analysis and recommendations. *The Future of Children, 9*(2), 4–20.

Lasch, C. (1977). The waning of private life. *Salmagundi, 36,* 3–15.

Lassonde, S. (1998). Should I go or should I stay? Adolescence, school attainment, and parent-child relations in Italian immigrant families in New Haven, 1900–1940. *History of Education Quarterly, 38*(1), 37–60.

Lee, J. (1912, August). Play for home. *The Playground,* pp. 1–6.

Lee, J. (1926). The way of growth. *Child Study, 4*(3), 3–5.

Lee, P. (1928). Children and leisure. *Child Study, 5*(5), 3–6.

Lindley, B., & Lindley, E. (1938). *A new deal for youth: The story of the National Youth Administration.* New York: Viking.

Littel, J., & Wynn, J. (1989). *The availability and use of community resources for young adolescents in an inner-city and a suburban community.* Chicago: Chapin Hall Center for Children.

Lofty, J. (2000). Reforming time: Timescapes and rhythms of learning. In P. Gandara (Ed.), *The dimension of time and the challenge of school reform.* New York: State University of New York Press.

Lyons, E. (2000). Creating an agency culture: A model for common humanity. *After-School Matters, 1*(1), 18–32.

Macleod, D. (1983). *Building character in the American boy.* Madison: University of Wisconsin Press.

Macleod, D. (1998). *The age of the child.* New York: Twayne

MacLeod, J. (1987). *Ain't no making it: Leveled aspirations in a low-income neighborhood.* Boulder: Westview Press.

Markely, M. (1987, October 10). After-school: Kids play it smart in week old program, *The Shreveport Times.*

Marris, P., & Rein, M. (1973). *Dilemmas of social reform*. London: Routledge & Kegan Paul.

Marshall, T. (1912). Address to a national Boys' Club Conference, Cleveland. *Work With Boys, 12*(6), 314.

Martin, L., & Ascher, C. (1994). Developing math and science materials for school-age child care programs. In F. Villaruel & R. Lerner (Eds.), *Community-based programs for socialization and learning*. San Francisco: Jossey Bass.

Mays, J. (1965). *The young pretenders*. New York: Schocken.

Marzke, C., & White, R. (2001). *Evaluation of the Baltimore Safe and Sound Youthplaces: Initial Report*. Washington, DC: Policy Studies Associates.

McDowell, M. (1914). *Draft manuscript for "Beginnings."* Chicago: Chicago Historical Society, University of Chicago Archives.

McLaughlin, M., Irby, M., & Langman, J. (1994). *Urban sanctuaries*. San Francisco: Jossey-Bass.

Medrich, E. (1983). *The serious business of growing up*. Berkeley & Los Angeles: University of California Press.

Merry, S. (n.d.). *Beyond home and school: The role of primary supports in youth development*. Chicago: Chapin Hall Center for Children.

Meyer, A. (1943). *Journey through chaos*. New York: Harcourt Brace.

Middlebrooks, S. (1998). *Getting to know city kids*. New York: Teachers College Press.

Midwest Division report. (1921). *Boys' Workers Roundtable, 2*(2), 24–25.

Miller, W. (1912). A plan for organized play in a city school. *Education, 32*(7), 409–412.

Miller, B., & Marx, F. (1990). *After-school arrangements in middle childhood: A review of the literature*. Wellesley, MA: School-Age Child Care Project, Wellesley College.

Miller, B., O'Conner, S., Sirignano, S., & Joshi, P. (1996). *I wish the kids didn't watch so much T.V.: Out of school time in three low-income communities*. Wellesley, MA: Center for Research on Women, Wellesley College.

Moore, W. (1969). *The vertical ghetto*. New York: Random House.

Moore, R. (1986). *Childhood's domain: Play and place in child development*. London: Croom Helm.

Moreo, D. (1997). *Schools in the Great Depression*. New York: Garland Press.

Moynihan, D. (1969). *Maximum feasible misunderstanding*. New York: Free Press.

Murao, S. (1954, June). *A study and analysis of factors related to boys dropping out of membership from the Lincoln Chicago Boys' Club*. Paper submitted to George Williams College, School of Social Work.

Nasaw, D. (1979). *Schooled to order: A social history of public schooling in the U.S.* New York: Oxford University Press.

Nasaw, D. (1985). *Children of the city*. New York: Anchor Press.

National Advisory Commission on Civil Disorders. (1968, March). *Report of the national advisory commission on civil disorders*. Washington, D.C.: Author.

National Governors' Association. (1999). *Making idle hours meaningful*. Advisory Committtee on Extra Learning Opportunities, Washington, D.C.

Nightingale, C. (1993). *On the edge: A history of poor Black children and their American dreams.* New York: Basic Books.

NIOST (National Institute on Out-of-School Time). (2001). Emerging roles in the field. *After-School Issues,* no. 3.

Olivet Items, Olivet Community Center. (1936). *Olivet Community Center Newsletter, 10,* 12.

Olivet Center Collection. (1960). *Letter to Mr. Philip Hampson,* Executive Director, Robert McCormick Trust.

Other workers' plans that may help you. (1918). *Boys' Workers Roundtable, 1*(3), 27.

Patri, A. (1925). *School and home.* New York: Appleton.

Pellegrini, A., & Bjorklund, D. (1996). The place of recess in school: Issues in the role of recess in children's education and development. *Journal of Research in Childhood Education, 11*(1), 5–13.

Pence, O. (1939). *The YMCA and social need.* New York: Association Press.

Pettit, G., Laird, R., Bates, J., & Dodge, K. (1997). Patterns of after-school care in middle childhood: Risk factors and developmental outcomes. *Merrill Palmer Quarterly, 43,* 515–538.

Petrie, P. (1996). School-age child care and the school: Recent European developments. In B. Bernstein & J. Brannen (Eds.), *Children, research and policy.* London: Taylor & Frances.

Phelps, E. (1995). *No turning back.* New York: Girls Inc.

Philpott, T. (1978). *The slum and the ghetto.* New York: Oxford University Press.

Postman, N. (1986). *Amusing ourselves to death.* New York: Penguin.

Proceedings. (1927, January). *Proceedings of the 3rd International Boys' Work Conference.* Chicago.

Pullum, N. (1985, January). Nancy Pullum, Manager of Child Care Services, Palm Beach County, *Personal interview with Wellesley School-Age Child Care Project.*

Raphael, J., & Chaplin, D. (2001). *Formative report on the Washington, D.C., 21st century Community Learning Centers after-school program.* Washington, D.C.: Urban Institute.

Reese, C. (1930). *Annual message of the director,* Abraham Lincoln Center Yearbook. Chicago: Chicago Historical Society Archives.

Reisner, L. (2001). *Building quality and supporting expansion of after-school projects: Evaluation results from the TASC after-school program's second year.* Washington, DC: Policy Study Associates.

Reiss, S. (1989). *City games.* Urbana: University of Illinois Press.

Resnick, L. (1990). Historical perspectives on literacy and schooling. *Daedalus, 119*(2), 15–32.

Riis, J. (1918). [Cited in Editorial]. *Boys' Workers Roundtable, 1*(1), 4.

Rivlin, L., & Wolfe, M. (1985). *Institutional settings in children's lives.* New York: Wiley.

Robinson, B. (1932). Why truancy. *American Childhood, 17*(7), 6–7.

Robinson, B., Rowland, B., & Coleman, M. (1989). *Home-alone kids.* Lexington, MA: Heath.

Roosevelt, T. (1920). Message to the boys of America. *Boys' Workers Roundtable*, *1*(4), 1.

Rose, E. (1997, April). *Essential patriatic service: Mothers and day care in World War Two Philadelphia*. Paper presented at the Annual Meeting of the Organization of American Historians, San Francisco.

Rothstein, R. (2002, January 9). In some ways the day only starts at 3. *New York Times*, p. A22.

Ruderman, F. (1968). *Child care and working mothers*. New York: Child Welfare League of America.

Safe and Sound Campaign. (n.d.). *Fact sheet and overview*. Baltimore: Safe and Sound Campaign.

Sapora, A., & Mitchell, E. (1961). *The theory of play and instruction*. New York: Ronald Press.

Schlossman, S., & Sedlak, M. (1983). *The Chicago Area Project revisited*. Santa Monica: Rand Corporation.

Schneider, K. (1982, January 24). Day care. *The Hartford Courant*, B1 & B4.

Schneider, E. (1992). *In the web of class: Delinquents and reformers in Boston, 1810s–1930s*. New York: New York University Press.

Scofield, R., & Page, A. (1982). *After-school care and the public schools*. Unpublished manuscript, School of Education, Tennessee State University.

Seligson, M. (1984, December). *School-age child care as a case study of cooperation between school and community*. Paper presented at the Spring Hill Conference.

Seligson, M. (1983). *School-age child care: A policy report*. Wellesley, MA: School-Age Child Care Project.

Seligson, M., & Allenson, M. (1993). *School-age child care*. Westport, CT: Auburn House.

Seligson, M., & Marx, F. (1989). *When school is out in New York City*. New York: Community Service Society.

Shannon, P. (1990). *The struggle to continue: Progressive reading instruction in the United States*. Portsmouth, NH: Heineman.

Sheley, J. (1984). Evaluation of the centralized, structured, after-school tutorial. *Journal of Educational Research*, *77*, 213–218.

Shevin, J., & Young, C. (2000). Naming common ground: Literacy and community. *After-School Matters*, *1*(1), 46–51.

Silberman, D. (1990). *Chicago and its children: A brief history of social services for children in Chicago*. Chicago: Chapin Hall Center for Children, University of Chicago.

Silverstein, B., & Krate, R. (1975). *Childen of the dark ghetto*. New York: Praeger.

Simkhovitch, M. (1904, September). The public school: Its neighborhood use, a recreational and social center. *The Commons*, pp. 406–417.

Simon, K. (1982). *Bronx primitive: Portraits in a childhood*. New York: Harper & Row.

Sochen, J. (1988). *Cafeteria America*. Ames: Iowa State University Press, 1988.

Sommerville, J. (1982). *The rise and fall of childhood*. Beverly Hills, CA: Sage.

Spear, A. (1967). *Black Chicago: The making of a ghetto*. Chicago: University of Chicago Press.

Spielberger, J., & Halpern, R. (2002). *The role of after-school programs in children's literacy development*. Chicago: Chapin Hall Center for Children, University of Chicago.

Spring, J. (1972). *Education and the rise of the corporate state*. Boston: Beacon Press.

Steinberg, L. (1986). Latch key children and susceptibility to peer pressure. *Development Psychology, 22*, 433–39.

Stipek, D. (1992). The child at school. In M. Bornstein & M. Lamb (Eds.), *Developmental psychology: An advanced textbook*. Mahwah, NJ: Lawrence Earlbaum.

Suransky, V. (1982). *The erosion of childhood*. Chicago: University of Chicago Press.

Sutton-Smith, B. (1975). The useless made useful: Play as variability training. *School Review, 83*(2), 197–214.

Sutton-Smith, B. (1990). School playground as festival. *Children's Environments Quarterly, 7*(2), 3–7.

Sutton-Smith, B. (1997). *The ambiguity of play*. Cambridge, MA: Harvard University Press.

TASC/The After-School Corporation. (n.d.). *Training and supervising after-school staff: A resource brief*. New York: Author.

Taylor, G. (1914). *The religious value of social work for children*. Graham Taylor Papers, Newberry Library, Chicago.

Taylor, J., & Randolph, J. (1975). *Community worker*. New York: Jason Aronson.

Trolander, J. (1987). *Professionalism and social change*. New York: Columbia University Press.

Tuttle, W. (1993). *Daddy's gone to war: The Second World War in the lives of American children*. New York: Oxford.

Tyack, D., & Cuban, L. (1995). *Tinkering toward utopia: A century of public school reform*. Cambridge, MA: Harvard University Press.

[Untitled comments]. (1922). *Boys' Workers Roundtable, 2*(3), 31.

U.S. Department of Education. (1983). *A nation at risk*. Washington, DC.: U.S. Government Printing Office.

U.S. Department of Education. (2001). *21st Century Community Learning Centers: Providing quality after-school learning opportunities for America's families*. Washington, DC: U.S. Government Printing Office.

Van Kleeck, M. (1908, January). Child labor in New York City tenements. *Charities and the Commons, 18*, [online]: http://tenantinet/community/LES/Kleeck9.html.

Vandell, D., Shumow, L., & Posner, J. (1997). Children's after-school programs: Promoting resiliency or vulnerability? In H. McCubbin et al. (Eds.), *Promoting resiliency in families and children at risk: Interdisciplinary perspectives*. Thousand Oaks, CA: Sage.

Varenne, H., & McDermott, R. (1998). *Successful failure: The schools America builds*. Greenwich, CT: Westview.

Villaruel, F., & Lerner, R. (1994). *Promoting community-based programs for socialization and learning.* San Francisco: Jossey-Bass.

A visit to the Chicago Boys' Club. (1923, April). *Boys' Workers Roundtable, 3*(1), 11–14.

Voelkl, K. (1997, May). Identification with school. *American Journal of Education, 105,* 295–318.

Wald, L. (1915). *The house on Henry Street.* New York: Henry Holt.

Walker, K., Grossman, J., Raley, R., Fellerath, V., & Holton, G. (2000). *The extended service schools interim evaluation report.* Philadelphia: Public Private Ventures.

Walters, P., & O'Connell, P. (1988, March). The family economy, work and educational participation in the U.S., 1890–1940. *American Journal of Sociology, 93,* 1116–1152.

Ward, C. (1978). *The child in the city.* New York: Pantheon.

Warren, C. (1999). *Evaluation of the New York City Beacons phase I findings.* New York: Academy for Educational Development.

Watson, E. (1911, February). Home work in the tenements. *The Survey, 25,* 772–781.

Weir, M. (1993). Urban policy and persistent urban poverty. [Background memo for a policy conference.] New York: Social Science Research Council, Program for Research on the Urban Underclass.

Wellborn, S. (1981, September 14). When school kids come home to an empty house. *U.S. News and World Report,* pp. 42, 47.

West, E. (1997). *Growing up in twentieth century America: A history and reference guide.* Westport, CT: Greenwood Press.

Whitaker, G., Cray, K., & Roole, B. (1998). *Developmental analysis of after-school programs for the governor's crime commission.* Chapel Hill: Center for Urban and regional Studies, University of North Carolina at Chapel Hill.

Wilgoren, J. (2000, January 24). The bell rings but the students stay and stay. *New York Times,* p. A1.

Wilhelm, J. (1997). *You gotta be the book.* New York: Teachers College Press.

Williams, M. (1985). Childhood in an urban black ghetto: Two life histories. In R. Hines & J. Hawes (Eds.), *Growing up in America: Children in historical perspective.* Urbana: University of Illinois Press.

Winn, M. (1981). *Children without childhood.* New York: Pantheon.

Wolfson, F. (1927). Opening the playground to the kindergarten child. *American Childhood, 12*(9), 17–20.

Woods, R., & Kennedy, A. (1970). *The settlement horizon.* New York: New York Times/Arno Press. (Work originally published 1922)

WSACCP (Wellesley School-Age Child Care Project). (1985). *Transcripts of interviews with school leaders.* Wellesley College.

Wukas, M. (1991). *The worn doorstep: An informal history of the Northwestern University Settlement, 1891–1991.* Chicago: Northwestern University Settlement.

Meeting the boy problem. (1912). *Work With Boys, 12,* 2.

The Morton, Pennsylvania, Boys' Club. (1914b). *Work With Boys, 14*(2), 56–59.

The Somerville Boys' Club. (1915). *Work With Boys, 15*(2), 56–61.

Tieing activities together in boys' clubs. (1914). *Work With Boys, 14*(6), 223–226.

Yost, A. (2000). Collaboration: The name of the game in after-school. *Making After-School Count, 3*(2), 1–5. Flint, MI: Mott Foundation.

Zald, M., & Denton, P. (1963). From evangelism to general service: The transformation of the YMCA. *Administrative Science Quarterly, 8*, 214–234.

Zane, S. (1990). *The boys' club of New York: A history*. New York: Boys Club of New York.

Zelizer, V. (1985). *Pricing the priceless child*. New York: Basic Books.

Index

About the Author

Robert Halpern is a Professor at the Erikson Institute for Graduate Study in Child Development in Chicago and a Faculty Associate at Chapin Hall Center for Children at the University of Chicago. He is the author of both *Fragile Families, Fragile Solutions: A History of Supportive Services for Families in Poverty* and *Rebuilding the Inner City: A History of Neighborhood Initiatives to Address Poverty*; he has also written numerous aricles on the effects of poverty on children and families and the role of services in poor families' lives. In recent years Dr. Halpern's research has focused on after-school programs. He recently completed a study of the role of after-school programs in fostering low-income children's literacy.